ENGAGING HEIDEGGER

One of the most important philosophers of the twentieth century, Martin Heidegger was primarily concerned with the 'question of Being.' However, recent scholarship has tended to marginalize the importance of the name of Being in his thought. Through a focused reading of Heidegger's texts, and especially his late and often overlooked Four Seminars (1966–1973), Richard Capobianco counters this trend by redirecting attention to the centrality of the name of Being in Heidegger's lifetime of thought.

Capobianco gives special attention to Heidegger's resonant terms Ereignis and Lichtung and reads them as saying and showing the very same fundamental phenomenon named 'Being itself.' Written in a clear and approachable manner, the essays in Engaging Heidegger examine Heidegger's thought in view of ancient Greek, medieval, and Eastern thinking, and they draw out the deeply humane character of his 'meditative thinking.'

RICHARD CAPOBIANCO is a professor and chair in the Department of Philosophy at Stonehill College.

WILLIAM J. RICHARDSON has been recognized for decades as one of the foremost Heidegger scholars in the world. He is a professor of philosophy at Boston College.

New Studies in Phenomenology and Hermeneutics

Kenneth Maly, General Editor

New Studies in Phenomenology and Hermeneutics aims to open up new approaches to classical issues in phenomenology and hermeneutics. Thus its intentions are the following: to further the work of Edmund Husserl, Maurice Merleau-Ponty, and Martin Heidegger – as well as that of Paul Ricoeur, Hans-Georg Gadamer, and Emmanuel Levinas; to enhance phenomenological thinking today by means of insightful interpretations of texts in phenomenology as they inform current issues in philosophical study; to inquire into the role of interpretation in phenomenological thinking: to take seriously Husserl's term *phenomenology* as 'a science which is intended to supply the basic instrument for a rigorously scientific philosophy and, in its consequent application, to make possible a methodical reform of all the sciences'; to take up Heidegger's claim that 'what is own to phenomenology, as a philosophical "direction," does not rest in being *real*. Higher than reality stands *possibility*. Understanding phenomenology consists solely in grasping it as possibility'; and to practise *phenomenology* as 'underway,' as 'the *praxis* of the self-showing of the matter for thinking,' as 'entering into the movement of enactment-thinking.'

The commitment of this book series is also to provide English translations of significant works from other languages. In summary, **New Studies in Phenomenology and Hermeneutics** intends to provide a forum for a full and fresh thinking and rethinking of the way of phenomenology and interpretive phenomenology, that is, hermeneutics.

For a list of books published in the series, see page 183.

Engaging Heidegger

RICHARD CAPOBIANCO

Foreword by William J. Richardson

UNIVERSITY OF TORONTO PRESS
Toronto Buffalo London

© University of Toronto Press Incorporated 2010
Toronto Buffalo London
www.utppublishing.com
Printed in the U.S.A.

Reprinted in paperback 2011

ISBN 978-1-4426-4159-4 (cloth)
ISBN 978-1-4426-1264-8 (paper)

Printed on acid-free paper.

Library and Archives Canada Cataloguing in Publication

Capobianco, Richard, 1957–
Engaging Heidegger / Richard Capobianco ; foreword by William J.
Richardson.

(New studies in phenomenology and hermeneutics)
Includes bibliographical references and index.
ISBN 978-1-4426-4159-4 (bound) – 978-1-4426-1264-8 (pbk.)

1. Heidegger, Martin, 1889–1976.   I. Title.   II. Series: New studies in
phenomenology and hermeneutics (Toronto, Ont.)

B3279.H49C36 2010   193   C2010-900192-3

University of Toronto Press acknowledges the financial assistance to its
publishing program of the Canada Council for the Arts and the Ontario
Arts Council.

  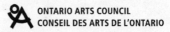

Canada Council   Conseil des Arts
for the Arts   du Canada

ONTARIO ARTS COUNCIL
CONSEIL DES ARTS DE L'ONTARIO

University of Toronto Press acknowledges the financial support of the
Government of Canada through the Canada Book Fund for its publishing
activities.

To the house, which is the world, the house-friend is friend. He tends to the whole and wide dwelling of humankind.

Martin Heidegger, Hebel – der Hausfreund

Contents

Foreword

In these engaging essays, Richard Capobianco engages the whole of Heidegger, if, indeed, not wholly. The whole of Heidegger begins, of course, with the first posing of the Being-question. This dates, not from the opening chapters of *Being and Time* (1927), but (as recalled in a letter of 1962) from the question that troubled the twenty-year-old *Gymnasium* student (circa 1909), who, after reading Franz Brentano's doctoral dissertation, *The Manifold Meaning of Being* [*des Seienden*] *in Aristotle*, asked (here in paraphrase): What is the meaning of Being (*Sein*) in its difference from beings (*Seiende*) that it lets be manifest in so many different ways?[1] This was the Being-question in its most rudimentary form, and it determined the way of Heidegger's thinking (*die Sache selbst*) up to the very end. To the extent that the following essays are polarized by this central core, they indeed engage the whole of Heidegger's enterprise; to say that they do not engage it 'wholly' means more than the obvious fact that they do not propose to exhaust the issues involved but rather that they take only certain ones among them as far as scholarship can go in order to set them free for further questioning.

The author presumes from the start the reader's familiarity with Heidegger's elaboration of his own question in the text of 1962 – a text that confirmed earlier hearsay about his Aristotelian beginnings. The method for pursuing the question as posed would be phenomenology, and the phenomenon of choice would be the being who posed the question, inasmuch as he must have had some intimation of an answer in order to ask it at all. Two additional elements marked the context in which the question matured: (1) the hint from Aristotle (e.g., *Nicomachean Ethics*, Book VI) that *aletheia*, the Greek word for 'truth,' literally means 'un-concealment'; and (2) the recognition that Being in the sense of 'presencing' (*Anwesen*) in whatever *comes*-to-presence clearly implies the dimension of time. With this much as baseline, the essays gathered here follow two different directions: the first focuses on the initially vague understanding of Being itself – did it change over the years? The second focuses on the conception of human being as its necessary correlate throughout the process. Both elements remain close to the core of Heidegger's thinking, but the former is the more comprehensive of the two and, perhaps, more revelatory of the author's own preference. Only a brief sketch of the results is possible here.

For most scholars, Heidegger's conception of Being remained fairly stable up through the so-called 'turn' (*die Kehre*) in his way of thought, which most associate with the early 1930s – that is, with the first public presentation in lecture form of 'On the Essence of Truth.' The earliest published expression of the effects of the turn seems to have been in *Introduction to Metaphysics* (1935). In that text, Being was considered under the guise of *physis, logos,* and *aletheia,* but these presented no great problem to the original formulation. Between 1936 and 1938, however, in an explosion of creative energy, Heidegger prepared a set of notes in secret (*Beiträge zur Philosophie [Vom Ereignis]*), the existence of which was known only to a chosen few and the text of which remained unpublished until 1989. Those notes introduced a new signifier, which he named *Ereignis* – an old word to which he now gave a uniquely new meaning. Flashes of the new term began to appear publicly around 1956, but it was not given centre stage until 1962 in the dramatically titled lecture 'Time and Being.'[2] How dramatic? The cognoscenti all knew that this was the proposed title of *Being and Time, Part III,* which had been projected in 1927 but had never appeared. How would the lecture relate to the long, turbulent hiatus in between?

For many, 'Time and Being' (hereafter TB), because of the central place given to the still strange terminology, was enigmatic and would remain so. The scholarly world would have to wait for the publication of *Beiträge* (*Contributions*) to have a good look at what Heidegger was getting at: *Ereignis* was to be thought of as the name for some kind of primordial Event out of which Being, beings, and human being all sprang, each unto its 'own' (*eigen*). Heidegger conceived of this aboriginal Moment as the coming-to-pass of 'Ap*propriation*,' or as the English translators put it, 'En-*own*-ment.' The consequent problem became immediately clear: Was this a new formulation implying that Being is somehow subsequent to, and hence subordinate to, a more original Event (*Ereignis*) from which it had sprung? Or did this term simply add further nuance (and if so, of what precise kind?) to the understanding of Being that had been in question all along? When all was said and done, what was *die Sache selbst* of Heidegger's thought at this point of time?

   After an exhaustive search through relevant texts, Capobianco embraces this position: Being and *Ereignis* are indeed the 'Same.' If it can be said that Being/*Ereignis* 'appropriates' 'Being' unto its 'own,' the sense must be that the 'Being' thus appropriated is 'Being' as metaphysics understands it, and its 'appropriation' but another name for the epochal destining (*Geschick*) of Being (in the sense of 'being-ness') that characterizes the metaphysical tradition as such. But does this interpretation stand up to scrutiny? The author's textual analyses are cogent and force the reader back to a re-examination of the original text of 'Time and Being' itself.

   What does Heidegger propose to do there? To think Being without its normal grounding in beings – that is, Being, so to speak, for itself alone. But it is impossible to do so without including a relation to time; and reciprocally, it is impossible to think time without including some reference to Being. This much had been clear from the very beginning of Heidegger's way. Being, to be sure, is not a being, no more than is time a being. At most we can say that 'there is' (*es gibt*) Being and 'there is' (*es gibt*) time. But what is It that does the giving – the giving of each to its 'own' and their complementarity to each other? Heidegger's answer: *Ereignis*, the Event of Appropriation. 'What lets [Being and time] belong together, what brings the two into their "own" [*eigen*] and, even more, maintains and holds them in their belonging together … is Appropriation' (19). And human being? 'Because Being and time are there only in Appropriating [*Ereignen*], Appropriating has the peculiar property of bringing man into his own as he who perceives Being by standing within true time. Thus Appropriated [*geeignet*], man belongs to Appropriation [*Ereignis*]' (23).

   In effect, these passages bring the entire reflection of 'Time and Being' to its conclusion. What more, indeed, needs to be said? Heidegger responds:

Only this: Appropriation appropriates. Saying this, we say the Same, in terms of the Same, about the Same … But what if we take what was said and adopt it unceasingly as the guide for our thinking, and consider that this Same is not even anything new, but the oldest of the old in Western thought: that ancient something which conceals itself in *A-letheia*. That which is said before all else by this first source of all the leitmotifs of thinking gives voice to a bond that binds all thinking, providing that thinking submits to the call of what must be thought. (TB, 24)

Surely these closing words reformulate in the most radical terms the Being-question as it had been understood from the beginning – adding explicitly, however, the two themes that had been part of the context of Heidegger's thinking all along: the insistence on the role of unconcealment (*aletheia*) as revelatory of Being; and the role of time, through its determination of Being, as constitutive of the epochal historicity of which the metaphysical tradition would be the prime analogate.

But is this way of speaking of *Ereignis* as the It that gives Being and time to themselves and to each other not dissonant from the earlier interpretation of *Ereignis* as Source of those dispensations (*Geschicke*) of Being that constitute Being as epochal history, of which the metaphysical tradition would be, perhaps, the prime analogate? Is it really possible to think of two such dissonant interpretations as somehow one and the Same?

Capobianco in fact leads the reader one step further as he pursues Heidegger's reflection through to the final *Four Seminars* of his career (1966–1973). Especially in the Seminar at Le Thor, France (11 September 1969), Heidegger returns to the issue of *Ereignis*. In meditating on the formula the 'Being of beings,' Heidegger insists on the difference between Being in the metaphysical sense of being-ness and the 'letting be' (*lassen*) quality of Being itself as a letting-come-to-presence. In this context, Capobianco twice cites Heidegger:

> It is a matter here of understanding that the deepest meaning of Being is *letting* [*das Lassen*]. Letting beings be, this is the non-causal meaning of 'letting' in 'Time and Being.' This 'letting' is something fundamentally different from 'doing.' The text 'Time and Being' attempted to think this 'letting' still more originally as 'giving.'
>
> The *giving* meant here speaks in the expression *Es gibt*. (20)

> If the emphasis is: *to let* presenc(ing) [come-to-pass], there is no longer room even for the name of Being [*Sein*]. *Letting* is then pure *giving*, which itself refers to the It [of *Es gibt*] that gives, which is understood as *Ereignis*. (21–2)

Accordingly, we are left to conclude that the two interpretations of *Ereignis* considered here are not as dissonant as it seems at first. If we take *Ereignis* to mean the ultimate dispensation of beings in such a way as to constitute a specific epoch of history, it is easy to think of any one dispensation as constituting the specificity – that is, the being-ness – of the beings that come-to-presence in that epoch, metaphysically.

If, however, we accept the conceit with which Heidegger begins 'Time and Being' – that is, his attempt to think Being 'without its being grounded in beings' – then the focus of the question shifts from the 'mode' of dispensation to its sheer givenness, the *Es gibt* as such. But we soon recognize here the absolute *aporia* of aletheic thinking in its ultimate consequence – or better, perhaps, in its primordial antecedence as the spontaneous givenness of pure *phainesthai*. Beyond this, aletheic thinking cannot go: this is indeed 'the ancient something which conceals itself as *A-letheia*.' For those who would follow his lead, Heidegger's only counsel is to 'submit to the call of what in this way may be thought' (TB, 24).

In a very valid sense, then, Capobianco's readings add up to what may legitimately be called an engaging of the 'whole' Heidegger. The remaining essays in this collection stay close to this essential core, and some move in another direction. They focus rather on Dasein as it passes through the high altitude of Heidegger's more challenging moments. The result is a much more humane conception of Dasein than the dark pages of *Being and Time* suggest. With special sensitivity to the affective disposition (*Befindlichkeit*) of Dasein, Capobianco traces, for example, the 'defining mood' of Dasein's 'authentic existence' from anxiety (BT) to awe and astonishment (Heidegger's translation of the Greek *thaumazein*) and even (with Hölderlin's help) to the spirit of a homecoming. Eventually, on the occasion of the seventh centenary of his hometown of Messkirch, Heidegger will talk of the serenity of 'releasement,' of 'gladness' and even 'joy.'

Taken in sum, these essays shine by reason of the thoroughness of their textual foundation, the clarity of their presentation, and the simplicity of their relatively jargon-free style. For those who find the author's engagement with the whole Heidegger not wholly Heidegger enough, the essays nonetheless offer the enormous advantage of leading readers back to the texts of Heidegger himself, where, perhaps, they may find the freedom to take a truly personal step along the way.

William J. Richardson, PhD
Boston College

Acknowledgments

I dedicate these essays to my teacher and mentor William J. Richardson, who has also generously contributed the foreword to this volume. Professor Richardson cleared a path to an understanding of Heidegger's thinking that generations of students and scholars have travelled. His book, *Heidegger: Through Phenomenology to Thought*, first published in 1963, is a work of sparkling clarity and immense learning that remains the surest guide to the essentials of Heidegger's thought.

Special thanks to Thomas Sheehan, with whom I have had the good fortune to have carried on a lively correspondence for over ten years. My *Auseinandersetzung* with his alternative 'paradigm' has sharpened the focus of several of the studies that follow, but more than that, I also thank him for his extraordinary collegiality and personal kindness. And to Professor Gábor Ferge, editor of the beautifully crafted international journal *Existentia* originating out of Budapest, I extend my deepest appreciation for his thoughtful support across the many miles.

I am grateful to my colleagues for their *disponibilité* and inspiration, and most especially to Antonio Barbagallo, Dieter Schönecker, Richard Velkley, Harold Brogan, Walter Brogan, Richard Polt, John Rose, Babette Babich, Tom Clarke, Anna Lännström, and Joe Velazquez; also to Marie Göbel for her beautiful gift of language and friendship; to Stonehill College Provost Katie Conboy and Dean Joe Favazza for their generous support of this project; and to all the students at Stonehill whom I have known over the years: both your good-heartedness and your good questions have brought me great joy.

And for my family – my wife Vivian, our sons Nicholas, Stefan, and Alex, and my brother Ken – my abiding thanks for their life-giving love, trust, and acceptance.

I also happily acknowledge the graciousness of Kenn Maly, the general editor of the series, and the gracious assistance of editor Len Husband and his colleagues at the University of Toronto Press.

Several of the chapters of this volume are somewhat revised and expanded versions of essays that have appeared earlier, and the author gratefully acknowledges these publications: 'The Fate of Being in Heidegger's *Four Seminars 1966–1973*,' *Existentia: An International Journal of Philosophy* 15, nos. 3–4 (2005): 161–83; '*Das Ereignis*: (Only) Another Name for Being Itself,' *Existentia: An International Journal of Philosophy* 16, nos. 5–6 (2006): 341–52; 'Heidegger's Turn toward Home: On Dasein's Primordial Relation to Being,' *Epoché: A Journal for the History of Philosophy* 10, no. 1 (2005): 155–73; 'Heidegger's *Die Lichtung*: From the "Lighting" to the "Clearing,"' *Existentia: An International Journal of Philosophy* 17, nos. 5–6 (2007): 321–35; 'Limit and Transgression: Heidegger and Lacan on Sophocles' *Antigone*,' *Review of Existential Psychology and Psychiatry* 26, no. 1 (2001): 17–26.

ENGAGING HEIDEGGER

Introduction

In his long lifetime of thinking, Heidegger safeguarded the originary word of Western philosophical thinking: Being. Several of the essays in this volume are intended to bring our attention back to this defining feature of his thought. The contemporary analytic and postmodern resistance and even hostility to the very word 'being' has no doubt contributed to the current tendency in Heidegger studies to shuffle the name of Being to the background, if not erase it altogether. Nevertheless, a careful consideration of the texts – a primary concern of the studies in this volume – reaffirms that Heidegger, right to the end of his life, continued to reserve and preserve in his thinking the ancient word 'Being' as the name for the fundamental matter for thought (*die Sache selbst*). The originary, fundamental, and unifying meaning of Being, the *Erfragte* from the outset of his *Denkweg*, was properly named by Heidegger as Beyng (*Seyn*), Being itself (*Sein selbst*), Being as such (*Sein als solches*), and Being as Being (*Sein als Sein*) in distinction from being as *beingness* (*Seiendheit*), which he always maintained to be the proper concern of the metaphysical tradition of thinking. The important but often neglected task of carefully parsing Heidegger's language of Being, beingness, and beings is taken up in a number of the essays.

Being remained a privileged name in Heidegger's thinking, which is not to say, of course, that he did not also call forth other names – some ancient, some poetic, some new and novel – in order to bring forth in language the *Ur*-phenomenon itself. What is this primordial phenomenon that he indicated was made manifest by the name of Being itself? It is the same phenomenon named *aletheia*, *physis*, *Logos*, *hen*; it is the same that is named the clearing, the fourfold, the holy; it is the same that is named *Ereignis*. And again, what is that? In the pages that follow,

I gather Heidegger's multiple, varied, rich, and resonant indications – the lifetime of work of a truly original thinker – into a basic description: the *Ur*-phenomenon that he always had in view, that he understood ancient Greek thinking to have originarily brought into view, albeit glancingly, with the word *eon*, Being, is *the temporal-spatial, finite and negatived, appearing of beings in their beingness, which calls forth and even compels from the human being (Dasein) a cor-respondence in language that allows both what appears – and appearing itself – to be made manifest meaningfully.*

This is the single, whole phenomenon – Being itself – that he named and renamed again and again over the course of his lifetime of thinking, and the abundant variety of names that he put into play succeeded in bringing into view the varied features of this one, simple phenomenon. So it is that we may also speak of the *unconcealing* of beings (*aletheia*), the *emerging* of beings (*physis*), the *laying out and gathering* of beings (*Logos*), the *unifying, unfolding* of beings (*hen*), the *presencing* of beings (*Anwesen*), the *lighting/clearing* of beings (*Lichtung*), the *freeing* of beings (*das Freie*); the *letting* of beings (*Lassen*), the *giving* of beings (*Es gibt*), and the *appropriating or enowning* of beings (*Ereignis*). All of these names, and still others, say (*sagen*) and show (*zeigen*), in somewhat different ways, the primordial phenomenon. Or to put this in Heidegger's terms, all of these names are the Same (*das Selbe*), but not simply identical (*das Gleiche*) in an empty, purely formal, logical sense.

Indeed, it is a principal aim of these essays to bring into sharper relief how all of these names *say* the Same and, therefore, *are* the Same. In particular, I focus on the terms *Ereignis* and *Lichtung*. To be sure, *Ereignis* has received considerable mention in contemporary scholarship, but the precise significance of this distinctive term in Heidegger's thinking has not received adequate consideration, especially with respect to how it relates to Being itself. My effort is to attend closely to his own words on the matter, and I think that we find – quite decisively, in fact – that he always understood *Ereignis* as another name for Being itself. *Lichtung*, though such an important word, especially for the later Heidegger, has received scant scholarly attention. Thus the two studies on this term included in this volume prove to be, I believe, a contribution not only towards understanding more clearly the place of this name in his thought but towards realizing the existential promise of this notion as well. In fact, let us keep in mind that all of his reflections have an existential dimension that speaks to our human sojourn between birth and death, as we dwell upon the earth and beneath the sky, always in the company of others and of other beings. In several of the essays, I attempt to draw out thematically the deeply humane character of his 'meditative thinking.'

Considered together, these studies reflect my abiding appreciation for the originality, power, and beauty of Heidegger's thinking. Even so, in certain places, I discuss particular problems or inconsistencies in his work, but always with the intention of clarifying and edifying – never merely to refute, dismiss, or set aside. One must remain ever mindful that all great thinkers are deserving of ample leeway. Overall, I would characterize my approach in these essays as engaging the most engaging thinker of the twentieth century in the specifics of his thinking – an effort that I am hopeful will yield for the reader fresh insights into his central ideas and terms along with a renewed appreciation for the astonishing richness and reach of his philosophical project.

1 The Fate of Being

We must emphasize again and again that the only question that has ever moved Heidegger is the question of Being: What does 'Being' mean?
Seminar in Zähringen, 1973

In philosophical discussion, where little is certain, there is at least the certainty that Martin Heidegger was the philosopher whose one defining thought concerned Being. Yet perhaps not? Some distinguished Heidegger scholars, such as Kenneth Maly, have made the case that Heidegger ultimately withdrew the name Being for *die Sache selbst,* that is, 'the fundamental matter for thought.'[1] Thomas Sheehan has gone one step further. He has been arguing provocatively that 'Heidegger's focal topic never was "being" in any of its forms.'[2] On the face of it, such a claim seems outrageous or at least outrageously overstated. Yet Sheehan, who reads Heidegger with admirable erudition, has marshalled a variety of texts to advance his argument that we should 'abandon the word "being" as a marker for *die Sache selbst.*' Nevertheless, though he and others may have shaken the certainty of scholars that the *Seinsfrage* was Heidegger's core concern, their readings are ultimately not convincing – in one form or another, the *Seinsfrage* remained central to all of Heidegger's reflections. To sharpen the focus, however, I propose that a close examination of his very late *Four Seminars* (1966–73), which have not been considered systematically up to this point, reveals that the task of clarifying the meaning of Being remained to the very end the fundamental concern of his thought.[3] No matter how many alternative formulations and poetic names Heidegger put into play over his lifetime to name Being – from *das Ereignis* to *die Lichtung* – his core philosophical task was defined from beginning to end by the question of the originary, fundamental, unifying meaning of Being.

I. Clearing the Way

On one point, there is no disputing Sheehan: too often the commentary on Heidegger's understanding of Being has been 'so freighted with confusion and absurdity that it cannot serve as a marker for Heidegger's focal topic.'[4] Mystifying translations and commentaries aside, Heidegger scholarship has often been beset by a tendency to confuse his core concern with *das Sein / das Seyn*, Being/Beyng (the finite and negatived *presencing* of beings in their beingness) with the traditional metaphysical core concern with *die Seiendheit*, the 'beingness' of beings. Sheehan longs for the time 'not long ago, when doing Heidegger [scholarship] did not mean sacrificing analytic precision, when terms had crisp edges as well as elegance.' And he justly cites William J. Richardson's 1963 commentary as perhaps the exemplar of such exacting scholarship.[5] So it is important to maintain some clarity and order in the universe of Heidegger's terms before proceeding to a discussion of the *Four Seminars*. The boxed text on the following pages is a helpful way of bringing into sharper relief the clearest thinking in a tradition of thinking (what Sheehan calls the 'classical paradigm') concerning Heidegger's understanding of Being, beings in their beingness, and Dasein.

The best commentary done within this so-called 'classical paradigm' has distinguished between Heidegger's principal concern, Being (*das Sein / das Seyn*) as the temporal-spatial, finite and negatived, presencing itself (*das Anwesen selbst*) of beings in their beingness, on the one hand, and 'being' traditionally understood either as what is present (*das Seiende, das Anwesende*) or as the beingness or essential presence (*die Seiendheit, die Anwesenheit*) of what is present, on the other. This decisive distinction – what separates Heidegger's thinking from all metaphysical formulations – is what has justified (and I think continues to justify) writing Being, Heidegger's primary concern, with a capital B. Understood properly, this convention has nothing to do with the hypostasization or mystification of *Sein/Seyn*. Being with a capital B (or, alternatively, written as 'be-ing') simply conveys in English Heidegger's distinctive understanding of the meaning of Being (*Sein/Seyn*) in contrast to the meaning of being (1) presupposed in the ontic sciences (*das Seiende*) and (2) articulated in the long history of metaphysical thinking (the being of beings, *das Sein des Seienden*, as the beingness of beings, *die*

I. Being/Beyng (*das Sein / das Seyn*); Being itself (*das Sein selbst*);
    Being as such (*das Sein als solches*); Being as Being (*das Sein als
    Sein*); (but also the Nothing [*das Nichts*]) is the Same (*das Selbe*)
    as:

    the finite, temporal-spatial

    unconcealing of beings (Gr., *Aletheia; die Unverborgenheit*)
    laying out and (fore)gathering of beings (Gr., *Logos; die
        (Ver)Sammlung*)
    emerging, arising, appearing of beings (Gr., *physis; das
        Aufgehen*)
    appropriating of beings or letting beings come into their own
        (*das Ereignis*)
    lighting, clearing of beings (*die Lichtung*)
    originating of beings (*der Ursprung, die Anfängnis, die Quelle,
        der Grund*)
    opening, freeing, and enabling of beings (*das Offene, das Freie,
        die Ermöchlichung*)
    granting and gracing of beings (*das Heilige*)
    sending, dispensing, destining of beings (*das Geschick*)
    regioning (opening, gathering, abiding) of beings (*die Gegnet*)
    unifying, joining, centering of beings (Gr., *hen; das Einzig-Eine,
        das Einfache, die Fuge/die Mitte* of *das Geviert*, the fourfold)
    drawing out, separating out of beings (*der Austrag, der
        Unter-Schied*)
    giving, letting of beings (*Es gibt, das Lassen*)
    essencing of beings (*das Wesen* understood verbally as *die
        Wesung*)
    presencing itself of beings (*das Anwesen selbst, anwesen selbst*)

    in which inheres a negatived dimension of concealment, clo-
    sure, opacity, inaccessibility (Gr., *lethe*); characterized further
    as absencing (Gr., *steresis; das Unwesen, die Abwesung*); also,
    withdrawal (*der Entzug*); retreating (*das Ausbleiben*); refusal (*die
    Verweigerung*); withholding (*der Vorenthalt*); mismeasurement
    (*die Vermessenheit*); errancy (*die Irre*).

II. (i) beings (*das Seiende*) in their (ii) beingness (*die Seiendheit*) =

(i) that which is; particular entities (Gr., *on, onta*; L., *ens, entia*; also *das Anwesende, das Seiend*)

(ii) the principal concern of metaphysics: the 'being,' 'real-ness,' 'is-ness,' or sheer 'presence' or 'presentness' of entities; the 'beingness' of beings (*die Seiendheit*, also *die Anwesenheit, das Seiendsein, die Präsenz*) construed in the history of meta-physics in various ways:

Gr., *eidos, idea, morphe* (essence, idea, form); Gr., *ousia* (substance, essence); Gr., *energeia* (actuality); L., *actus, actualitas* (act, actuality); L., *quidditas* (quiddity or whatness); L., *es-sentia/esse* (essence/existence; *das Was-sein / das Daß-sein* in Heidegger's rendering); Gr., *hypokeimenon* (subject, substrate); the objectiveness or objectness (Heidegger uses both *die Gegenständlichkeit* and *die Gegenständigkeit*) of objects present to a subject in the various forms of subjectness (*die Subjektität*) in modern philosophy: *cogito* (Descartes), transcendental uni-ty of apperception (Kant), infinite Ego (Fichte), Absolute Spir-it (Hegel), will (Schopenhauer), will to power (Nietzsche), transcendental ego (Husserl).

III. Dasein = the human being as the ek-sisting, ek-static 'there' of Being; the being that cor-responds (Gr., *legein/noein*; *homolo-gein*) to Being by letting beings be meaningfully in language (*die Sprache*). Dasein and Being are cor-relative and co-dis-closive.

Seiendheit des Seienden). *Sein/Seyn*, Being/Beyng (and note that through-out this volume I reserve the capital B in English for this usage only), is Heidegger's word that marks or manifests the finite and negatived emerging / unfolding / coming-to-presence of beings in their being-ness; it is his word that unifies the multiple senses of being discussed by Aristotle; it is, for Heidegger, the word that names the most important (glancing) insight of the ancient Greek thinkers Parmenides and Hera-clitus at the very dawn of Western thinking.

II. Heidegger's Four Seminars

In the last decade of his life, Heidegger led four seminars with a small group of French colleagues, including Jean Beaufret, to whom the 1947 'Letter on Humanism' had been addressed. Three of the seminars – in 1966, 1968, and 1969 – were held in Le Thor, France, in the home region of the poet René Char, Heidegger's friend, who occasionally joined the group in conversation.[6] The final seminar was held in 1973 in Heidegger's home in Zähringen near Freiburg. The texts of these seminars are not in Heidegger's hand; rather, they are 'protocols' written in French by one or more of the participants at the time of the conversations (except for the summaries of the 1966 seminars, which were written sometime after). In almost every case, the protocols were read in Heidegger's presence and apparently approved by him. The French text of the protocols was translated into German by Curd Ochwadt, 'monitored' in some fashion by Heidegger himself. Apparently, Heidegger wanted these seminars to be included in his *Gesamtausgabe*, and eventually they were published (in the German version) as *Vier Seminare* in *Gesamtausgabe, Band* 15, in 1986. For the German edition, the editor Curd Ochwadt included a brief but important statement on Parmenides that Heidegger himself authored and read at the last seminar in 1973. An English translation of the *Four Seminars* by Andrew Mitchell and François Raffoul appeared in 2003.

The *Four Seminars* are of special interest because they offer us an insight into what themes engaged Heidegger in the last years of his lifetime of thinking. I am not suggesting that these texts represent his most complete thoughts on any of the issues raised in the seminars or that his remarks are more significant than his published work. Nevertheless, the seminars are exceptionally helpful in illuminating his thinking in these latter years, and they are also of value in revealing Heidegger, the man and the thinker, at his very best: collegial, generous, and engaging; brilliant, compelling, and boldly original.

For our purposes, what is most striking about these seminars is that Heidegger gives central place to the theme of *the meaning of Being*. His thinking returns to where it began, with the task of clarifying 'the meaning of Being.' But admittedly, his elaborations on this theme are sometimes quite challenging and puzzling, and the issues need to be sorted out carefully. An examination of the relevant seminar sessions will bring these issues into sharp focus.

III. Seminar in Le Thor, 1966

5 September 1966

Heidegger reprises his lifelong consideration of the fragments of Heraclitus and Parmenides in light of his lifelong consideration of the *meaning of Being*. He translates the opening line from Fragment 1 of Heraclitus in the following way: *'Now of logos, of beings in their Being [vom Seienden in seinem Sein], human beings never have an understanding'* (2:273). In other words, it is constitutive for human beings to fall upon beings and away from Being. He emphasizes the relatedness of *logos* and *eon* (the archaic form of the word *on*). *Eon* is the decisively important Greek word, which he translates here as Being (*das Sein*) – and we need to make special note of his translation because he will return to this word *eon* in the last seminar in 1973. He recalls (in his own words) Parmenides' saying that 'thinking' (*Denken*) and 'Being' (*Sein*) are 'the same' (cor-related). The seminar protocol notes (2:273) that Heidegger had discussed this theme in his 1957 *The Principle of Reason*, in which he stated that 'a belonging to Being [*Sein*] … speaks in all that is said in the Greek word *logos*' – in other words, that '*logos* names Being' or that 'though it had other names in early Western thinking, Being means *logos*.' This is a familiar theme in Heidegger's work: Being means *Logos* as the primordial laying out and gathering together of beings. Human thinking (*legein/noein*) is the cor-relative or cor-responding laying out and gathering together of beings meaningfully in language (*homologein*).

8 September 1966

Being as *Logos* is also to be understood as *to diapheromenon* – that is, the differentiating and gathering together of beings as contraries. Yet, Heidegger warns, this unfolding of contraries is not to be understood in a rigidly '*dialectically* determined' manner as in Hegel's thinking. Referring to Heraclitus, he observes: 'The house of Being is that of day-night taken together' (4:276). 'There is no day "alone," nor night "apart from itself," but rather the co-belonging of day and night, which is their very Being [*Sein*].' We recognize in such statements not only Heidegger's basic theme of the originary (ontological) difference (*Differenz*) between Being and beings, but also his later understanding of Being as the unifying 'drawing out' (*der Austrag*) or 'separating out' (*der Unter-Schied*) of beings as contraries.[7] Understood in this light, Being is the 'jointure' (*die Fuge*) or the 'middle' (*die Mitte*) that unfolds as the co-belonging of contraries. As he puts it in this seminar: 'What truly *is*, is neither the one [day] nor the other [night], but the co-belonging of the two as the concealed middle between them' (4:277).

He also recalls and restates the theme that human thinking is most profoundly understood as a cor-respondence (*homologein*) with Being (*Logos*). Thus: 'Human thinking itself, its *noein*, belongs to the *logos* and determines itself from this [*logos*] as *homologein* (Fragment 50)' (6:279). The protocol concludes with Heidegger saying: 'All thinking is "for the sake of Being," which is certainly not to say that this would be only an object of thought' (6:280).

IV. Seminar in Le Thor, 1968

30 August 1968

Heidegger takes up a close reading of a text by Hegel. In his commentary, he once again takes up the matter of 'opposites,' and he brings Hegel's position closer to his own view that opposites are both separated out and held together in a unitary emerging:

> We then return to conjoining [*Vereinigung*] in order to show its difference from *unification*. In the conjoining – insofar as it is the work of the Absolute – the oppositions *do not disappear*. There is a unity of opposites that remain as opposites. What, then, is this conjoining? It is the power that holds the opposites together *for one another:* in this holding together, there is no longer room for the autonomy or separateness of the opposites each for itself (which characterizes the scission [*Ent-zweiung*]). (12:289–90)

31 August 1968

The discussion concerning Hegel continues, but in the midst of this, Heidegger makes a reference to *das Sein* that is central to our discussion because it illuminates a frequent confusion about his understanding of Being – a confusion that we must admit is generated in part by Heidegger's own way of articulating the fundamental matter for thought over the many years of his philosophical work. The essence of philosophy, he says, is thinking towards 'conjoining' or 'unity,' what both Heraclitus and Parmenides named *hen*. And he adds:

Listening to the tradition of philosophy, that is, to metaphysics, we learn that philosophy is concerned with the being of beings [*das Sein des Seienden*]. What is then the relation between the *hen* and the being of beings? The relation between *hen* and *ousia*? (15:295–6)

The seminar members make note of the several ways in which 'being' appears according to Aristotle, including as *dynamis-energeia* and as *ousia-symbebekos*, and the question is asked and answered: 'What is the unity of being, that single realm? Aristotle does not say.' This question – What is the unifying meaning of being in Aristotle? – is precisely Heidegger's original and fundamental question, and for him the meaning of being that unifies Aristotle's multiple meanings of being is *Sein/ Seyn* as the temporal emerging of beings in their beingness. But – and here is the complication in his discourse that has given rise to confusion – he uses the key phrase *das Sein des Seienden* in this passage and in other places in the seminar to refer specifically to the metaphysical 'beingness' (*Seiendheit*) of beings, and *not* to the Being of beings in their beingness (that is, the presencing of *Seienden* in their *Seiendheit*), which was his primary concern. Now, if *das Sein des Seienden* refers only to the 'beingness of beings,' then certainly *Sein* could never have been *die Sache selbst* for Heidegger. However, he was not always helpful in his use of this particular phrase over the many years of his discourse; often he used it to name the fundamental matter for thought, yet just as often – and especially in the later work – he used it as a shorthand way to refer to the core concern of metaphysics.

Here is not the place to document in detail the history of this small but significant expression in Heidegger's thinking, but it is important to cite several texts that highlight his often inconsistent use of the phrase. In *Being and Time* (1927), he opens his inquiry into the meaning of Being by insisting that Being cannot have 'the character of some possible being.' In stating this, he uses this phrase *das Sein des Seienden* to name his proper concern: 'The Being of beings "is" not itself a being.'[8] In another important early text, *On the Essence of Ground* (1929), he maintains the following: 'Ontic and ontological truth always concern different [aspects of the one phenomenon], *beings in* their Being [*Seiendes in seinem Sein*] and *Being of* beings [*Sein von Seiendem*].'[9] In other words, he correlates 'ontic' truth (including metaphysical truth), which is focused on beings (as beings), with the phrase '*beings in* their Being'; and he correlates 'ontological' truth – his fundamental concern and the fundamental task for thought – with the phrase '*Being of* beings.'

In *Introduction to Metaphysics* (1935), he states that the expression 'the being of beings' (*das Sein des Seienden*) has traditionally named the metaphysical concern with the beingness (*Seiendheit*) of beings, but he nonetheless repeatedly uses this same phrase to pose his own question and concern – for example:

> We encounter beings everywhere; they surround us, carry and control us, enchant and fulfill us, elevate and disappoint us, but in all of this, where is and wherein consists the Being of beings?[10]

In his 1942 lecture course and commentary on Hölderlin's poem 'The Ister,' he identifies the 'hearth' named in Sophocles' *Antigone* as Being (*Sein*) 'in whose light and radiance, glow and warmth, all beings have in each case already gathered.' Being/Hearth is his name for what is most thoughtworthy – the emerging, unfolding, gathering of beings – and he refers several times to the 'knowledge of the hearth' as the 'knowledge of the Being of beings [*das Sein des Seienden*].'[11] Here, again, the phrase *das Sein des Seienden* marks the fundamental matter for thought.

Soon after the course on 'The Ister,' he gave a lecture course on Parmenides (1942–3). Throughout the course, he uses *das Sein* or *das Sein selbst* to name his ownmost concern, namely, the emerging of beings into unconcealedness, Being as *aletheia*; but he also uses the phrase *das Sein des Seienden* in this way. In Section 6, he begins a reading of Plato's *mythos* of 'the essence of the *polis*' in the *Republic*.[12] He clarifies the fundamental insight into Plato's understanding of the *polis* in this way:

> In truth it is the insight that the Being of beings is 'really' nowhere within beings and is not, as it were, on hand as one of their parts ... The *polis* itself is only the pole of *pelein* [the ancient Greek word for 'to be'], the way the Being of beings, in its disclosure and closure, disposes for itself a 'where' in which the history of a human people is gathered. (P, 95–6:141–2)

In this section, then, Heidegger uses the expression *das Sein des Seienden* as a marker for the fundamental matter.

Nevertheless, in a later place in this same lecture course, he gives this same phrase a different significance. In Section 7(b), he discusses how Plato narrowed the Greek experience of unconcealedness (*Unver-borgenheit*; Gr., *aletheia*) to the experience of 'the sight and the aspect that something offers' (*Sicht, Anblick, Aussehen*; Gr., *eidos, idea*), and he states:

> Thought in Plato's sense, unconcealedness happens as *idea* and *eidos*. In

these and through these, beings, that is, what is present [*Anwesende*], come to presence. The *idea* is the countenance by which at any time self-disclosive beings look at human beings. The *idea* is the presence [*Anwesenheit*] of what is present [*Anwesenden*]: the being of beings [*das Sein des Seienden*]. (P, 124:184)

Here, he uses *das Sein des Seienden* to mean specifically and unequivocally the beingness of beings (*die Seiendheit des Seienden*) – the fundamental concern of metaphysics. In one and the same text, therefore, he uses this key phrase in two different ways – and note that he does so without any helpful qualification or clarification.

In the 1951–2 lecture course *What Is Called Thinking?* (published in 1954), he frequently uses the phrase *das Sein des Seienden* to highlight the theme of the (ontological) difference. He maintains that this formulation has traditionally referred to the metaphysical 'difference' between particular beings in their beingness. Yet he also uses the same phrase when framing his own concern: the originary difference or twofold (which grounds any metaphysical difference). So, for example, he poses *die Sache* in this ambiguous manner: 'The Being of beings is the most apparent; and yet, we normally do not see it – and if we do, only with difficulty.'[13] In the later work of the 1950s and especially the 1960s, Heidegger more often employed the formulation *das Sein des Seienden* to refer exclusively to the proper concern of metaphysics.[14]

In the *Four Seminars* we are discussing, he repeatedly uses this phrase in the ontic, metaphysical sense, which is no doubt confusing to those readers who are familiar with the history of his using this same phrase to name his own concern, 'the Being of beings.' In any case, the point is that we should not be misled by his particular use of this phrase in the *Four Seminars*. The significance is not that he abandoned the word *Sein/Seyn* as the marker for *die Sache selbst*; rather, it suggests only that in much of the later work he apparently did abandon (or at least subordinate) *this particular formulation*, which included the word *Sein*, as a marker for *die Sache*. This little phrase, *das Sein des Seienden*, certainly has a long and interesting history in Heidegger's thinking, as even this brief review reveals. But we may be justifiably dismayed that he did not make a greater effort to be more precise with the principal terms of the phrase and that he did not call sufficient attention to his change in the *primary* use of it in the work of the later years. Regrettably, the elusive and shifting meaning of this key phrase in his work has contributed to a good deal of the confusion that has plagued efforts to understand and state clearly the difference between his inquiry into 'the Being of beings' and the traditional metaphysical inquiry into the 'being-ness of beings.'

2 September 1968

Heidegger asks about the 'unity' that human beings are in cor-relation with, 'which is neither day nor night [nor any of the contraries], even if [this unity] is not expressly thematized' (19:301). He rules out the answers 'world,' 'light,' 'space,' and even 'time' as 'all too general.' He identifies the 'unity' as *hen* as Being (*Sein*): 'If we consider that, since Heraclitus, this unity is called *hen*, and that, since this origin, the One is the other name for Being, then we are referred back to the "understanding of Being" spoken of in *Being and Time*' (19:302). Being (*Sein*) is the 'unity' that calls forth thinking and that thinking is seeking. In Heidegger's view, this is also the meaning of Being that unifies the multiple ways that being is spoken of by Aristotle.

4 September 1968

The issue is raised by Heidegger concerning whether 'the question of Being [*Sein*] is the question of metaphysics' (21:305). He maintains, as he had in earlier sessions, that metaphysics inquires into 'the being-ness of beings,' which, he adds, is equivalent to the question of 'What is a being as a being [*das Seiende als Seiendes*]?' But metaphysics 'does not inquire into Being itself [*Sein selbst*].' Once again, then, he explicitly names the fundamental matter for thought Being itself (*Sein selbst*).

He insists that the 'question of Being' that defines his own path of thinking is *'entirely other'* than the question asked in metaphysics. His own question 'does not inquire into being insofar as it determines beings as beings; it inquires into Being as Being [*Sein als Sein*]' (22:307). *Being as Being* is another way of naming *die Sache*. Furthermore, he warns that thinking about what he had named the 'ontological difference' is most 'dangerous' because there is always the tendency to think about the difference merely in metaphysical terms. In other words, metaphysical thinking always tends to represent the 'being' of beings in terms of *a* being, namely, as *eidos*, *actualitas*, ego, nature, Spirit, and the like. Metaphysics merely 'raises the being of beings to the second power,' and by this he apparently means that the metaphysical version of the 'ontological difference' is always in terms of *die Seiendheit des Seienden*, the beingness of beings, which is no more than a difference in the consideration of *beings*. Metaphysics does not move beyond this kind of thinking to think the ontological difference in its primordiality: Being (namely presencing itself) and beings (that which comes-to-*presence* in any form).

5 September 1968

Heidegger considers further the theme of the 'danger of the ontological difference.' He restates the central point from the last seminar that 'all metaphysics indeed moves within the [ontological] difference (this is constantly stressed, in particular by Aquinas), but no metaphysics recognizes this difference in the dimension that it unfolds *as* difference.' (24:310). That is, all metaphysics, in one way or another, thinks the difference between beings in their beingness, but metaphysics does not think the *originary* difference between Being (No-thing) unfolding *as* beings in their beingness.

V. Seminar in Le Thor, 1969

2 September 1969

In the opening seminar of a new year, Heidegger again poses the central question: 'What does the "question of Being" mean?' And again, he distinguishes his concern from the proper concern of metaphysics:

> One says 'being' and from the outset one understands the word metaphysically, i.e., from out of metaphysics. However, in metaphysics and its tradition, 'being' means: that which determines a being [*das Seiende*] insofar as it is a being. As a result, metaphysically the question of Being means: the question concerning a being *as* a being [*Seienden als Seiendem*]. (35:326)

He explains that the originary Greek experience of a being was as *phenomenon*, pure appearing or 'what shows itself from itself.' In the most fundamental sense, a being is 'pure phenomenon' that is 'named' or made manifest in language by the human being. But when naming becomes 'making a proposition,' a being becomes the about-which-something-is-said; a being becomes (in the Greek) *hypokeimenon*, the subject of predication (or the subject of attributes). In modern philosophy, as in Kant's philosophy, 'phenomenon' is narrowed further to mean a mental 'object' for a 'subject.' Heidegger sums up this difference simply:

'For the Greeks, things appear. For Kant, things appear to me' (36:329).

The Greeks experienced the 'overabundance' (*die Überfülle*) and 'excess' (*das Übermaß*) of the appearance or presence of beings (38:331). They resided generally 'in the midst of phenomena,' and philosophy – what he calls a 'hyper-Greek' way of existing – was born of the 'wonder' about this overwhelming thrust of presencing. The Greek philosophers were 'compelled to ask the question concerning what is present *as* what is present [*Anwesenden als Anwesendem*].' But even among the Greeks, this question soon devolved into the fundamental metaphysical question about 'the being of beings,' which he again renders as *das Sein des Seienden* (rather than more precisely as *die Seiendheit des Seienden*). Even among the Greeks, the question concerning 'Being as Being' – his question, *die Sache* – was never posed as such. Yet, though the Greek thinkers did not come 'so far as to pose the *question of aletheia* (as such),' or the question of 'Being *as Being*,' still, *aletheia* was 'visible' to them 'as *logos*, and *logos* means, much more originarily than 'to speak': *to let* presenc(ing) [*Anwesen lassen*]' (39:332). I translate *Anwesen* as 'presenc(ing)' here because Heidegger uses *Anwesen* in this particular formulation *not as the name for Being as Being (Being itself)*, but rather, as the marker for *what* emerges into presence – beings in their beingness. Thus, Heidegger's position is that Being as Being *lets* presenc(ing), that is, *lets* beings. The Greek thinkers, who in their attentiveness were 'more Greek than the Greeks,' had a glancing insight into Being *as Being*, Being as *Aletheia*, Being as *Logos* – and that also meant Being as *Anwesen lassen*.

But with Plato this insight gave way to a metaphysical way of seeing. Plato names the 'being of beings' *eidos*, and though this is a metaphysical answer to 'the metaphysical question,' it remains nonetheless related to the originary Greek experience of a being as phenomenon in the sense of what shows itself from itself. In other words, *eidos* must be understood as the pure, 'never absencing' presence (*Anwesenheit*) of what becomes present. Plato's (in)sight thus became fixed on the sheer appearance of what appears, and he named the 'being of beings' (or more precisely said, the beingness of beings) *eidos* or pure appearance (*Aussehen, Anwesenheit*). Furthermore, Plato's understanding of the 'difference' between *eidos* (the essential feature of something) and *eidolon* (the particular entity) is no more than a metaphysical difference in the consideration of *beings* and by no means the originary (ontological) difference. *Eidos* (as *Seiendheit*) is *a being*, Heidegger insists, but a being understood more in the verbal sense of *das Seiend* (retaining an aspect of dynamic appearing) than in the later static, substantive metaphysical sense, which he refers to simply as *das Seiende* (40:333).

4 September 1969

A lengthy discussion, but for our purposes two comments deserve highlighting. In the first, Heidegger articulates clearly and explicitly that the phrase *das Sein des Seienden* means *die Seiendheit des Seienden*:

> According to the [philosophical] tradition, the 'question of Being' means the question concerning the being of beings [*das Sein des Seienden*], in other words: the question concerning the beingness of beings [*die Seiendheit des Seienden*], in which a being is determined in regard to its being-a-being [*Seiendseins*]. This question is *the* question of metaphysics. (46:344)

We have, then, confirmation that for the Heidegger of these seminars the phrase *das Sein des Seienden* had become no more than a marker for the essential matter for thought in metaphysics, *die Seiendheit des Seienden*. Nevertheless, as we noted earlier, this does not *also* mean that he had abandoned the word *Sein* for *die Sache selbst*, for in the very next passage he maintains that 'the question of Being as Being [*Sein als Sein*]' has been his fundamental question going all the way back to *Being and Time*:

> With *Being and Time*, however, the 'question of Being' receives an entirely other meaning [from the metaphysical tradition]. Here it concerns the question of Being as Being. The question becomes thematic in *Being and Time* under the name of the 'question of the meaning of Being.'

He may have abandoned the phrase *das Sein des Seienden* as a marker for *die Sache selbst* in these seminars, but certainly not the name *Sein*.

The second comment of special interest offers some confirmation of the 'classical' reading of his much debated 'turn' (*die Kehre*) in thinking after *Being and Time*. Heidegger observes, according to the protocol:

> The thinking that proceeds after *Being and Time*, in that it gives up the word 'meaning of Being' in favor of 'truth of Being,' henceforth emphasizes the openness of Being itself, rather than the openness of Dasein in regard to this openness of Being. This signifies 'the turn' [*die Kehre*], in which thinking always more decidedly turns to Being as Being. (47:345)

11 September 1969

This session is especially important, and it challenges us with some puzzling statements that need clarification. The discussion opens with Heidegger restating a familiar theme: Being and Nothing are the 'same' in the sense that Being is not a being, no-thing. He expresses this paratactically in the following way: 'Being: Nothing: The Same' (58:363). Being is 'entirely other than a being,' but at the same time, Being is that 'through which alone the particular being *is*.' He adds that we can name Being as origin, 'assuming that all ontic-causal overtones are excluded.' Being is 'the appropriating event [*das Ereignis*] of Being [that is, as belonging to Being] as condition for the arrival of beings: Being lets beings come to presence [*das Sein läßt das Seiende anwesen*]' (59:363). This line of thinking is perfectly clear: Being *as* origin (*Ursprung*) *as* appropriating event (*Ereignis*) lets all beings appear or become present.

He adds another layer to his understanding of Being:

> It is a matter here of understanding that the deepest meaning of Being is *letting* [*das Lassen*]. Letting beings be, this is the non-causal meaning of 'letting' in 'Time and Being.' This 'letting' is something fundamentally different from 'doing.' The text 'Time and Being' attempted to think this 'letting' still more originarily as 'giving.'
>
> The *giving* meant here speaks in the expression *Es gibt*. (59:363)

Let us take careful note of Heidegger's words – and he could not have been more explicit: The 'deepest meaning' of Being is *as* letting beings and, thus, in turn, *as* giving beings (Being *as Es gibt*). Being is *letting* beings; Being is *giving* beings. Now he goes on to warn that the expression '"*Es gibt*" is not safe from an ontic conception.' If it is construed with an emphasis on the sheer presence or presentness (*Anwesenheit*) of beings, then the expression is ontically understood as the giving of *something*. On the other hand, the emphasis may fall on the 'letting itself.' The expression then 'has the precise meaning of *letting* presenc(ing) [*Lassen das Anwesen*].' Again, I translate *das Anwesen* as 'presenc(ing)' in this formulation because Heidegger once more uses this word in a particular way, that is, not as the name of Being itself (presencing itself) but as a marker for *what* becomes present in presencing. He is highlighting the *letting* (*Lassen*) of presenc(ing) so that, in his words, 'it is no longer the presence [*Anwesenheit*] of a being which draws one's attention, but the ground which that being covers over, in order to make itself independent from it: letting as such' (59:364). And the *letting* of presenc(ing) – letting as such – is precisely Being itself, Being as Being. Again, I must highlight what he has explicitly stated in this session (some six years *after* his oft-cited lecture 'Time and Being'): 'the deepest meaning of Being is letting.'

Thus, his unfolding of the meaning of Being in this seminar, carefully and properly understood, is altogether consistent with the 'classical paradigm.' Being, or *Being as Being* – as Heidegger repeatedly names *die Sache* in these seminars – is to be understood as *letting* (*das Lassen*) beings be. He summarizes three meanings of 'letting be.' The first meaning 'refers to that which is,' the particular being that appears. The second meaning draws attention more to the appearance itself of what appears, and this 'concerns an interpretation of being of the sort given by metaphysics.' In other words, in the second sense, one is more concerned with *die Seiendheit des Seienden*, traditionally construed as the 'essence' of things, which is the core concern of metaphysical thinking. The third meaning, the one that he apparently identifies as his own, maintains that:

> the stress is now decisively placed upon the *letting* itself, that which *lets* presenc(ing). Since it lets (releases?) presenc(ing), which means that it lets being [*es läßt das Sein*], this third emphasis falls on the *epoché* of Being [itself]. In this third meaning, one stands before Being *as* Being, and no longer before one of the forms of its dispensation [*Geschicks*]. (60:365)

Here is where another difficulty arises. Heidegger's sense is clear, but his language is not helpful. In effect, he is stating his position in a mind-aching way: Being as Being allows being; in the German, it would be rendered *Sein als Sein läßt das Sein*. This is not just gibberish, of course. His meaning is apparent enough: Being as Being (also understood as the *epoché* of Being itself)[15] allows all forms of beings, all beings (*das Seiende*) in their beingness (*die Seiendheit*), to come to presence. Even so, we must admit that he certainly risks unintelligibility by letting the word *Sein* (in the formulation *es läßt das Sein*) stand in for both *Seiende* and *Seiendheit* (likewise *Anwesende* and *Anwesenheit*). This confusion is brought to a head in an additional comment he makes, a comment that has received attention by Sheehan and other commentators. According to the protocol, Heidegger adds:

> If the emphasis is: *to let* presenc(ing), there is no longer room even for the

name of being [*Sein*]. *Letting* is then pure *giving*, which itself refers back to the It [of *Es gibt*] that gives, which is understood as *Ereignis*. (60:365)

Does this comment reveal that Heidegger ultimately abandoned 'the name of being' for *die Sache selbst*? No, not at all. We must consider the remark in the context of the whole discussion of this seminar. Insofar as he sometimes uses *Sein* (and *Anwesen)* in the seminar to refer to the various forms of *Seiendheit* (and *Anwesenheit*) that came to pass in the history of metaphysics, then indeed there can be no 'room' for the name 'being' in thinking the fundamental matter of the *letting* or *giving* of beings in their beingness. But insofar as he explicitly and precisely names his ownmost concern *Being as Being* (*Sein als Sein) as letting and as giving – which in turn is to be understood as appropriating event (das Ereignis) –* then quite clearly he did not abandon the name Being for *die Sache selbst*. What this seminar discussion reveals more than anything else is how Heidegger struggled – but also persisted – right to the very end of his life to set apart in language his understanding of the originary, fundamental, unifying meaning of Being (Being as Being, Being itself) from the long-standing and deeply ingrained metaphysical understanding of being(ness).

The discussion continues with Heidegger further clarifying the meaning of *das Ereignis*, and the same considerations we have addressed come into play. To think *das Ereignis* is to 'step back' from thinking about 'the various epochs of the history of being [*Geschichte des Seins*].' Here again, he means more precisely that the 'history of being' is the history of the epochal renderings of the beingness (*Seiendheit*) of beings because he explicitly adds that these 'are the epochs of the various ways in which *presence* [*Anwesenheit*] dispenses itself to Western human beings' (61:367) from the Greek period to the contemporary period (and continuing forward). As he sees it, then, thinking must 'go beyond' this history in order to think 'Being *as* Being,' which even the Greeks could not quite achieve (61:367). Thinking that goes beyond metaphysics thinks *das Ereignis* as the temporal giving – which also withdraws itself from view – of beings (including human beings) in their beingness as this comes to pass (in language) in all the different historical epochs. Thus, thinking *das Ereignis* is thinking Being as Being. And by virtue of this thinking, we become aware that 'the history of being[ness] has not so much reached its end, as that it now appears *as* the history of being[ness].' One important lesson we must take away from this seminar discussion is that Sheehan, Maly, and several other Heidegger commentators, especially more recently, have simply claimed too much for the notion of *das Ereignis*. Thinking *das Ereignis* is not more fundamental than thinking Being as Being; rather, fundamental thinking is mindful of Being as Being (Being itself) *as das Ereignis*.[16]

The seminar concludes with Heidegger reflecting on the special significance of the human being – and restating an old theme:

> Thus, the human being necessarily belongs to, and has the place in, the openness (and currently in the forgottenness) of Being. Being, however, for its opening, needs the human being as the there [*das Da*] of its manifestation. (63:370)

VI. Seminar in Zähringen, 1973

The group resumed the seminars for the last time in 1973 in Heidegger's home in Zähringen, on the western slope of the Black Forest. They met on Thursday, Friday, and Saturday, 6, 7, and 8 September. Heidegger was nearly eighty-four at the time; he died in May 1976 at the age of eighty-six.

6 September 1973

What is striking is that yet again, the *Grundfrage* for Heidegger as well as for the seminar members is 'the question of Being' (64:372). Heidegger attempts to answer two questions posed by Jean Beaufret. The first concerns the question of Being in Husserl's thinking; the second asks Heidegger to assess the significance of his 'analysis of the world-around' (*Umweltanalyse*) in *Being and Time*.

The group begins with the second question. According to the protocol, Heidegger makes the point that his analysis of the 'worldhood of the world' in *Being and Time* was an essential advance because 'for the first time in the history of philosophy, being-in-the-world is discovered as the primary mode of encountering beings.' Yet he restates his previous assessment (from the 1929 *On the Essence of Ground*) that this analysis 'remains of subordinate significance' in the context of the larger project of *Being and Time*; and he recalls that the 'guiding aim' of *Being and Time* was 'to raise anew *the question of the meaning of Being.*' The protocol states firmly: 'It is therefore necessary to return always to the core of this thinking [in *Being and Time*], namely, the question of Being' (64:373).

Heidegger explains that the 'question of Being' means 'the question concerning the meaning of Being,' and according to the protocol:

> Heidegger explains still more precisely: after *Being and Time*, the expression 'meaning' is replaced by 'truth' – so that the question of Being, now understood as the question concerning the truth of Being, can no longer be taken as a metaphysical question. (64:373)

He appears to make it perfectly clear that the defining question of his lifetime of thought concerned Being and that his question about Being was never the same as the metaphysical question about the beingness of beings, *Sein* as *Seiendheit*, as he suggests some had (persistently) construed it over the years. The protocol clarifies that 'metaphysics investigates the being of beings [*Sein des Seienden*],' and we know from the previous seminars that by this expression is meant precisely the 'beingness of beings' (*Seiendheit des Seienden*). According to the protocol, what is proper to Heidegger's concern is 'the *truth* of Being, where truth is to be understood from preserving, in which Being as Being [*Sein als Sein*] is safeguarded' (65:373). In other words, his question was always concerned with thinking *through* the metaphysical question in order to ask about the meaning of Being that encompasses or enfolds the metaphysical meaning of the beingness of beings. As Heidegger himself puts this in the discussion:

> In the question concerning the meaning of Being, what one asks about [*das Befragte*] is being, that is, the being[ness] of beings [*das Sein des Seienden*]; that toward which one is inquiring [*das Erfragte*] is the meaning of Being – which later will be called the truth of Being. (67:377–8)

Let us sharpen the point by way of summary: Heidegger's fundamental matter for thought, from the beginning to the end of his path of thinking, concerned the *Being (Sein/Seyn) of beings (Seiende) in their beingness (Seiendheit)*.[17] His overriding concern was to clarify the unifying meaning of Being that remained implicit and unquestioned in the meaning of the beingness of beings made manifest by Plato and Aristotle long ago, and thereby to arrive at the 'ground' of the ancient and venerable tradition of metaphysical thinking. The seminar protocol, read aloud in Heidegger's presence, states the matter of his defining question simply and emphatically:

We must emphasize again and again that the only question that has ever moved Heidegger is the question of Being: What does 'Being' mean? (67:377)

7 September 1973

Heidegger engages the question: 'What is the relation between consciousness and Dasein (better yet: between the being-of-consciousness and being-the-there-of-the-open-expanse)?' As in earlier seminars, he credits Husserl for opening new possibilities for thinking; but he concludes that in the end, Husserl could not break through the Cartesian model of subjectness. 'Thus,' Heidegger observes, 'despite intentionality, Husserl remains trapped in immanence – and the consequence of this position is the *Méditations cartésiennes*' (70:382). He takes a stronger stand against Marx and the Marxist understanding of 'the self-production of man and society.' This is an understanding of the human being that is entirely shaped by the contemporary dispensation of Enframing (*das Gestell*) characterized by 'the totality of all the modes of positing that are imposed upon the human being to the extent that it [the human being] ek-sists today' (74:388). The next day, 8 September, he adds that 'it is from this perspective and from this vision that I can say that regarding Marx, the position of the most extreme nihilism is reached.' And he emphasizes that this means only that 'Being as Being is *nothing* (*nihil*) anymore for human beings' (77:393).

According to Heidegger, the significance of his own understanding of Dasein in *Being and Time* is that 'immanence, here, is broken through and through.' And he adds:

> Da-sein is essentially ek-static. One must understand this ek-static character not only with respect to that which presences, in the sense of what holds its place over against us, but also as ek-stasis in relation to the having-been, to the present, and to the future. (71:383–4)

He believes that he has thought Husserl's notion of intentionality 'through to its ground' by uncovering 'the ek-stasis of Da-sein.' 'In a word,' he observes, 'one needs to recognize that consciousness is grounded in Da-sein.' Yet he adds that he 'would no longer speak simply of ek-stasis, but [also] of in-standing in the clearing [*Inständigkeit in der Lichtung*].' Dasein must be understood as both 'standing in the three ek-stases' and 'preserving and maintaining Being through the entirety of Dasein' (71:384). We hear once more of the special cor-relation of Dasein and Being.

8 September 1973

According to the protocol, the final session returned to 'the question concerning access [*Zugang*] to Being' (77:394). To proceed, Heidegger read a short paper on Parmenides that he had composed. The protocol summarizes his remarks and the ensuing discussion. The text authored by Heidegger was included (as an appendix) in the German edition of the *Four Seminars* along with a brief preface provided by him. These formal written remarks were among his last before his death, so it is understandable that some commentators attempt to find in them some significant breakthrough. There is the temptation to read into his brief commentary one last dramatic revelation just as the final curtain was coming down. But such a theatrical script is not supported by the manuscript itself, I think.

Heidegger returns to the fragments of Parmenides that he had engaged so many times over the course of his life. In particular, this brief elucidation recalls his extended commentary on the fragments in one of his most important lecture courses, *What Is Called Thinking?* (1951–2, published in 1954). In Part II of this earlier discussion, he gave close attention to Parmenides' words in Fragment 6: *chre to legein te noein t' eon emmenai*, which speaks of *eon* ('being') and *emmenai* ('to be'), the archaic Greek forms of *on* and *einai*. Heidegger rewrites the line paratactically so that the final two words appear as *eon: emmenai*. As he sees it, *eon*, 'being,' the participle, is the key word; it is 'the participle which gathers all other participles into itself' (WT, 221:225). As a participle, it has both a nominal meaning (a being) and a verbal meaning (be-ing). Parmenides' words, then, remind us to take to 'heart' (*noein*) both senses of the word *eon*, or as Heidegger puts it, the '*emmenai* in *eon*, the Being of beings' (WT, 224:228). *Eon emmenai* means 'beings in their Being.' Properly understood, this Parmenidean fragment brings into view the originary twofold of Being and beings, which grounds the twofold of the beingness of beings that has structured metaphysical thinking ever since Plato.

But Heidegger takes another step. In order to get closer to the Greek experience of 'beings in their Being,' he further elucidates the meaning of the Greek words *eon* and *emmenai* (and the later form *einai*). 'Heard with Greek ears,' *eon* means *das Anwesende*, that which appears or is present, and *emmenai* means *anwesen*, presencing (WT, 233:237). That is, *eon emmenai* means what is present (to Dasein) in its presencing or in its 'rising from unconcealedness' – and this is the primordial meaning of 'the Being of beings' or of 'beings in their Being' that was glimpsed and hinted at by Parmenides and Heraclitus at the dawn of Western thinking. Yet 'in subsequent European thinking,' the focus shifted to a consideration of what is present in its sheer 'presence' (*Anwesenheit*) or later in its 'objectness' (*Gegenständigkeit*) or in its 'realness' (*Wirklichkeit*) (WT, 238:241). Precisely this consideration is at the core of the metaphysical tradition of thinking. Metaphysics considers, in one way or another, the beingness of beings and not 'the Being of beings' as *'das Anwesen des Anwesenden,'* the presencing of what is present. Metaphysics lost sight of the Being of beings as

> unconcealedness, the rising from unconcealedness, the emergence into unconcealedness, the coming and going away, the lingering, the gathering, the radiance, the rest, the hidden suddenness of possible disappearance. (WT, 237:241)

We now move ahead twenty years to the Zähringen seminar in 1973 and the text on Parmenides that Heidegger presented, and we ask: Is there anything in his brief elucidation that is *fundamentally* different from the earlier one in *What Is Called Thinking?* Not at all; there are only minor modifications in his discourse. Let us first focus our attention on Heidegger's text. He reflects on Parmenides' words *esti gar einai* from Fragment 6 and observes that a translation such as '(it) is: namely being' misses the 'Greek saying of the words.' 'Thought in a Greek manner,' he states, *'einai* says: "presencing" [*anwesen*]' (95:405).[18] Therefore, Parmenides' words *esti gar einai* mean 'presences, namely presencing' (*anwest nämlich anwesen*) or 'presences, presencing (itself)' (*anwest anwesen [selbst]*), which is a profoundly meaningful 'tautology.' That is, these words convey the most primordial Greek glancing insight into presencing (emerging, unfolding) *itself*. Not simply what emerges into presence, but presencing itself.

According to Heidegger, Parmenides' 'fundamental word' that expresses the fundamental matter for thinking is *eon*, the verbal participle that says simultaneously *'anwesend: anwesen selbst,'* 'presenc(ing): presencing itself' (95:405).[19] *Eon* names (1) what-is-present (*anwesend*, presenc[ing]) in (2) its very presencing (*anwesen selbst*, presencing itself), and this *Ur*-phenomenon was also named by the Greeks *aletheia*. He adds that this same matter for thought is said again by Parmenides in Fragment 6: *eon emmenai*. *Eon emmenai* is an explicitation of the meaning of the participle *eon;* that is, *eon emmenai* means 'anwesend: anwesen,' 'presenc(ing): presencing' (96:406). Thinking is thus most profoundly and most originarily a 'glimpsing' (*Erblicken*) of what comes-to-presence (*anwesend*) in its very *coming*-to-presence (*anwesen*). As he puts it further:

> Pure glimpsing: 'presenc(ing): presencing itself' – or not-glimpsing, that is here – at the origin of Western thinking – the question. (97:406)

But is not the glimpsing of 'presenc(ing): presencing itself' the glimpsing of beings in their Being, of Being itself, of Being as Being, the single defining thought of Heidegger's lifetime of thinking? Indeed, I think this is precisely how the text is to be read. Yet Kenneth Maly, for one, does not think so. He proposes that Heidegger's final position is that *Sein* is no longer the appropriate name for *die Sache selbst*. Regarding this particular text, Maly concludes that for Heidegger, 'in fact, the word *being* no longer names the *Sache*.'[20] His position rests primarily on one passage in Heidegger's text:

> According to Parmenides, the name of the core issue of the matter for thinking is: *to eon*. This fundamental word of his thinking names neither 'beings' [*das Seiende*] nor simply [*bloß*] 'being' [*das Sein*]. *To eon* must be thought verbally as [a] participle. Then it says: 'presenc(ing): presencing itself.' (95:405)

It seems, however, that Maly overreads this one statement to make the case that Heidegger ultimately withdrew the name Being for *die Sache*. Again, we must consider Heidegger's comment in the context of the seminar and of the series of seminars. As we have discussed, throughout the seminars he uses *das Sein des Seienden* and sometimes simply *das Sein* to refer to the beingness (*die Seiendheit*) of beings, the core concern of metaphysics. Yet when he speaks *strictly* about the fundamental matter for thinking, *die Sache selbst*, he uses the expressions *das Sein selbst* (Being itself) or especially *das Sein als Sein* (Being as Being). His comment in question must be read, then, with these considerations in mind. He states that Parmenides' fundamental word *eon*, which names the fundamental matter for thought, names neither 'beings' nor simply 'being.' Note carefully: Heidegger writes, and I emphasize, 'nor *simply* "being."' That one qualifying word *bloß* – simply or merely – is crucial and must not be overlooked. In the protocol, this same qualification is made, but the word used is *lediglich*.[21] These qualifiers are the important clues that Heidegger's meaning here is more likely that *die Sache* cannot be named *das Sein* understood *simply* or *merely* or even *purely* as beingness (*die Seiendheit*) as variously named in the long history of metaphysical thinking, what he calls elsewhere 'the history of being[ness],' *die Geschichte des Seins*.[22] And therefore, his statement asks us to consider that Parmenides' word *eon* does not name *simply* beingness in any form from any epoch, but rather Being itself, Being as Being, Being as *aletheia*, Being as 'presenc(ing): presencing itself.' In fact, significantly, Heidegger goes on to say, according to the protocol, that one finds in the words of Parmenides' Fragment 8, verse 29, 'a letting-be-seen [*Zeignis*] that shows Being [*das Sein*]' (79:398). We realize, then, that Heidegger's text certainly does not renounce the name Being; rather, it invites us to consider yet one more way of articulating the 'meaning' of Being, the 'truth' of Being, the 'place' of Being, namely, as 'presenc(ing): presencing itself.'[23]

Conclusion

The protocol states that after Heidegger finished reading and commenting on his text, he added a few remarks, including this observation: 'I name the thinking here in question tautological thinking. It is the primordial meaning of phenomenology' (80:399). What is most reasonable to conclude is that this 'tautological' thinking, this primordial phenomenological thinking that holds in view 'presenc(ing): presencing itself,' is none other than *thinking about Being – Being itself, Being as Being* – the focal point of all *Four Seminars* – and indeed, the focal point of Heidegger's lifetime of thought. The protocol tells us further that when Heidegger finished speaking there was 'silence' among the members of the group. Jean Beaufret then posed to him a final question about Heraclitus in relation to Parmenides. We should not be surprised that Heidegger's concluding response as recorded in the seminar protocol was – fittingly enough – a thought that names Being:

> But if one is able to read Heraclitus on the basis of the Parmenidean tautology, then he himself appears very near to the same tautology; he himself appears on the path of a singular approach offering access to Being. (81:400)

Appendix
Last Reflections on the *Seinsfrage:*
Heidegger's letter, 11 April 1976

In the *Four Seminars* (1966–73), Heidegger and the seminar participants repeatedly reaffirmed that the question of the originary, fundamental, unifying meaning of *Being* was the central question of his lifetime of thinking and that Being (Being itself, Being as such, Being as Being) is the name for the fundamental matter for thought (*die Sache Selbst*). Furthermore, if we consider Heidegger's public correspondence over the last several years of his life, his statements are equally clear. So, for example, in an open letter to Prof. Frings, who presided over the Heidegger Symposium in Chicago in 1966, Heidegger maintained unequivocally:

> I would be very glad if it were possible to orient the discussion at once – in the first moments of the symposium – purely and decisively toward the matter [*die Sache*; for thought]. In that way, there would develop, instead of a 'Heidegger Symposium,' a *Colloquium on the Question of Being.* For it is this question – and it alone – that determines the way of my thought and its boundaries.[1]

In November 1974, he sent a 'Greeting' to the participants at a symposium held in Beirut, Lebanon, who had gathered to honour him in the year of his eighty-fifth birthday. In his letter, Heidegger wrote that our coming to understand the origin of the 'danger' posed by modern technicity 'requires that we ask the question about the proper character of Being as such.'[2] He repeated almost the entire text of this letter – including this very same line – in another 'Greeting' he sent to a Japanese publication, also in November 1974.[3] And in an open letter written just before his death in 1976, he once again put the matter decisively: 'The question with which I greet you is the only question that, even up to the present hour, I seek to inquire into ever more inquiringly. One knows this question under the title of the "question of Being."'

Heidegger dated this letter, one of his very last written statements, 11 April 1976 from Freiburg im Breisgau.[4] Six weeks later, on 26 May 1976, he died at the age of eighty-six. Since, as we have noted, in recent years some Heidegger scholars have put into question the centrality of the name and theme of Being in his thought, his reflections on the *Seinsfrage* in this letter take on a special importance and significance today that they did not have thirty years ago and in subsequent years.

Thus, the time is ripe for another look at this letter, a new translation of which follows below. I offer several brief observations on its content that are relevant to the current discussion about the place of the *Seinsfrage* in his thought: (1) Heidegger clearly and emphatically identifies 'the question of Being' as the fundamental question of his lifetime of thinking; (2) he distinguishes between 'the being of beings,' the core concern of metaphysical questioning, and 'Being itself,' his own proper concern, which metaphysical thinking, from its origins, has not been capable of addressing as such; (3) he makes the point that to think the question of Being properly is also to think *'aletheia* as such'; (4) he does not mention *das Ereignis* in this particular context of naming the fundamental matter for thought; and (5) he does not suggest, in any manner, that there is a matter for thought more originary or fundamental than 'Being itself'/*'aletheia* as such.'

The letter was sent to the participants of the tenth annual Heidegger Circle meeting held at DePaul University in Chicago.

Greetings to the participants of the 10th Colloquium
May 14–16, 1976 in Chicago

Thinking people greet one another by posing to each other questions.

The question with which I greet you is the only question that, even up to the present hour, I seek to inquire into ever more inquiringly. One knows this question under the title 'the question of Being.'

For us, this question can be asked, first of all, only by way of a discussion of Western-European metaphysics, and in particular with respect to the forgottenness of Being that has held sway in metaphysics from the beginning.

In the metaphysical question concerning the being of beings [*Sein des Seienden*], Being itself [*das Sein selbst*] conceals itself regarding its own proper character and locality.[5]

This self-concealing of Being is different in the individual epochs (cf. *Holzwege, Der Spruch des Anaximander*, p. 296ff).[6]

The forgottenness of Being in the age of the world civilization imprinted by technology is especially pressing for the posing of the question of Being.

From the variety of questions that are necessary here, the following one may be stated:

Is modern natural science – as it is maintained – the foundation of modern technology or is it itself already the basic form of technological thinking, the determining fore-conception of technological representing and its constant intrusiveness in the implementing and establishing machination of modern technicity?[7]

Whose[8] increasingly accelerating 'efficiency' drives the forgottenness of Being in the extreme, and thus lets the question of Being appear as insignificant and superfluous.

In the few days of the Colloquium, you will not be able to answer, nor probably even be able to pose adequately, this question concerning the relation of the modern natural sciences to modern technicity.

But it would be already sufficient and beneficial if each of the participants gave attention, each in his own way, to this question and took it up as a suggestion for his area of research.

So, in this way, the question of Being may become more pressing and experienceable as what it is in truth:

To think in its own proper character – *aletheia* as such – which in the legacy from the beginning of the history of Being has remained necessarily still unthought in and for this beginning; and thereby [by bringing *aletheia* into such thoughtfulness] to prepare the possibility of a transformed sojourn in the world for human beings.

Martin Heidegger
Freiburg i. Br.
am 11. April 1976

Notes for Translation

1 *Gesamtausgabe* (hereafter GA), *Band 16, Reden und andere Zeugnisse eines Lebensweges* (Frankfurt am Main: Vittorio Klostermann, 2000), 684. Translation by William J. Richardson in *Heidegger and the Quest For Truth*, ed. Manfred S. Frings (Chicago: Quadrangle, 1968), 17 (slightly modified).
2 Ibid., 743. In Günther Neske and Emil Kettering, eds., *Martin Heidegger and National Socialism*, trans. Lisa Harries (New York: Paragon House, 1990), 254 (modified).
3 Ibid., 745.
4 Ibid., 747–8. The present translation follows the formatting of the letter in this volume. Heidegger's letter in the German and an earlier English translation (unsigned) appeared over thirty years ago in *Research in Phenomenology* 7 (1977): 1–4. There are several imprecisions in this earlier translation; the letter is also formatted differently.
5 In this context, the phrase 'the being of beings' (*Sein des Seienden*) in this line means more precisely the beingness of beings (*die Seiendheit des Seienden*), the core concern of metaphysical questioning from its origins. For Heidegger, the fundamental task for thought is to think 'Being itself' (*das Sein selbst*) – that is, the Being of beings in their beingness. Note also that the earlier translation omitted the significant word 'itself' in his naming of '*das Sein selbst*' in this line.
6 Heidegger included this citation.
7 He uses both words – *die Technologie* and *die Technik* – in the letter. Some scholars, with some justification, discern a difference in the meaning of these terms in Heidegger's thinking and prefer to translate *die Technologie* as 'technology' and *die Technik* as 'technicity.' I follow this convention, though admittedly, the difference is hardly apparent in this letter.
8 His reference beginning this sentence ('*Deren*'; 'Whose') is not clear, so I leave it simply as it is written.

2 *Ereignis*: (Only) Another Name for Being Itself

The word, wherein the essence of the historical human being is given over to itself, is the word of Beyng.

Lecture course on Heraclitus, 1943

Since the publication of Heidegger's 1936–8 collection of reflections titled *Beiträge zur Philosophie (Vom Ereignis)* in 1989, there has been a trend in Heidegger studies towards overstating the significance of the notion of *das Ereignis* in his thought.[1] To be sure, Heidegger considered that his arrival at the name *Ereignis* was an important event in his thinking and that this particular word had a special power and nuance to make manifest *die Sache selbst*, the fundamental matter for thought.[2] Even so, there is neither sufficient nor convincing textual evidence to maintain that he ever considered *Ereignis* as a *more* fundamental matter for thought than *das Sein* – that is, Being thought in an originary and fundamental way as the temporal-spatial, finite and negatived, unconcealing of beings (*das Seiende*) in their beingness (*die Seiendheit*) as made manifest meaningfully by *Dasein* in language.[3] (Again, note that I retain the convention of writing Being (with a capital B) for this usage only.)[4] In fact, to the contrary, he was clear and emphatic right to the end of his life that the single, defining concern of his path of thinking regarded the originary, fundamental, unifying meaning of Being, named by him over the many years as Beyng (*das Seyn*), Being itself (*das Sein selbst*), Being as such (*das Sein als solches*), and Being as Being (*das Sein als Sein*).[5] Certainly, there is no denying the importance of the notion of *Ereignis* in his thought, but its *significance* has been overworked and overstated by several Heidegger scholars in recent years. In other words, I think that if we examine Heidegger's words carefully, we find that he understood *Ereignis* to be (only) another name for Being itself.

I. The Word

How shall we translate this word *das Ereignis*, with all of its resonances, into English? The discussion has continued for decades now and there is no end in sight. We have many options to choose from (along with the additional option of capitalization in each case): 'e-vent,' 'event,' 'appropriation,' 'event of appropriation,' 'appropriating event,' 'appropriative event,' 'the disclosure of appropriation,' and even 'the disclosive appropriating event.' Of course, there is also the coinage 'enowning,' which is preferred by the translators of *Beiträge* (*Contributions*) and thus currently much in vogue. With so many translations in play, the reasonable solution moving forward, I suggest, is simply to leave Heidegger's word untranslated and allow it to resonate as it will, just as it has become acceptable in the scholarship to leave untranslated certain words such as Angst and Dasein. The difficulty with this solution, though, seems to be that though there is something like a consensus about what is suggested by Angst and Dasein, there does not appear to be a similar agreement about the word *Ereignis*. That is, I suspect that the continuing need to find the right translation for *Ereignis* reflects our continuing need to try to circumscribe its meaning and significance in Heidegger's thought. I will come back to this issue in the chapter's conclusion, but in what follows, I am concerned with presenting the textual evidence of how Heidegger related *Ereignis* to Being. And for this purpose, it makes the most sense just to let the word be.

II. Overview

To begin, a few general observations on the history of the term *Ereignis* in Heidegger's thinking are in order. Recent scholarship has taken into account the appearance of the word in his very early 1919 lecture course and in scattered places in his work of the 1920s.[6] Nevertheless, by Heidegger's own testimony, he worked out the notion especially during the years 1936–8 in the series of unpublished meditations we know as *Beiträge*. In the following years, from roughly 1938 to 1944, he continued to feature the term *Ereignis* in a number of reflections, none of which he saw fit to publish in his lifetime. In recent years, most of these writings have been published in the *Gesamtausgabe*, and as I see it, their appearance has tended to skew the scholarly discussion about the development of his thought. That is, the intense focus on these sometimes brilliant, sometimes inscrutable musings featuring the notion of *Ereignis* has relegated to the background his other writings and commentaries of this same period that address the meaning of Being – indeed, with barely a mention of *Ereignis*. These texts include the important commentaries on Aristotle and Plato, 'On the Essence and Concept of *physis* in Aristotle's *Physics* B 1' (1939, published 1958) and 'Plato's Doctrine of Truth' (1940, published 1942), and the lecture courses and commentaries on Parmenides (1942–3) and on Hölderlin's poetry (in particular, the poem 'The Ister,' 1942). Therefore, we must be careful to keep the picture broad enough to see that in these years 1936 to 1944, during which Heidegger was privately working out the set of themes related to *Ereignis*, he was also composing major statements that primarily posed and pursued the question of the originary, fundamental, and unifying meaning of Being.

In addition, Heidegger did not marginalize the *Seinsfrage* in favour of the thematization of *Ereignis* in the years following his burst of private *Ereignis*-writings. Quite to the contrary, between 1944 and 1956 he made only occasional formal references to *Ereignis* while he focused more intensely on the originary meaning of Being in an array of reflections, including the essays 'The Determination of Nihilism in Terms of the History of Being' (1944–6), 'Anaximander's Saying' (1946), 'Letter on Humanism' (1947), 'The Way Back into the Ground of Metaphysics' (1949), '*Logos* (Heraclitus, Fragment B 50)' (1951), and *On the Question of Being* (1956); his important lecture courses *What Is Called Thinking* (1951–2) and *The Principle of Reason* (1955–6); and the public lecture 'What Is That – Philosophy?' (1955). Now, it is true that in a period of a few years from roughly 1957 to 1962 he brought the term *Ereignis* into full public view and thematized the notion more frequently while speaking less about Being. This is the case in such major statements as 'The Principle of Identity' (1957) and 'The Way to Language' (1959), culminating with the lecture and seminars on 'Time and Being' in 1962. Yet even in these years, he did not neglect the question of Being altogether as, for example, in his lecture 'Kant's Thesis About Being' (1961).

Some commentators, focusing especially on the 1962 lecture 'Time and Being,' have suggested that from the early 1960s until his death in 1976 Heidegger subordinated the theme of Being to the notion of *Ereignis*; but again, I do not think that the textual evidence supports such a claim. In particular, he made the question of the meaning of

Being the central topic of his series of seminars with French colleagues during the years 1966 to 1973. As I highlighted in chapter 1, in these seminars – known as the *Four Seminars* – we find him returning again and again to the task of clarifying the meaning of Being, and the protocol text for one of the last sessions in Zähringen in 1973 sums up the matter clearly and firmly: 'We must emphasize again and again that the only question that has ever moved Heidegger is the question of Being: What does "Being" mean?'[7] In the *Four Seminars*, Heidegger made few references to *Ereignis*, and this is also true in his public correspondence over the last decade of his life, in which he continued to insist that the *Seinsfrage* was the single, defining question of his path of thinking. Indeed, in a public letter – one of his very last written statements before his death in May 1976 – he stated in no uncertain terms: 'The question with which I greet you is the only question that, even up to the present hour, I seek to inquire into ever more inquiringly. One knows this question under the title "the question of Being."'[8]

From my perspective, all of this suggests that Heidegger always considered *das Ereignis* to be only another name – a 'refreshed' name, a metaphysically untainted name – for Being (*eon*) as it was glimpsed and named by Parmenides and Heraclitus at the dawn of Western thinking. From the beginning to the end of his lifetime of thinking, he was concerned with illuminating Being in an originary and fundamental sense, which along the way he properly named Beyng, Being itself, Being as such, Being as Being; but he also arrived at other names – resonant names like *Ereignis* and *Lichtung* – that brought the same matter for thought into view. So, to adapt one of Heidegger's favourite rhetorical turns, I put it this way: Being and *Ereignis*: the Same (*das Selbe*), but not necessarily identical (*das Gleiche*) in all respects in a formal logical sense. However, it is not enough simply to state this; the textual evidence is both compelling and convincing.

III. The Early *Ereignis*-writings: 1936–1944

A. Beiträge zur Philosophie (Vom Ereignis), GA 65 (1936–8)

This manuscript, which has received so much attention in recent years, reads as a *private* work in progress, and one can certainly understand why Heidegger did not think of it as a finished, publishable text. His series of meditations rework and develop earlier themes in a boldly new and experimental (and strange) philosophical language that prominently features the word *Ereignis*. There are flashes of brilliance and clarity in the text, but also many dense and cryptic passages, not to mention a number of metaphors gone terribly awry, such as 'mood is the spraying [*Versprühung*] of the trembling [*Erzitterung*] of Beyng' (*Gesamtausgabe* [hereafter GA] 65, 21).

Given the difficulty of the manuscript's language and syntax, one must consider Emad and Maly's English translation a splendid achievement; on the other hand, their translation strategy often compounds the difficulties of the text. Their penchant for choosing the most idiosyncratic English equivalents makes the oddity of Heidegger's German read even more oddly in English. But this reservation aside, there is also the more important matter of their translating the oft-repeated *Wesen* and *Wesung* (especially in the phrase *Wesen / Wesung des Seyns*) as 'essential sway' and 'essential swaying.' The chief difficulty, it seems to me, is that these translations depart too fundamentally from the meaning of this key word *Wesen*, 'essence,' as Heidegger took it up into his own thinking. As he often noted, his effort was to draw out and emphasize the originary verbal sense of the word *Wesen*, and for this reason the English word 'essencing' may well be the most satisfactory translation. But if we keep in mind that over the course of his thinking he consistently understood 'essencing' in the fundamental phenomenological sense of 'presencing' (*anwesen*) *to Dasein*, then I think that the best case can be made for translating *Wesen/Wesung* as 'presencing,' understood properly (as Heidegger often maintained) in the full sense of positive *and* negatived appearing. 'Presencing' also has the advantage of staying close to his own words about the matter, such as in his statement in '*Das Wesen der Sprache*' (1957–8) that '"*Es west*" *meint: Es west an, während geht es uns an, be-wëgt und be-langt uns.*' ('"It essences" means: It presences, and abiding, it concerns us, moves us along the way, and summons us.')[9]

In addition, 'presencing' seems to me less problematical than other translations that have been adopted in recent years. 'Emerging,' a frequent choice, more properly translates *Aufgehen*. 'Unfolding' is better reserved to translate *Entfaltung*; also, the word poses the difficulty of hinting at a making explicit of what is implicit, which might confuse Heidegger's meaning with something like a Neoplatonic philosophical position. Similarly, 'happening' and 'prevailing' translate other important words in Heidegger's discourse (*das Geschehen* and *das Walten*) and are better employed for this purpose. Finally, all phrases that turn the key word into an adjective such as 'essential happening,' 'essential unfolding,' 'essential swaying,' and so forth, not only take too much liberty with the text, but also introduce the unwanted implication that there is in contrast something like an *inessential* happening, unfolding, swaying of Beyng – which is certainly not Heidegger's meaning. For all these reasons, then, I think that 'presencing' is the preferable translation, but I admit that there is ample room for further discussion.[10]

In any case, our present concern is specifically with how Heidegger related *Ereignis* to Beyng (*das Seyn*). Throughout his manuscript, he uses the word *das Seyn*, the older spelling of the German word *das Sein*, to name the fundamental matter for thought – that is, Beyng understood not metaphysically but rather in an originary and fundamental way as the temporal granting of the various historical epochs in which being – or more precisely 'beingness' – has been given to be thought. What we find throughout the text is that whenever Heidegger speaks of Beyng and *Ereignis* together, he invariably elucidates one *in terms of the other* and, even more significantly, he also simply links the two with the copula 'is.' The citations are numerous; highlighting several key lines will suffice.[11] (Translations are my own, but I also include the page references to the Emad and Maly translation.):

> *Das Seyn west als das Ereignis.* (GA 65, 30)
> Beyng presences as *das Ereignis.* (*Contributions to Philosophy [From Enowning]* [hereafter CP], 22)

> *Das Seyn (als Ereignis) braucht das Seiende, damit es, das Seyn, wese.* (GA 65, 30)
> Beyng (as *Ereignis*) needs beings so that Beyng may presence. (CP, 22)

> *Der <u>Anfang</u> ist das <u>Seyn selbst</u> als Ereignis, die verborgene Herrschaft des Ursprungs der Wahrheit des Seienden als solchen.* (GA 65, 58)
> The *beginning* is Beyng itself as *Ereignis*, the hidden reign of the origin of the truth of beings as such. (CP, 41)

> *Der Anklang des Seyns will das Seyn in seiner <u>vollen Wesung</u> als Ereignis durch die Enthüllung der Seinsverlassenheit zurückholen.* (GA 65, 116)
> The echo of Beyng wants to retrieve Beyng in its *full presencing* as *Ereignis* through the disclosing of the abandonment of Being. (CP, 81)

> *Das Seyn aber west als das Ereignis, die Augenblicksstätte der Entscheidung über Nähe und Ferne des letzen Gottes.* (GA 65, 230)

But Beyng presences as *das Ereignis*, the site for the moment of decision about the nearness and farness of the last god. (CP, 163)

Das Seyn west als das Ereignis der Dagründung, in der Abkurzung: als Ereignis. (GA 65, 247)
Beyng presences as *das Ereignis of the grounding of the there*, in a word: as *Ereignis*. (CP, 174)

Das Seyn west als das Ereignis. (GA 65, 256)
Beyng presences as *das Ereignis.* (CP, 181)

Denn das Da-sein 'ist' eben die Gründung der Wahrheit des Seyns als Ereignis. (GA 65, 455)
For Da-*sein* 'is' precisely the grounding of the truth of Beyng as *Ereignis*. (CP, 320)

Das Seyn ist – das will sagen: das Seyn west allein das Wesen seiner selbst (Ereignis). (GA 65, 473)
Beyng is – that is to say: Beyng presences only the presencing of it itself (*Ereignis*). (CP, 333)

Das Seyn ist das Er-eignis. (GA 65, 470)
Beyng is *das Er-eignis.* (CP, 330)

B. Besinnung, GA 66 (1938–9)

This volume, *Meditativeness*, appeared in the *Gesamtausgabe* in 1997.[12] Heidegger's manuscript dates from the years 1938–9, and in a series of loosely connected reflections he continues to pursue the themes of *Beiträge* and, in particular, his understanding of *das seynsgeschichtliche Denken* – that is, Beyng-historical thinking. But, again, let us remain precise in our focus; in the course of his meditations, Heidegger often refers to Beyng *as Ereignis*, and he also simply identifies the two. So, among several instances:[13]

Das Seyn selbst ist als das Er-eignis dieser Entscheidung und ihres Zeitspiel-Raumes. (GA 66, 93)
Beyng itself *is* as *das Er-eignis* of this decision and of its timeplay-space.

Seyn ist das Er-eignis der Wahrheit. (GA 66, 98)

Beyng is *das Er-eignis* of truth.

Das Seyn ist Er-eignis. (GA 66, 100)
Beyng is *Er-eignis*.

C. *'Die Überwindung der Metaphysik,' GA 67 (1938–9) and 'Die Geschichte des Seyns,' GA 69 (1938–40)*

Volume 67 of the *Gesamtausgabe*, titled *Metaphysik und Nihilismus* (published in 1999; not yet translated) includes the manuscript *'Die Überwindung der Metaphysik'* ('The Overcoming of Metaphysics'), which belongs to the group of writings related to *Beiträge*.[14] In this collection of meditations, Heidegger makes similar references to the relation of *Ereignis* and Beyng. For example, he refers to 'the *echo* of Beyng as *Ereignis*' (GA 67, 99), and he explicitly states:

Ereignis ist das Seyn. (GA 67, 62)
Ereignis is Beyng.[15]

The two manuscripts collected in GA 69 (published in 1998; not yet translated) are also related in content and style to the meditations of *Beiträge*.[16] The first (and longer) piece is titled *'Die Geschichte des Seyns'* ('The History of Beyng'), composed 1938–40; the second is *'Koinon: Aus der Geschichte des Seyns'* ('*Koinon*: From the History of Beyng'), which dates from 1939–40. In the first composition, we find a number of relevant and revealing epigrams, among them the following:

Das Er-eignis. (Seyn). Austrag. (GA 69, 28)
Das Er-eignis. (Beyng). Drawing out.

Das Seyn ist – Er-eignis. (GA 69, 106)
Beyng is – *Er-eignis*.

Das Seyn ist Er-eignis. (GA 69, 134)
Beyng is *Er-eignis*.

Das <u>Ereignis</u> als das Seyn.
  <u>Das Seyn als die Wahrheit</u>.
  <u>Das Seyn nur ist</u>. (GA 69, 141)

Das Ereignis as Beyng.
  Beyng as truth.
  Only Beyng is.

Aber wie 'ist' das Seyn? <u>*Das Ereignis*</u>. (GA 69, 144)
`But how 'is' Beyng? *Das Ereignis*.[17]

D. *Über den Anfang, GA 70 (1941)*

The manuscript *Über den Anfang* (*On the Beginning*) dates to 1941 and has been published recently in the *Gesamtausgabe* (2005).[18] We will have to wait for the publication of the remaining *Ereignis*-writings composed by Heidegger in the years 1936 to 1944. According to the plan of the *Gesamtausgabe*, two additional volumes are forthcoming: volume 71, *Das Ereignis* (1941–2), and volume 72, *Die Stege des Anfangs* (1944). I think that we can expect no major surprises in these volumes, simply further elaborations on the same set of themes.

In *Beiträge* and in related reflections, he had proposed the notion of 'the first beginning' (*der erste Anfang*) and 'the other beginning' (*der andere Anfang*). As with other ideas and terms put into play by Heidegger in these *Ereignis*-writings, his account of the 'first' and 'other' beginning is not altogether clear or fully worked out. Yet as we can gather, he names the earliest Greek thinking of Being (as *physis* and *aletheia*) as the 'first' beginning, and the thinking of Beyng as *Ereignis* – that is, thinking that is emerging for Dasein in the present day – as the 'other' beginning. But he emphasizes that to think the first beginning in the proper way is *also* to think the other beginning, and that conversely, to think the other beginning is *also* to recall and meditate on the first. Therefore, there is really only one 'beginning' to be thought – that is, only one fundamental matter for thought. In *Beiträge*, he had put it this way: 'The *beginning* is *Beyng itself* as *Ereignis*, the hidden reign of the origin of the truth of beings as such' (GA 65, 58/CP, 41). In the 1941 manuscript *Über den Anfang*, he uses an obscure, antiquated German word to name this unifying 'beginning' (Beyng itself as *Ereignis*) that holds sway over both historical 'beginnings' (*die Anfänge*). The unusual word he uses, which can be traced back to Early New High German (roughly 1350–1650), is *die Anfängnis*, which I translate as 'the Originating.'[19] According to Heidegger, then, '*Die Anfängnis bestimmt und "ist" die Wesung des Anfangs*' / 'The Originating determines and "is" the presencing of the beginning' (GA 70, 13). Furthermore, he proceeds to identify the Originating with *Ereignis* and, in turn, to identify *Ereignis* with Beyng.

Thus, for our purposes, the decisive statement in his discussion culminates with his *identification* of *Ereignis* and Beyng:

> *Das Er-eignis ist die Anfängnis des Anfangs, sofern dieser sich gegen das Seiende als das anfänglich Nichtslose scheidet und in solchem 'gegen' das Seiende in das Da aufstehen läßt. Das Ereignis ist das Seyn.* (GA 70, 16)

> *Das Er-eignis* is the Originating of the beginning, in so far as this [beginning] separates itself against beings, as the initial eclipse of Nothing, and in such 'against,' beings are let to arise in the there. *Das Ereignis* is Beyng.[20]

For Heidegger, then, *das Ereignis* 'is' the Originating (*die Anfängnis*) 'is' Beyng. But I would like to make one further observation regarding the significance of Heidegger's choice of the word *die Anfängnis*. Some commentators have rightly noted that Heidegger is sometimes explicit in the early *Ereignis*-writings that he understands *der Anfang* to be a more fundamental word than *der Beginn*. What has been overlooked, though, is that he also appears to have considered *die Anfängnis* to be the *most* fundamental word insofar as it makes manifest what is *most* primordial – that is, the unitary and unifying temporal emerging or 'originating' from out of which we must think even an *Anfang*. There is perhaps another clue to this in the very structure of the word *Anfängnis*, which bears the same ending as *Ereignis*. In German, the *–nis* ending may convey neutrality or impersonality; therefore, in the case of the word *Anfängnis*, the ending emphasizes the sheer im-personality of the temporal 'originating,' thereby more decidedly stripping away any onto-theological sense of a divine agency or a subjective (or subject-ist) divine 'origin' or 'beginning,' which the word *Anfang* might still convey. In my view, it seems altogether reasonable to suggest that Heidegger retrieved the antiquated word *die Anfängnis* with his signature word *Ereignis* fully in mind. In other words, this 'originating' (*die Anfängnis*) that he describes is quite simply the primordial temporal emerging/ arising of beings (and epochs) that is *das Ereignis*, which, in turn, is precisely Beyng (Beyng itself).

IV. The Later *Ereignis*-writings, 1957–1962

My concern is not to give a complete account of Heidegger's use of the term *Ereignis* in his work of these later years, but rather to focus on how in certain major statements he related *Ereignis* to Being. As noted earlier, in the late 1950s and early 1960s he brought his notion of *Ereignis* into fuller public view. Though he often remarked in these years that he had been employing the term *Ereignis* in his thinking for over twenty-five years, it remains that he began to feature and thematize the notion before a wider audience beginning only in the late 1950s.

Generally speaking, his discussion of *Ereignis* in his later thought is calmer, more mature, and more genial than in the earlier writings; gone is the extravagant rhetoric and almost apocalyptic tone that marked the *Beiträge*-related reflections. He no longer highlights *Ereignis* as the dramatic – even traumatic – event-fulness of history, but rather now as the 'most gentle of laws' that allows the gathering of each being into what it properly is and into a belonging with other beings[21] – a characterization, we might note and emphasize, that is remarkably similar to his long-standing description of Being as the primordial *Logos*. Yet if Heidegger's understanding of *Ereignis* matures and comes into its own, so to speak, in the later reflections, it is in the earlier *Ereignis*-writings that he is more precise in distinguishing between the fundamental matter for thought, *das Seyn / das Seyn selbst* (Beyng / Beyng itself), and *das Sein* as *die Seiendheit*, being as beingness, the proper concern of metaphysical thinking (*eidos*, *essentia*, essence, and all other forms of 'perduring presence').[22] Unfortunately, in the later work of the 1950s and 1960s, he is far less careful to make this critical distinction consistently explicit and clear. Often he simply refers to *das Sein*, and the reader is left with the task of gathering from the context whether he is referring to Being, his proper concern, or to beingness, the core concern of metaphysics. As we shall document in a moment, this difficulty is precisely what so often complicates his later comments on the relation of *Ereignis* and Being. Regrettably, at least from the reader's standpoint, in his later work Heidegger did not always maintain the kind of terminological discipline and clarity that he employed in his earlier *Ereignis*-writings in distinguishing between *das Seyn* and *das Sein* as *die Seiendheit*.

A. 'Der Weg zur Sprache' / 'The Way to Language' (1959)

In the lecture 'The Principle of Identity' delivered at the University of Freiburg on 27 June 1957, Heidegger spoke at length about *Ereignis* and noted that the word 'should now speak as a key term in the service of thinking.'[23] Though this lecture is an important statement on *Ereignis*, it does not pose the issue of the relation between *Ereignis* and Being as sharply as does a somewhat later lecture, 'The Way to Language.'

He gave this lecture in January 1959 in both Munich and Berlin and revised and slightly expanded the original lecture text later the same year. I readily admit that every effort at the daunting task of translating a text by Heidegger deserves our admiration; unfortunately, the widely read English translation of 'The Way to Language' by Peter Hertz in the volume *On the Way to Language* (hereafter OWL) is so fundamentally inaccurate on the precise issue we are investigating that it has no doubt contributed to a serious misunderstanding of Heidegger's position.[24]

First, let us focus on Heidegger's words. In Section III, he introduces the notion of *Ereignis* and makes some clarifying remarks. He characterizes *Ereignis* as irreducible; it is the fundamental matter for thought:

> *Es gibt nichts anderes, worauf das Ereignis noch zurückführt, woraus es gar erklärt werden könnte. Das Ereignen ist kein Ergebnis (Resultat) aus anderem, aber die Er-gebnis, deren reichendes Geben erst dergleichen wie ein 'Es gibt' gewährt, dessen auch noch 'das Sein' bedarf, um als Anwesen in sein Eigenes zu gelangen.* (GA 12, 247)

> There is nothing else whereupon *das Ereignis* could be grounded or even whereby it could be explained. *Das Ereignen* is not the outcome (result) of something else, but rather the giving-forth, whose reaching giving first grants something like a 'there is,' which also even 'being' needs in order to come into its own as presence.[25] (my translation)

At issue is the relation of *Ereignis* to Being. A quick first reading might lead us to think that Heidegger is saying that *Ereignis* 'gives' or 'grants' Being, and therefore that Being is subordinated in importance to *Ereignis*. But we must read more carefully. He encloses *'das Sein'* in quotation marks, and this tells us that he is not speaking about *Being itself*, but rather about 'being' as this has been generally understood over the long course of metaphysical thought. In other words, *'das Sein'* in this passage is tantamount to 'being' as beingness, *die Seiendheit*. Here is a perfect example of how in his later work Heidegger often leaves the reader unsure about the precise meaning of *das Sein*; nevertheless, he *does* provide a crucial clue: he encloses the word in quotation marks to signal that the name 'being' is here limited to the meaning of being as determined in metaphysics (beingness, essence). Understood aright, then, his statement says only that *Ereignis* 'grants' metaphysical beingness. It says nothing at all about the relation of *Ereignis* to 'Being itself,' which is Heidegger's proper name for the originary and fundamental meaning of *das Sein*. However, this is precisely where Hertz's translation goes awry. His version of the last line reads: 'which even Being itself stands in need to come into its own as presence' (OWL, 127). Not only does he leave out the telling quotation marks around the word being, but he also inexplicably translates '*das Sein*' as 'Being itself,' thereby significantly distorting the meaning of Heidegger's statement and thoroughly confounding readers.

The problem with Hertz's translation does not end here, but again, let us first attend to Heidegger's words. Shortly after this passage, he appends a significant and illuminating footnote that speaks directly to his understanding of the relation of *Ereignis* to Being. He remarks that he has been using the word *Ereignis* in his 'manuscripts' for over twenty-five years to name the fundamental matter (*die Sache*) under consideration in the essay. What follows is decisive:

> *Diese Sache, obzwar in sich einfach, bleibt vorerst schwer zu denken, weil das Denken sich zuvor dessen entwöhnen muß, in die Meinung zu verfallen, hier werde 'das Sein' als Ereignis gedacht. Aber das Ereignis ist wesenhaft anderes, weil reicher als jede mögliche metaphysische Bestimmung des Seins. Dagegen läßt sich das Sein hinsichtlich seiner Wesensherkunft aus dem Ereignis denken.* (GA 12, 248–9)

> This matter, although simple in itself, still remains difficult to think, because thinking must first overcome the habit of falling back on the opinion that what is thought here is 'being' as *Ereignis*. But *das Ereignis* is essentially different because it is richer than any possible metaphysical determination of being. Nevertheless, Being, regarding its originating of presence, may be thought of in terms of *Ereignis*. (my translation)

Note that in his first mention of *das Sein*, Heidegger again encloses the word in quotes. This detail is most important, and what I proposed earlier about its significance appears confirmed here. That is, he states that *Ereignis* cannot be understood as '"*das Sein*"' because *Ereginis* is 'richer than any possible metaphysical determination of being.' Thus, the word *das Sein* enclosed in quotes = the metaphysical determination of being (beingness). A careful reading reveals that '*das Sein*' is simply Heidegger's shorthand for beingness (*die Seiendheit*). But again, this is entirely lost in Hertz's translation because here he omits the word 'metaphysical' in Heidegger's sentence. Readers in English are misled by Hertz's version, which states that *Ereignis* 'is richer than any conceivable definition of Being' (OWL, 129). This is not Heidegger's meaning at all, and one omitted word – 'metaphysical' – makes all the difference.

But to return to the footnote. In the very following sentence, Heidegger frees the word *das Sein* of its limiting quotation marks and thereby frees it up for its originary and fundamental meaning. So, to think Being in a non-metaphysical way is to think Being regarding its 'originating of presence' (*Wesensherkunft*), and this characterization echoes his earlier (1941) description of Beyng as the Originating, *die Anfängnis*. Of particular significance is that Heidegger's word *Wesensherkunft* says the *origin-ating of presence (essence)*; that is, Being, thought in a fundamental way, originates (gives, grants) beings (that is, what-is-present) in their beingness (that is, in their sheer presence or essence). Hertz misses (and even reverses!) the meaning of this crucial word *Wesensherkunft* by translating it as 'essential origin,' and unfortunately, Krell follows suit with his translation 'essential provenance.' But the key point of this clarification is this: Heidegger concludes that *if* Being is thought 'regarding its originating of presence,' then indeed Being and *Ereignis* may be thought together. In other words, Being/*Ereignis* originates (gives, grants, lets, enables, allows) beings in their beingness.[26] Being and *Ereignis:* the Same. Or to be more exact, Being (Beyng, Being itself, Being as such, Being as Being) and *Ereignis:* the Same.

B. *'Zeit und Sein' / 'Time and Being'* (1962)

Heidegger delivered this much anticipated lecture on 31 January 1962 at the University of Freiburg. In September of the same year in Todt-nauberg he led six seminar sessions on the text of the lecture. Summaries or protocols of the seminars were written by one of the participants, Dr Alfred Guzzoni, and these were checked and slightly supplemented by Heidegger for publication. Both the lecture and protocol texts were published in a small collection titled *Zur Sache des Denkens* in 1969.[27] This volume, with the same title, has recently appeared as volume 14 of the *Gesamtausgabe* (2007).

The lecture attempts to gloss what might have been said in the proposed third section of the first part of *Being and Time*, which, of course, Heidegger never wrote. He freely admits, though, that the lecture is really no more than a series of indications because 'written three and half decades later, [the lecture text] can no longer be a continuation of the text of *Being and Time*' (SD, 91/TB, 83). At the time, Heidegger and those in attendance thought the lecture to be an important statement of his later thinking. No doubt this is so, but from the perspective of the present, I do not think that it can be considered an altogether satisfying philosophical reflection. Principal terms are unclarified, the language is especially cryptic, and the major themes are only loosely developed. It is arguable that he addressed the key ideas more carefully in other reflections from these years. Nonetheless, we certainly cannot ignore this well-known and oft-mentioned lecture in investigating our concern.

Again, the focus must be precise, so we cannot consider the text as a whole. Instead, let us target one key line for discussion. Near the end of the lecture, he states: 'The sole purpose of this lecture is to bring into view Being itself [*das Sein selbst*] as *Ereignis*' (SD, 22/TB, 21). This one line certainly would be decisive and definitive for the purpose of this study were it not that Heidegger does not helpfully clarify this conclusion. He immediately shifts to a consideration of how this is *not* to be thought – that is, he warns that the 'as' in this statement is especially 'treacherous' because the metaphysical habit of thinking reflexively construes what follows the 'as' to be only a 'mode' of being. He observes that if his statement were considered in this metaphysical manner, *Ereignis* would be no more than a subset of being and therefore 'subordinated' to being as 'the main concept,' and he emphasizes that this is certainly not his meaning. Metaphysical thinking simply misses the fundamental matter to be thought in saying 'Being itself as *Ereignis*.' This may be so, but he offers no careful elucidation of how his conclusion *is* to be understood, though his meaning is perhaps apparent enough that Being itself as *Ereignis* names the Same, namely, the *giving* of the epochal or historical renderings of being *qua* beingness. Yet more to the point, he does not directly address the apparent tension in the lecture between two claims: on the one hand, he states throughout that *Ereignis* 'gives' *das Sein* (*Es gibt Sein*), but on the other hand, he concludes with the indication that the whole point of the lecture is precisely to bring into view 'Being itself as *Ereignis*.'

The root of the problem lies with his uncertain use of the word *das Sein*. In those places where he speaks of *Ereignis* giving or granting *das Sein*, he appears to be referring to being as beingness (*die Seiendheit*), but unlike in 'The Way to Language,' in this text he does not enclose *das Sein* in quotation marks to give the reader a telling clue that he is limiting the meaning of being in such formulations to the many forms of metaphysical beingness or 'presence' (*Anwesenheit*). As noted before, one of the chief difficulties in reading the later Heidegger is that he often leaves the reader uncertain about the precise meaning of *das Sein* in certain contexts, and here is a particularly vexing instance of this. On the other hand, this is certainly not the case with his use of the name *das Sein selbst*, Being itself, because he is always careful and precise in reserving this name for the fundamental matter for thought. So in 'Time and Being,' we find that he does not state that *Ereignis* gives or grants *Being itself*; in fact, as far as I can determine, there is *no* place in any of Heidegger's texts – early, middle, or late – where he allows that *Ereignis* gives Being itself (nowhere, in other words, where he use the phrase *Es gibt Sein selbst*). Therefore, if we sort out the terminology of the lecture, we can make better sense of his fundamental position: *Ereignis* as *Es gibt* gives (grants, allows, enables) beingness; but *Ereignis* and Being itself: the Same.

This reading is strengthened when we turn to the protocol of the fourth seminar on the lecture text that Heidegger led several months later in Todtnauberg. According to the protocol, the participants addressed the problem of the apparent contradiction that we have highlighted. The response – and I think we can presume that it was principally Heidegger's response – was that the name 'Being itself' always had a special significance in his thinking. The participants cite the 'Letter on Humanism' (1947), and it is observed that though the word *Ereignis* is not mentioned in this statement, nonetheless the term '"Being itself"' already names *Ereignis*' (SD, 46/TB, 43). In other words, for Heidegger, the name Being itself *also names Ereignis*.

Consequently, as the protocol observes, this reminder should make it clear that there is no contradiction in 'Time and Being.' Unfortunately, the protocol clarifies this crucial point in an all too cryptic way: 'it is precisely a matter of seeing that *das Sein*, in coming into view as *Ereignis*, disappears as *das Sein*' (SD, 46/TB, 43). We can dispel the mystery and confusion by restating the line more carefully: it is precisely a matter of seeing that if we are able to bring into view *Being itself* as *Ereignis*, then there is no contradiction in also saying that being *qua metaphysical beingness* recedes in visibility and importance for thinking.

In turn, this reading is supported by a brief response that Heidegger made to a question posed to him by Joan Stambaugh (and editors) during the summer of 1970, while they were preparing the volume *The End of Philosophy*. The third question made in writing to Heidegger asked, in part, whether 'Being itself [should] be thought as the Appropriation [*Ereignis*].' Stambaugh provides only a translation of his written response, so regrettably, we cannot examine his own words. Nevertheless, even in translation, his answer clearly echoes the cryptic statement from the 1962 seminar – and also clarifies the issue as I have suggested:

> 'Being itself' means: The Appropriation [*Ereignis*] can no longer be thought as 'Being' in terms of presence. 'Appropriation' no longer names another manner and epoch of 'Being.' 'Being' thought without regard to beings (i.e., always only in terms of, and with respect to, them) means at the same time: no longer thought as 'Being' (presence).[28]

To put a finer point on the matter, I gloss his response as follows:

> *Being itself* means *Ereignis*. *Being itself* and *Ereignis* cannot be thought in terms of beingness. *Ereignis* does not name another historical form of beingness. Thinking *Being itself* means that all metaphysical thinking about beingness must recede in importance.

Carefully considered, then, Heidegger's lecture 'Time and Being' does not reveal a radical departure in his thinking at all, but rather only a radical reformulation of the fundamental matter for thought in terms of *Ereignis* as *Es gibt*. The task for thinking abetted by this new and different language is to get into view what metaphysical thinking simply could not: the pure appropriating, giving, letting of what appears. Nonetheless, as he observes at the end of the lecture, this task is really no more than 'to think Being without regard to metaphysics.'[29]

Conclusion: Translating *Ereignis*

Thus, as Heidegger was wont to do, we might state our finding paratactically:[30]

> *das Sein selbst*: *das Ereignis*: *das Selbe*
> Being itself: *das Ereignis*: the Same

This formulation, I suggest, says succinctly and elegantly what Heidegger's words repeatedly bear out: Being itself characterizes *Ereignis* and *Ereignis* characterizes Being itself. These names are the Same insofar as they *both name the fundamental matter for thought*, that is, the temporal-spatial, finite and negatived, appearing (unconcealing, presencing, emerging, originating, giving, letting) of beings in their beingness as made manifest meaningfully by Dasein in language. Yet insofar as each name may convey or emphasize a particular aspect of *die Sache des Denkens*, we need not say that these names are 'identical' in all respects (*das Gleiche*).

What, then, of the issue of translating *Ereignis*? If we are to translate this word in the *fundamental* sense that Heidegger often discussed, then we must cross-over (*über*-setzen) in our thinking to what he essentially said by *Ereignis*. To do so is to realize that the proper 'translation' is – Being itself. Heidegger meditated a lifetime on what was first named in the West by Parmenides and Heraclitus as *eon* – Being; and in attending to it so closely, he allowed it to come anew, renewed, in the name *Ereignis*. If we gather and hold this in our thinking, then, if we must have an English word or phrase to translate *Ereignis*, any of the thoughtful options that have been offered by commentators and translators over the years will do.

3 The Turn towards Home

In the midst of the unhomely we are making a turn back into the homely.
'Messkirch's Seventh Centennial,' 1961

Is Dasein primordially – that is, at the very core of its being – 'at home' or 'not at home' in Being? One of the more overlooked or understated issues in Heidegger studies is how Heidegger, over the course of a lifetime of thinking, transformed his answer to such a question about Dasein's fundamental relation to Being.[1] This significant development in his thought is fascinating in itself, but it also helps us better understand why his thinking has been appropriated in such different ways serving such different ends and purposes. The story of this development moves from the early Heidegger of the 1920s, who insisted that 'from an existential-ontological perspective, not-at-homeness must be understood as the more primordial phenomenon'; through the middle Heidegger of the early 1940s, who elaborated the theme of 'becoming at home in being-not-at-home'; to the later Heidegger of the 1950s and 1960s, who claimed with conviction that 'a return home has the power of overtaking again and again everything that sweeps us up into the unhomely.' In what follows, I examine several key texts from the period 1925 to 1961 that offer a compelling if not comprehensive account of these developments in his thinking. The decisive text in illuminating his 'turn towards home' is his 1942 commentary on Hölderlin's poem 'The Ister,' which also offers, in my estimation, Heidegger's most satisfying phenomenological account of being human.

I. The Angst of Being Unsettled: *The History of the Concept of Time* (1925) and *Being and Time* (1927)

The Prolegomena to The History of the Concept of Time (hereafter HCT) is the text of a lecture course Heidegger delivered at Marburg University in the summer semester of 1925 and is 'a text that is clearly in transition toward *Being and Time*,' as the translator Theodore Kisiel observes.[2] Most of the lecture course text anticipates Division One of *Being and Time*, which lays out a phenomenological analysis of Dasein's being-in-the-world. Of special interest to us is Heidegger's discussion of *Angst* and *Unheimlichkeit*. Kisiel translates these key terms as 'dread' and 'uncanniness,' and he is not alone; but I make the argument in the next chapter that we opt for the word 'anxiety' over 'dread' in translating *Angst* – if we must translate the word at all.[3] In any case, I will use the words 'Angst' (unitalicized) and 'anxiety' interchangeably in the discussion that follows. The German words *unheimlich* and *die Unheimlichkeit* mean more literally 'not-at-home(ness),' and Heidegger often plays on this literal sense; so to convey this sense in English, I prefer to translate these key words as 'unsettled' and 'unsettledness' rather than as 'uncanny' and 'uncanniness.'[4]

In this 1925 lecture course, Heidegger already makes clear the fundamental distinction between the affective dispositions of fear and Angst that he works out so famously in *Being and Time* (1927). In fear, one feels threatened by something 'definite' in the 'environing world in its meaningfulness'; yet in anxiety, 'what threatens is nothing definite and worldly.' Anxiety leaves us feeling profoundly 'unsettled'; one 'no longer feels at home [*zu Hause*] in his most familiar environment, the one closest to him.'[5] This unsettledness is not related to any modification or change in the environment or world itself. Rather, Dasein is anxious about no-thing, 'nothing' in the world; it is anxious about '*being-in-the-world as such.*' Dasein is anxious and unsettled in the face of its radically negated existence, the hallmark of which is death (finitude). 'In anxiety,' he states, 'being-in-the-world is totally transformed into "not-at-homeness" [*Nicht-zu-Hause*] purely and simply.'[6]

The significance of this statement is that Heidegger understands Dasein's 'not-at-homeness' to be *fundamental*. Dasein is primordially 'not at home' in its 'facticity,' or radically negated finite existence, and is therefore anxious and unsettled at the core of its being. He expresses this again with even greater clarity: 'That *of which* anxiety is anxious is the *in-which of being-in-the world*, and that *about which* one is anxious is this *very same being-in-the-world*, specifically in its primary uncovered-ness as "not-at-homeness" [*Unzuhause*].'[7]

Dasein may be primordially 'not at home,' but he observes that Dasein is for the most part in 'flight' from this difficult truth of its existence and that it clings to familiar modes of being in order to evade or cover over the Angst and unsettledness that define its being. 'What is at stake in the flight from unsettledness is precisely a cultivation of Dasein itself as being-in-the-world, so much so that it lets itself be determined for the most part from the world.' In falling, in flight from itself, Dasein cultivates ways of 'being-at-home' (*Zuhause-seins*) that Heidegger ultimately characterizes as Dasein's 'deceitful way of not wanting to see' itself in its essentially anxious and unsettled existence.[8] Thus, his position in the 1925 lecture course emerges clearly: Dasein is primordially – at the core of its being – 'not at home' as being-in-the-world.

In *Being and Time* (hereafter BT), Heidegger repeats and reworks this entire thematic.[9] In Section 40, he draws the phenomenological distinction between the affective disposition of fear and the fundamental affective disposition (*die Grundbefindlichkeit*) of Angst. Fear 'always comes from beings within the world,' but one is anxious about no-thing, 'nothing,' and this is so because '*that in the face of which one is anxious is being-in-the-world as such.*' Or again, '*the world as such is that in the face of which one is anxious,*' and once more, '*being-in-the-world itself is that in the face of which anxiety is anxious*' (all italicized by Heidegger).[10] He privileges the mood of Angst because it is the mood that brings Dasein face to face with its radically negatived finite existence as such and, consequently, gives to Dasein the possibility of taking hold of itself resolutely and authentically. 'Anxiety thus takes away from Dasein the possibility of understanding itself, as it falls, in terms of the "world" and the way things have been publicly interpreted. Anxiety throws Dasein back upon that which it is anxious about – its authentic potentiality-for-being-in-the-world.'[11]

One minor difference with his discussion in HCT is that in *Being and Time* he more explicitly frames the analysis in terms of the distinction existentiell-ontic / existential-ontological. He characterizes the mood of fear primarily as an existentiell-ontic phenomenon that is derivative of the more primordial or existential-ontological disposition of Angst. Another notable difference is that he adds another layer to the analysis, emphasizing that Dasein's average everyday dealing with 'moods' is for the most part 'inauthentic' insofar as these moods disguise or cover over Dasein in its very being. So, for example: 'Fear is anxiety, fallen into the "world," inauthentic, and, as such, hidden from itself.'[12] Only by confronting the ontological mood of Angst and taking it up reso- lutely can Dasein take hold of itself and live 'authentically': 'Anxiety brings Dasein face to face with its *being-free for* ... (*propensio in* ...) the authenticity of its being, and for this authenticity as a possibility which it always is.'[13] Admittedly, there is a difficulty with his tendency in this phenomenological analysis to conflate the neutral structural distinction ontic/ontological with the qualitative existential distinction inauthen- tic/authentic, but we must leave such a discussion for another time.

In any case, the principal point is that Heidegger's discussion of Angst in BT is essentially a continuation of his analysis in HCT, and this includes his discussion of *die Unheimlichkeit*, which is of special im- portance for the present essay. In BT he again highlights that 'in anxiety one is "unsettled" [*unheimlich*],' and once more he plays on this German word to bring out the essential 'not-at-homeness' of Dasein's being-in- the-world. 'But here,' he states, 'unsettledness also means being-not- at-home [*Nicht-zuhause-sein*].'[14] Constitutively, Dasein is 'not at home,' and he derisively refers to the 'tranquillized,' 'obvious,' 'being-at- home' (*Zuhause-sein*) modes of being of the 'they.' Angst brings Dasein back from its absorption in the world of the they. Dasein is shaken to the core of its being, and 'being-in assumes the existential "mode" of *not-at-homeness* [*Un-zuhause*].'[15]

Also, he restates that Dasein is for the most part in flight from itself and seeks refuge in the 'tranquillized familiarity' of ontic and inauthen- tic modes of being. 'When in falling, we flee *into* the at-homeness [*Zu- hause*] of the public world, we flee *from* not-at-homeness [*Unzuhause*].'[16] In average everydayness, 'unsettledness' and 'not-at-homeness' get 'dimmed-down'; but make no mistake about it, Heidegger insists – this is so only because Dasein is ontologically – at the core of its being – un- settled. He sums up his position in one emphatic, italicized sentence: '*From an existential-ontological perspective, not-at-homeness [das Un-zu- hause] must be understood as the more primordial phenomenon.*'[17]

II. Expelled from the Hearth: The Reading of *Antigone* in *Introduction to Metaphysics* (1935)

In turning our attention to *Introduction to Metaphysics* (hereafter IM) – arguably Heidegger's major work of the 1930s – our focus remains on the issue of his characterization of the essential cor-relation of Dasein and Being.[18] Thus far, we have determined that his position in the two related texts HCT and BT is that Dasein is primordially 'not at home' as being-in-the-world. In IM his fundamental position does not change, though it is articulated in a new way, especially in the context of his remarkably original (albeit debatable) commentary on the first choral ode in Sophocles' *Antigone*. The *Antigone* commentary in IM not only goes to the heart of our concern but also helps bring into sharper relief his striking change in thinking by 1942, when he revisits the choral lines in his commentary on Hölderlin's 'The Ister.'

In IM, Heidegger does not privilege the mood of Angst as he had in his work of the 1920s, yet he does reprise the theme of Dasein's not-at-homeness. In his commentary on the first choral ode (lines 332 to 375), he translates Sophocles' word *deinon* as 'unheimlich,' and again, I think that the word 'unsettled' better conveys Heidegger's wordplay. The human being is intrinsically 'unsettled,' he tells us, by 'that which throws one out of the "settled" [*Heimlichen*], that is, the homely [*Heimischen*], the customary, the usual, the secure. The unhomely [*das Unheimische*] does not allow us to be at home.'[19] As he sees it, all 'at home' modes of being add up to nothing more than the customary and familiar, what he had called 'ontic' and 'inauthentic' modes of being in BT. The human being in its very being is 'unsettled' (*unheimlich*) and 'not at home' (*unheimisch*) in its relation to Being as the Overpowering and therefore *must* 'transgress' (*überschreitet*) the limits of at-home modes of being in order to exist authentically in relation to Being. So, he states, 'the most unsettled (the human being) is what it is because, most fundamentally, it cultivates and guards what is close to home [*das Einheimische*] only in order to break out of it and to let what overpowers it break in.'[20] Human beings are not true to their being-in-the-world who seek refuge in 'at home' modes of being, who get 'bogged down in their routes, get stuck in ruts, and by getting stuck they draw in the circle of their world, get enmeshed in seeming, and thus shut themselves out of Being.'[21] The human being is true – and a true creator – who, like Antigone, accepts that he or she is without a home in Being; who stands out into the *polemos*, the strife with Being as the Overpowering; who violently wrestles Being into beings; and who unflinchingly and heroically accepts the possibility that its 'venture' into Being may result in 'disaster.'

Heidegger's language in IM is different from in HCT and BT, but the message remains fundamentally the same: Dasein is primordially not at home in Being. As he puts it poetically, glossing the lines of the choral ode, the human being, the most unsettled, must 'embark on the groundless deep, forsaking the solid land.' Dasein cannot sail 'upon bright, smooth waters,' but only amid 'the storms of winter.'[22] More plainly, he states: 'Thus, *Da-sein is the happening of unsettledness itself*' (my italics).[23] This is the difficult truth that human beings generally seek to avoid, finding false tranquillity and security in the inessential (*Unwesen*), 'at home' modes of being that keep them out of their own 'essence' (*Wesen*). And once more he states this for emphasis: 'How far the human being is not at home in its ownmost essence ...'[24]

He concludes his commentary on the choral ode by addressing lines 372 to 375. This is especially significant, for he will come back to these lines in his 1942 commentary on Hölderlin and offer a strikingly different reading. According to the Loeb translation, the lines read in English: 'May he who does such things never sit by my hearth or share my thoughts!'[25] Heidegger renders them as 'Let him not become a companion at my hearth, nor let my knowing share the delusions of the one who works such deeds.'[26] He finds in these lines only the chorus's contempt for the 'daring,' 'unsettled' one who upsets the familiar and customary. The chorus, representing the average everydayness of inauthentic Dasein, 'turns *against* the most unsettled one' and banishes him or her from 'hearth and counsel.' He declares: 'There is nothing surprising about these concluding words; indeed, we should have to be surprised if they were lacking.'[27] For Heidegger, the chorus cannot accept that the human being is primordially not at home in Being; yet paradoxically, their rejection of one like Antigone is in fact 'a direct and complete confirmation of the unsettledness that is the essence of being human.'[28] Indeed! But when he revisits these very same lines in 1942, he will work out a very different characterization of the essential correlation of Dasein and Being.

III. (Re)turning Home: The (Re)reading of *Antigone* in 'Hölderlin's Hymn "Der Ister"' (1942)

Heidegger's turn towards 'home' is perhaps best illuminated in his 1942 lecture course on Hölderlin's poem 'The Ister.'[29] In this commentary, which features a rereading of the first choral ode of Sophocles' *Antigone*, he works out with great care and subtlety the position that Dasein is primordially *at home* in Being – and it is this theme that we recognize as so prominent in his later work. Two other Hölderlin commentaries of the early 1940s, one on the poem 'Remembrance' and the other on the poem 'Homecoming / To Kindred Ones' are close in spirit to the commentary on 'The Ister' and are also of special significance.[30]

Of course, Heidegger had engaged Hölderlin's poetry throughout the 1930s. In 1934–5, he had offered a lecture course on the poems 'Germania' and 'The Rhine' and had already begun to thematize the 'homeland' (*Heimat*). Even so, his preoccupation with the 'power' (*Macht*) and 'violence' (*Gewalt*) of poetic creation in relation to Being (*Seyn*) links these earlier commentaries more closely to the fundamental themes of *Introduction to Metaphysics*.[31] In any case, the commentary on 'The Ister' deserves special recognition and attention because of the striking difference we find in his rereading of Sophocles' words as he works out the theme of Dasein's 'return home.'[32]

In the summer semester of 1942, he gave a lecture course on an unfinished poem by Hölderlin that was given the title 'The Ister' by the first editor, Norbert von Hellingrath. 'Ister' was the ancient Greco-Roman name for the lower course of the Danube, and as he observes at the beginning of his commentary, 'Hölderlin ... names precisely the upper course of the Donau with the Greco-Roman name for the lower course of the river, just as if the lower Donau had returned to the upper, and thus turned back to its source.'[33] For this reason, Heidegger finds the title of the poem appropriate, and he takes up the lengthy task of elucidating the hymn.

A large part of this lecture course is given over to an *Auseinandersetzung* between Hölderlin and Sophocles. Specifically, he is interested in illuminating the meaning of Hölderlin's poem by way of an elucidation of the first choral ode in *Antigone* because this 'singular poetic work of a singular poet resonates repeatedly in Hölderlin's poetic telling.'[34] Thus, Heidegger returns to the same choral lines in *Antigone* that he had addressed in IM in 1935. But is this return no more than a repetition, as some have suggested? Certainly not. We discover in his renewed engagement with Sophocles' words a significant departure from the earlier reading – though unacknowledged by Heidegger – and, along with it, evidence of the turn towards 'home' in his thinking.

As his commentary on *Antigone* unfolds, he returns to an explication of Sophocles' word *deinon*, which had been central to his earlier reading in IM. Again, he translates *deinon* as *unheimlich*, and the translation of this word remains an issue; the case can be made for 'uncanny,' 'strange,' or 'awesome.' Yet since he pointedly continues to link *unheimlich* with *unheimisch*, it makes sense to continue with 'unsettled' to translate *unheimlich* in order to give resonance to his wordplay.

Initially, Heidegger shifts his concern to Being itself in discussing *to deinon*. Sophocles' word may be understood in the first place as *das Un-*

heimliche or *das Ungeheure*, the Unsettling or Extraordinary – names for Being itself, as his remarks suggest. In thinking about *das Unheimliche*, we must think three aspects in their 'unity': 'the fearful, the powerful, and the unusual.'[35] Now, with respect to human *being*, Dasein is *unheimlich*, unsettled, in the following ways: as frightened only in the sense of being in awe and in admiration before that which commands respect and awe; as powerful in the sense of standing out into the powerful itself; and as unusual in the sense of going beyond the habitual and accustomed to stand out into what is extraordinary. The human being is *'das Unheimlichste,'* 'the most unsettled,' and, therefore, *'unheimisch,'* 'not at home' or 'unhomely.' And he underscores this by adding that 'we are hereby pointing to a connection that presumably extends beyond the merely extrinsic resonance of the words *"unheimisch"*and *"unheimlich."*'[36]

He thus restates an important theme from the *Antigone* commentary in IM: In an essential way, the human being is 'not at home' (in Being). The human being is the being that in its essencing goes beyond the ordinary to the extraordinary, the being that is cast out from being at home among the homely. In a key passage, he observes:

> We mean the unsettled in the sense of that which is not at home – not homely in that which is homely. It is only for this reason that the un-home-ly [*das Un-heimische*] can, as a consequence, also be 'unsettled' [*unheimlich*] in the sense of something that has an alienating or 'frightening' effect that gives rise to anxiety. In that case, Sophocles' word, which speaks of the human being as the most unsettled being, says that human beings are in a singular sense, not at home, ...[37]

We find in these words everything that is consistent with his reading of the choral lines in IM and with his fundamental position in that work that the human being is primordially not at home in Being. Yet when we complete the last line of the above passage, we discover a striking departure from the earlier reading that he does not acknowledge as such. The complete last line reads (italics mine):

> In that case, Sophocles' word, which speaks of the human being as the most unsettled being, says that human beings are, in a singular sense, not at home, *and that their care is to become at home.*

'Their care [*Sorge*] is to become at home [*Heimischwerden*].' Nowhere in the 1935 *Antigone* reading did Heidegger use such words or suggest any such idea; yet here, and in a most matter-of-fact way, he maintains this to be Sophocles' meaning. He does not give any clue whatsoever that he has made a significant addition or modification to his earlier reading of Sophocles' 'word.' He simply adds that 'the task is now to show to what extent the choral ode itself justifies this interpretation.' He moves on to a detailed reading of the choral ode with this (unacknowledged) new and very different aim in view: to show how the human being, the unhomely one, is nonetheless primordially *at home* in Being.

His commentary that follows is lengthy and exceedingly dense, and we cannot do justice to all the particulars of his discussion. So let us focus on the points in his reading that go to the heart of our present concern. He comes back to a further elucidation of the Greek word *deinon*. Among beings, the human being is in a special way 'unsettled' (*unheimlich*) and therefore 'unhomely' (*unheimisch*). Being 'unhomely' is not the same as being a mere 'adventurer' who romantically wanders in the 'wilderness' of beings, venturing heroically, and who 'thus becomes acquainted with everything' under the sun. Such being-not-at-home among beings, no matter how exhilarating, still comes to 'nothing' because 'no skillfulness, no acts of power, and no artfulness can stave off death.'[38] Human beings are finite, and this kind of 'adventuring' among beings is in fact only a kind of flight from this truth.

The essential meaning of being 'unhomely' is different from adventuring. Human beings 'alone [among beings] stand in the midst of beings in such a way as to comport themselves toward beings as such.'[39] Only the human being 'knows of beings themselves and knows of them as beings, addressing them and articulating them.' For this reason, only the human being can 'forget' the source of beings, the Being (*Sein*) of beings. Only the human being in its relation to beings can *forget* Being. Consequently, the human being is intrinsically 'unhomely' because it constitutively forgets Being in the engagement with beings (what Heidegger had called 'falling' in *Being and Time*). What is more, the human being, who ultimately founders upon death, can find no 'home' – no ultimate ground or meaning – among beings.

The human being is 'unsettled' among beings and, therefore, 'not at home' among beings. Of course, this is a hard truth, and for the most part, human beings 'evade' this truth of their being: 'As venturing forth in all directions, human beings arrive everywhere and yet everywhere come to nothing, insofar as what they attain in venturing forth is never sufficient to fulfill and sustain their essence.'[40] But this is precisely *not* the case with Antigone. She is resolute in taking up and taking upon herself the *deinon*, the unsettledness, that is constitutive of being human; she is the 'supreme unsettled' and therefore also the 'utterly unhomely.'[41] According to Heidegger, the fundamental dramatic action of the play is precisely Antigone's noble '*pathein*' – her 'experiencing' and 'enduring' and 'suffering' in an extreme way the 'unsettledness' and 'unhomeliness' of the human being among beings.[42] Antigone represents an 'intensification' of this truth about being human.[43]

But this is not the only truth – or the most important truth – about being human that Heidegger wants to articulate in this lecture course, which brings us back to the issue of the 'turning' in his thinking about the meaning of *Antigone*. He introduces the new twist on the old reading – again without acknowledging it as such – with a rhetorical question: 'What if that which were most intrinsically unhomely [like Antigone], thus most remote from all that is homely, were that which in itself simultaneously preserved the most intimate belonging to the homely?'[44] This leads him to a consideration of the concluding lines of the first choral ode, lines 372 to 375, which speak of expelling the daring one from the 'hearth.' As we discussed, in IM he read these lines to mean that the chorus, representing average everyday thinking, could not tolerate the likes of an Antigone, whose boldness and daring revealed the essential 'unsettledness' of being human. Her expulsion from 'hearth and counsel' by the chorus was inevitable, he had maintained, and a 'direct and complete confirmation of the unsettledness that is the essence of being human.' And there his commentary ended. But not so in 'The Ister' commentary.

These lines speak differently to Heidegger in 1942. *The 'hearth' is no longer the site of inauthentic Dasein; now it is 'the site of being-at-home' in a primordial and authentic way.*[45] He states that '*Hestia* is the hearth of the house, the locale at which there stand the gods of the hearth. [It is where there is] the fire in the manifoldness of its essence, which essentially prevails as lighting, illuminating, warming, nourishing, purifying, refining, glowing.' In other words, the 'hearth' is the warmth of home; it is Being itself. The 'hearth' is Being, the source of all beings, and becoming 'at home' in Being is the aim, the destination of the journeying of the 'unsettled' and 'unhomely' one.

The 'Theban elders' expel the *deinotaton*, the most unsettled, from the hearth, and this rejection confirms that 'unsettledness' and 'unhomeliness' belong intrinsically to being human. *But*, in this rereading, Heidegger adds that 'this insight brings us only to the place where understanding can genuinely begin.'[46] The chorus's words lead us to think 'beyond' the *deinon*. 'But in what direction?' he asks rhetorically. His reply: 'In the direction of the homely, the hearth.' The Theban elders in their expulsion of Antigone from the hearth have an *implicit* understanding of the hearth. They have a *'phronein,'* a knowing, about the hearth itself and about human beings who are primordially at home at the hearth. 'For someone to be able to expel the most unsettled of all beings from the homely hearth, they must know of the hearth itself.'[47] And this implicit knowing of the hearth is an implicit knowing of Being itself: 'This knowledge that expels from the hearth must know the Being of all beings [*Sein alles Seienden*].'[48]

Thereby, Heidegger completes a remarkable transformation of his earlier reading of these choral lines. In the 1935 reading, he understood the chorus's expulsion of the *deinotaton* to be the firmest confirmation that Dasein is *not at home* at the core of its being. Yet in this 1942 reading, he understands the chorus to be pointing 'beyond' the human being's 'unsettledness' unto the *hearth* – unto Being, the 'place' where human beings primordially belong. Earlier, Sophocles' words testified only to the noble estrangement of human beings; for Heidegger in 1942, these same words also point the way *home*.

Home is the 'hearth' and the 'hearth' is Being itself, the emerging-appearing-unfolding of all beings. Heidegger finds confirmation for this understanding of the hearth in Plato's description of the life of the gods in the *Phaedrus*. '*Hestia* alone,' he translates Plato's words, 'always remains steadfastly behind in the homestead [*Heimstatt*] of the gods.'[49] Ancient Greek poetizing and thinking had 'the insight into the essential connection between *Hestia* and Being.' He expresses this insight in his own poetic words: 'The hearth, the homestead of the homely, is Being itself in whose light and radiance, glow and warmth, all beings already have gathered.'[50] And in another place: 'The hearth is the word for Being; it is that appearing that is named in Antigone's word and that determines everything, even beyond the gods.'[51]

The ultimate destination of the human being is *home*, dwelling near the Source, the Origin, Being as such. Heidegger repeatedly refers to this journey as 'becoming at home in being-not-at-home' (*das Heimischwerden im Unheimischsein*).[52] This phrase sums up the lesson of Sophocles' poetic work, and 'Antigone herself *is* the poem of becoming at home in being-not-at-home.'[53] Again, what is decisively different in his 1942 elucidation of *Antigone* is this theme of the *(re)turn home*. The human being is primordially at home in nearness to Being, the source of all beings. Even so, it is also true that the human being is 'unsettled' and 'unhomely.' We might summarize Heidegger's nuanced position this way: The human being is primordially at home in Being but in the beginning is not aware of Home *as* Home. Because of this 'forgetting' of Being, human beings are lost among beings and founder among beings, 'the foreign land,' and for this reason, they are intrinsically 'unsettled' and 'unhomely' among beings. Nonetheless, some, like Antigone, take up this unsettledness and unhomeliness resolutely; they choose a 'bold forgetting' as they journey through the 'foreign land.' Such passing through the foreign land is necessary for human beings if they are to come to re-cognize Being *as* Home and to dwell at the Source in 'thoughtful remembrance' (*Andenken*). For Heidegger, the Ister, the river of Hölderlin's poem, is 'the river proper to the home of the poet.' It is the river that flows away from its source but that also, according to the poem, appears 'to go backwards.' And this tells us that the truth of the river is the truth of being human:

> The Ister whiles by the Source and is reluctant to abandon its locale because it dwells near the Origin. And it dwells near the Origin because it has returned home to its locality from its journeying to foreign parts. The Ister satisfies the law of becoming at home as the law of being-not-at-home.[54]

To recap our analysis. What is so fascinating about this 1942 lecture course on Hölderlin's poem 'The Ister' is that we find Heidegger working out a reading of Sophocles' *Antigone* that is markedly different from the one he had offered in 1935 in IM. He brilliantly refashions (without admitting so) his reading of Sophocles' words in light of a significant turning in his own thinking in the early 1940s, a turning towards *home*, towards the theme of the human being's primordial existential 'at homeness' in relation to Being. Indeed, in 1942–3 Heidegger makes the theme of the joy (*Freude*) of 'homecoming' central in two additional reflections on Hölderlin's poetry, the commentaries on the poems 'Homecoming / To Kindred Ones' and 'Remembrance.' And after these essays, we find him returning to this motif again and again in the work of the 1950s and 1960s – but with yet another important difference that we will discuss.

Before moving on to a later text, we should also take note of what is so compelling about his account in this 1942 commentary that we have been discussing. He works out a subtle phenomenological understanding of the human being that describes the 'counterplay' (*Gegenspiel*) or 'counterturning' (*Gegenwendigkeit*) between the existential truth of being 'unsettled' (*unheimlich*) and that of 'returning home' (*Heimkehr*). To put this somewhat differently, Heidegger does not abandon his earlier insistence that the de-centring ('unsettling') of the they–self (everyday Dasein) is necessary to achieve an authentic existence; in a poetic way, he continues to maintain that such unsettling is structurally 'essential' to being human. Nonetheless, in his revised view the de-centring or 'unsettling' of the they–self (which had revealed the authentic self to be home-less) is no longer the 'destination'; it now represents a necessary *passage*, an existential precondition, to a re-centring ('returning home') of the self in relation to Being as sheltering Home. As he puts it: 'Coming to be at home is thus a passage [*Durchgang*] through the foreign.'[55] The re-centred self finds safe harbour in Being but also harbours no illusions about mastery over beings or about fulfilment among beings. The re-centred self finds astonishment, joy, and serenity in dwelling thoughtfully in relation to all that comes to be and ceases to be, what the Greeks called *physis*, and what Heidegger calls the Being of beings. His poetic phenomenological description of being human is admirably complex in the 1942 commentary – and it is precisely this complexity that arguably begins to slip away in the later work.

IV. At Home Undisturbed by Unsettledness: '*Gelassenheit*' (1955)

On 30 October 1955, Heidegger gave a talk in Messkirch to celebrate the 175th birthday of the composer Conradin Kreutzer. This speech was later given the title '*Gelassenheit*' or 'Releasement,' though it is better known as 'Memorial Address' to English readers.[56] This brief and elegant address is best-known for the distinction he makes between 'calculative thinking' (*das rechnende Denken*) and 'meditative thinking' (*das besinnliche Nachdenken*). Our primary interest concerns how in this 1955 statement he employs the word *unheimlich*, a word that has a long history in his thinking.

He opens the talk with thanks to his homeland (*Heimat*) 'for all that it has given me along the path of my life.' But he warns that there is something deeply disturbing and even dangerous about the contemporary world. A 'thoughtlessness' has taken hold of the times, he cautions: 'Thoughtlessness is an unsettling [*unheimlicher*] visitor who comes and goes everywhere in today's world.'[57] This is the first time in the text that he uses the word *unheimlich*. Again, we may translate this as 'uncanny,' but the contrast with *Heimat* is obvious enough for us to prefer the translation 'unsettling.' In other words, the unwelcome visitor *unsettles* the home and those who are at home. We also must take careful note that he pointedly says that this thoughtlessness, this unsettling visitor, is everywhere to be found in *'today's world'* (my italics). This suggests that what is 'unsettling' is specifically characteristic of the modern or contemporary world and not an *essential* feature of being-in-the-world. If this is the case, then Heidegger's thinking has taken yet another turn since the early 1940s. In the 1942 commentary, the *unheimlich* remains constitutive of being human; but in this 1955 statement, the *unheimlich* is apparently relegated to a principal feature of the *present age,* which is dominated by 'calculative thinking.'

This reading is certainly strengthened by what follows in the address. Heidegger evokes a time in the past when human beings dwelt 'calmly between heaven and earth.'[58] Calmly, not unsettled. And in this time, human beings were nourished by the life-giving 'roots' of the homeland. They were 'grounded' or 'rooted' at home. Indeed, this 'rootedness' (*Bodenständigkeit*) defines the being of human beings; but then he declares that 'the *rootedness* of human beings today is threatened at its core.'[59] Rootedness (in Being itself) has given way to a disturbing and dangerous uprootedness, an unsettledness, that specifically 'springs from the spirit of the age into which all of us were born.'

The sway of 'calculative thinking,' which defines the essence of the technological age, has made us 'unsettled.' The dangers of the proliferation of technological developments are obvious enough, he observes, yet even 'if the hydrogen bombs do *not* explode and human life on earth is preserved, an unsettling [*unheimliche*] change in the world moves upon us.'[60] What is truly unsettling is not the vast array of technologies, but rather our being unaware of what is shaping and forming and dominating our times, and this is the sway of calculative thinking. Now, what precisely he understands to be the provenance of this sway of calculative thinking may be open to debate, but it seems quite clear that he understands Dasein's 'unsettledness' in the world to be exclusively characteristic of the present age. It is not Dasein itself that is constitutively unsettled; it is only Dasein in the present age that is *unheimlich*.

Heidegger proposes that the domination of calculative thinking can and must be challenged by a 'releasement toward things' (*Gelassenheit zu den Dingen*) and a 'meditative thinking' that lets beings be and that is open to the 'mystery' of the coming to be and ceasing to be of all things.

Meditative thinking is the fundamental manner of thinking, and it is also originary because in a former time, in the 'old rootedness' (*alte Bodenständigkeit*), human beings dwelt meditatively and serenely on the earth and under the sky. The present age has brought with it a peculiar unsettledness, but this unsettledness is by no means constitutive of human dwelling; it does not touch 'our inner and real core,' he says.[61] In fact, he clearly suggests that it ultimately can be overcome so that we can dwell 'in the world in a completely different way': 'Releasement toward things and openness to mystery give us a vision of a new rootedness, which someday even might be fit to recover the old and now rapidly disappearing rootedness in a different form.'[62] Thus, he offers a 'vision,' a vision of human beings *once again* dwelling at home in relation to Being altogether undisturbed by the unsettledness of the present age. Apparently, the journey home for Dasein no longer *essentially* and *necessarily* passes through the *unheimlich*.

V. At Home Everything Is Gladdened: 'Messkirch's Seventh Centennial' (1961)

In the evening of 22 July 1961, Heidegger delivered a talk in Messkirch to celebrate the town's seven hundredth anniversary.[63] Once again, the topic for reflection is the 'homeland' (*Heimat*). He takes note of the many technological innovations that have transformed life for contemporary human beings. Nevertheless, these technological developments appear to 'offer no abiding, reliable, resting place; they change unceasingly from the new to the newest.' Human beings have become captivated by all that is new, and he characterizes this as a movement 'from the homely into the unhomely' (*aus dem Heimischen ins Unheimische*).[64] He returns, therefore, to another earlier theme, the theme of being 'not at home' or 'unhomely,' *unheimisch*, which also has a long history in his thinking. Yet again there is a difference. He speaks of the unhomely in this address in much the same way as he had spoken of the unsettling in the 1955 address on *Gelassenheit*; that is, he clearly appears to characterize the existential unhomeliness of human beings as a phenomenon specifically of the present 'technological age.' Dasein's unhomeliness is not constitutive of being-in-the-world as such; rather, it is the constitutive affliction of the present age dominated by 'modern technicity' (*die moderne Technik*).

In the present age, human beings are 'in flight into the unhomely,' and this flight takes the form of the rush to fill up time with gadgets and activities that, in the end, leaves us profoundly bored and bewildered. A 'puzzling' and 'unsettling' (*unheimlich*) way of life has overtaken human beings in the technological age, and this has left us 'unhomely' and suffering from 'homesickness' (*Heimweh*). Nonetheless, this very homesickness confirms the abiding presence of home. We are longing for home. We are seeking to restore our primordial relation to the 'homeland,' to the Origin, to Being itself (though Heidegger does not explicitly mention Being in this address). The Origin seeks human beings, too. No matter how 'not at home' human beings are in the present age, 'there yet comes towards us the homeland that we seek, even though it is wrapped in disguise. Because it touches us again and again in such a form, we must go out and meet it.'[65]

Such cryptic pronouncements make it difficult to decipher precisely his meaning; yet it emerges clearly enough that the search for home is a search that will lead us *beyond* the unhomely and unsettling to what he calls 'rest and in-gathering.' Dasein's recovery of Home will overcome the unhomely and the unsettling, which are the determinative features of the technological age. How else can we understand the following words?

> In the midst of the unhomely we are making a turn back into the homely. Such a return home has the power – if we abide carefully and without haste on its way – such a return home has the power of overtaking again and again everything that sweeps us up into the unhomely.[66]

Our return home (in relation to Being as the temporal unfolding of all beings) has the power to overcome the existential unhomeliness that afflicts us. Indeed, he adds, by gathering ourselves once again into meditative thinking, 'everything is gladdened, everything becomes clear and transparent.'[67]

Conclusion

In several important texts of the 1920s and 1930s – *The History of the Concept of Time*, *Being and Time*, and *Introduction to Metaphysics* – Heidegger maintained the position that Dasein is primordially *unheimlich*, 'unsettled,' and thus also *unheimisch*, 'not at home' at the core of its being. However, we discover a significant turning in his thinking towards *home*, especially in the early 1940s. The 1942 commentary on Hölderlin's poem 'The Ister' stands out as a bridge text between the early and later Heidegger on this issue; in particular, we find a striking and significant difference in his reading of Sophocles' *Antigone* compared with the better-known reading in the 1935 *Introduction to Metaphysics*. In 'The Ister' commentary, he engaged both Sophocles and Hölderlin to work out the motif – so prominent in his later work – that human beings are primordially 'at home' in Being, the sheltering source and origin of all beings. Even so, in this commentary he continued to maintain that confrontation with the 'foreign,' with the 'unsettled,' with the 'unhomely,' belongs to the very essencing of human beings. The journey home for human beings must pass through the 'foreign land'; only those, like Antigone, who resolutely confront the 'unsettled' and 'unhomely' that we essentially *are* – only these can return home and authentically dwell at home in relation to Being.

We find yet another development in his thinking on this issue in his work of the 1950s and 1960s. In two representative texts, *'Gelassenheit'* ('Memorial Address'; 1955) and 'Messkirch's Seventh Centennial' (1961), he no longer speaks about 'unsettledness' and 'not-at-homeness' as belonging constitutively to Dasein's being; rather, he speaks of *das Unheimliche* and *das Unheimische* as afflicting Dasein in the modern technological age. In Heidegger's later view, Dasein must struggle against the prevailing unsettling and unhomely spirit of the present age in order to recover its primordially at-home relation to Being and to dwell, calm and gladdened, in nearness to Being – Home, Source and Origin of all beings.

From a phenomenological standpoint, each of Heidegger's descriptions – early, middle, and late – of Dasein's fundamental relation to Being has compelling features that resonate powerfully, and this surely testifies to the richness of his thought. Even so, I would suggest that it is his account in the middle years – the period when he composed the commentary on 'The Ister' – that is most compelling because of its depth and complexity. Once again, to recast Heidegger's language in somewhat different terms, we might say that the emphasis in his early work was on 'de-centring' the they–self that Dasein (always) is and that the emphasis in the later work was on 're-centring' Dasein in relation to Being. Yet in the middle period, he worked out a more complex phenomenological description of Dasein that keeps fully in view both the 'de-centring' and the 're-centring' of Dasein. This is one way of understanding his central motif in the commentary on 'The Ister' of 'becoming at home in being-not-at-home' (*das Heimischwerden im Unheimischsein*). That is, Dasein is structurally 'de-centred' ('not at home') for all of the existential reasons that he had laid out in the early work: Dasein's existence is contingent, unfounded, dispersed, and finite ('factical,' 'thrown,' 'fallen,' and 'being-towards-death'). In the face of its radically negatived finitude, Dasein is no longer able to maintain its identity in terms of the they–self; nonetheless, such de-centring makes possible a re-centring of the self in relation to Being as Home. Dasein is re-centred ('becomes at home') and finds *joy*, *calm*, and *rest* in meditatively wondering and marvelling about its being in relation to Being, the temporal giving and flowing forth of all beings.

Thus, as I hope has been made clear, Heidegger's early view of Dasein's gritty and resolute acceptance of its anxious, unsettled, and unhomely being-in-the-world gave way – especially in the work of the early 1940s – to the much more sanguine and serene view of Dasein's 'return home' to Being. Nevertheless, his poetic phenomenological description of the human being in relation to Being, such as we find in the commentary on 'The Ister,' is nuanced and retains important insights of his earlier thinking. In the later thinking of the 1950s and 1960s, his account of Dasein's being at home in relation to Being appears to flatten and lose the complexity and depth of his perspective of the middle years. This impression – and I say impression because I do not want to overstate the case – is based on several later texts, but one observation will do for the present. In the commentary on 'The Ister,' Heidegger speaks of the joy of Dasein's returning home: 'Joy is a safeguarding and guarding over the return home to one's own.'[68] But he also tempers that joy with the reminder that 'mourning pervades the Ister ... it pervades the poet himself in his poetic essence.'[69] Sadness attends the 'knowing of the necessity of patient whiling "near the origin."' After all, we may say, our journey home that passes through the 'foreign land' is a difficult and painful one that leaves us all wounded – and mournful. Yet in the 1961 address this sobering truth is missing from his description of Dasein's return home: 'Meditation is not melancholy but gladsomeness [*die Heiterkeit*] in which everything is gladdened, everything becomes clear and transparent.'[70]

Such statements from the later Heidegger certainly have their appeal, but they also leave us somewhat puzzled and wondering. How do we understand that Dasein's thoughtful dwelling at home in relation to Being leaves all melancholy and mourning behind? How is it possible that 'everything is gladdened'? What does it mean to say that 'everything becomes clear and transparent'? These remain fair and important questions to put to Heidegger's later thought.

4 From Angst to Astonishment

Among all beings, only the human being, called upon by the voice of
Being, experiences the wonder of all wonders: *that* beings *are*.
Postscript to 'What is Metaphysics?' 1943

One dimension of our being-in-the-world is affective, so over the years
the question has been asked in existential philosophy and psychology:
How shall we name and characterize the affective disposition that most
defines our being-in-the-world? Or to put this question another way:
What is the defining mood of our authentically taking up our situation?
In *Being and Time*, Heidegger identified Angst as the mood that brings
the human being (Dasein) most squarely face to face with the sobering truth of its radically finite existence.[1] In inauthenticity, Dasein finds
multiple ways of fleeing Angst and the truth it reveals; yet in authenticity, Dasein brings an end to the flight and resolutely accepts its finitude
and the accompanying mood of Angst. Thus, as he worked it out in
Being and Time, the mood of Angst is more fundamentally constitutive
of Dasein than any other mood, and confronting and resolutely taking
up Angst is a defining feature of authentic existence.

Heidegger's discussion of Angst in *Being and Time* has become a core
component of existential thinking over the years. Even so, a closer examination of his account would help clarify several issues that are of
importance not only to philosophers but also to those working theo-
retically or clinically in the general area of existential or phenomenological psychology. Moreover, we need to give an account of how after
Being and Time he increasingly moved away from his early emphasis on

Angst as he worked out more clearly his ownmost matter for thought. After 1930, Heidegger became reluctant to identify one fundamental, defining mood; even so, we find that in his later thinking he gave greater attention to 'awe' (*die Scheu*) and 'astonishment' (*das Erstaunen*) in describing the prevailing affective disposition of Dasein's authentic existing, thereby recalling the importance of the mood of 'wonder' spoken of long ago by the ancient Greek philosophers. I do not propose to offer a comprehensive analysis of the issue of affective disposition in Heidegger's work; I wish only to highlight certain notable points of development in his thinking with the overarching aim of illuminating how his reflections continue to be of value in thinking about authentic modes of human existing.

I. *Being and Time* (1927)

In Section 29, Heidegger identifies 'affective disposition' (*die Befindlichkeit*) as an *existentiale;* that is, it is a fundamental structural component of Dasein.[2] The human being (Dasein) always-already finds itself affectively disposed in a certain way because Dasein is always-already open to the world, 'thrown' and 'delivered over' to it. Because Dasein is structurally this thrown-openness, it is always-already affectively 'disposed' or 'attuned.' According to his terminology, 'affective disposition' (*Befindlichkeit*) names the ontological-existential dimension of human affectedness that is distinguishable from specific ontic-existentiell 'moods' (*Stimmungen*). Though this distinction between the ontic and the ontological dimensions is meaningful and useful (as we shall discuss shortly), it remains that in either case, the human being is always-already 'affectively disposed' or 'mooded' in a certain way. Consequently, I will use the terms affective disposition, mood, and attunement interchangeably.

In Section 30, he gives a phenomenological description of one particular mood, fear, with the end in view of contrasting fear and Angst later in Section 40 (and again in 68b). Fear is always fear of something definite within the world. As he puts it: '*That in the face of which* we fear, the fearsome, is in every case something that we encounter within the world and that may have either readiness-to-hand, presence-at-hand, or Dasein-with as its kind of being.'[3] Since fear is always related to some entity within the world, this particular mood does not and cannot disclose the world *as such* to Dasein. Heidegger is interested in identifying an affective disposition that has more disclosive power, a mood that lights up for Dasein its being-in-the-world as such or, put another way, its radically finite openness as such. That mood is Angst.

In Section 40, he draws the contrast between the affective dispositions of fear and Angst. But first, a serious difficulty presents itself for English readers. How shall we translate this word Angst? We know that Heidegger's discussion of Angst was deeply indebted to Kierkegaard's own analysis of this phenomenon (*Der Begriff der Angst*, 1844). Generally speaking, the word Angst as Kierkegaard used it has been translated into English as 'dread,' and several translators of Heidegger's work have followed suit in preferring this word. In fact, in a recently published new (and elegant) translation of Heidegger's 1929 lecture 'What Is Metaphysics?' Thomas Sheehan also makes the case for 'dread.'[4] Yet as I hope to make clear shortly, I think there are more compelling reasons to translate Angst – if we must translate it at all – as anxiety. To be sure, translating Angst as anxiety has its own difficulties, but the word 'dread' ultimately proves to be more problematical.

In Section 40, he restates that fear 'always comes from entities within the world,' but in marked contrast, 'that in the face of which one has anxiety is not an entity within the world.'[5] Anxiety is not anxious before *this* or *that* or any-*thing*. What Dasein is anxious about is 'nothing and nowhere within the world.' Dasein's anxiety is not related to any particular entity or entities within the world; rather, it relates to being-in-the-world as such. If heeded, anxiety leads Dasein past its involvements with beings in the world and lights up the 'world as world,' but it also discloses to Dasein its peculiar predicament: its thrownness, facticity, fallenness, and mortality (being-towards-death). In short, anxiety reveals to Dasein its radically finite and negatived existence. In anxiety, Dasein experiences itself as exiled from beings and from the world; it feels 'estranged,' 'uneasy,' 'unsettled,' 'uncanny' (all possible translations of Heidegger's word *unheimlich*). Even so, it is precisely anxiety that 'brings Dasein face to face with its *being-free for* ... (*propensio in* ...) the authenticity of its being, and for this authenticity as a possibility that it always-already is.'[6] Authentic existing requires that Dasein resolutely take up the Angst constitutive of its radically finite existence.

This much about Heidegger's analysis is clear, but several clarifications remain to be made. First, it would seem that his phenomenological analysis of anxiety is not completely drawn. Towards the end of Section 40, he makes an important observation that he does not work out with much precision. He notes that insofar as Dasein is under the sway of falling and publicness, 'authentic Angst' (*eigentliche Angst*) is 'rare.' Nonetheless, everyday Dasein often experiences anxiety in the form of 'physiological' symptoms. He adds: 'This fact, in its facticity, is a problem *ontologically*, not merely with regard to its ontic causation and course of development. Only because Dasein is anxious at the core of its being, does it become possible for anxiety to be manifested physiologically.'[7] In effect, Heidegger is saying that in analysing the phenomenon of Angst, we need to make a crucial distinction between the ontic and ontological dimensions, but he does not draw this out precisely or state it explicitly. Consequently, though there is no explicit textual warrant for this, I believe that such observations justify our making an important and useful distinction between what I will call 'ontic anxiousness' (the ontic dimension of Angst) and 'ontological anxiety' (the ontological dimension of Angst).

On the basis of Heidegger's textual clue, I use the term 'ontic anxiousness' to refer to 'average, everyday' anxiousness or to the kind of neurotic anxiousness that is burdensome to human beings and that manifests itself in a wide variety of psychic confusions and physiological symptoms such as rapid heart beat, palpitations, aching and twitching muscles, excessive sweating, stomach aches, and headaches. This 'ontic anxiousness' can be bearable or crippling and, depending upon its severity, is what leads people to seek out psychoanalysis or psychotherapy for help or, as is (regrettably) becoming more and more common, to simply secure one of a host of new medications to 'treat' such 'disorders.'

It is apparent that such 'ontic anxiousness' is *not* what Heidegger has in mind when he speaks about Dasein resolutely taking up the 'authentic' Angst of its radically finite existence. Yet in Section 40 and in *Being and Time* generally, he is not as clear about this as he might have been, and the result is that the difference between the ontic and ontological dimensions of the phenomenon of Angst becomes blurred or uncertain. Unfortunately, this uncertainty in the text has given rise over the years to a variety of misunderstandings about the significance of his emphasis on the mood of Angst. For example, for some, the neurotic anxiousness of a Woody Allen serves as a model of Heideggerian anxious resoluteness! However, a more serious and perhaps even tragic misunderstanding is that for others, neurotic anxiousness is mistaken for (or misdiagnosed as) 'ontological anxiety' (authentic Angst) with the consequence that debilitating anguish is endured unnecessarily in the name of 'authenticity.'

This lack of clarity or precision in the text is related to another limitation in his analysis. His sharp contrast between the dispositions of Angst and fear seems too neat. Consider that phenomenologically, 'ontic anxiousness' may manifest the features of *both* Angst and fear as he discusses these. That is, neurotic anxiousness (resembling authentic Angst) is often about 'nothing'; one who is gripped by such 'generalized' anxiousness cannot say exactly 'what' he or she is anxious about. Yet as Freud helped us understand, such neurotic anxiety *is* nonetheless an anxiousness (resembling fear) before some definite 'entity within the world' – but an entity that has not yet been brought into view. In other words, Dasein may be suffering from a diffuse, 'generalized' anxiousness that stems from a 'repressed' trauma, and though there *is* a specific 'entity' in the face of which Dasein is anxious/fearful, Dasein has not yet brought this entity into word, and therefore, 'within the world.' By bringing the 'repressed' entity into word and world, Dasein also brings itself relief from such debilitating anxiousness.

Of course, as Heidegger obliquely observes in Section 40, 'ontic anxiousness' (to use my terms) is *related* to 'ontological anxiety' (authentic Angst) precisely because ontic anxiousness ultimately *discloses* to Dasein the fundamental 'unsettledness' (*Unheimlichkeit*) that is constitutive of being-in-the-world. Thus, because ontic anxiousness and ontological anxiety are related phenomenologically, it is preferable to translate Angst – again, if we must translate it at all – as 'anxiety.' I suggest that this word better captures and preserves the relatedness and tension between the ontic and ontological dimensions of the phenomenon that Heidegger is describing than does the word 'dread.' In addition, 'dread' introduces some other difficulties. First, 'dread,' like 'fear,' is most often used in English in a way that emphasizes the specific object or term, as in expressions in the general form of 'I dread *that*!' Second, 'dread' connotes a much more specific, powerful, and arresting affect than does 'anxiety.' Third, 'dread' misses altogether the peculiar 'calm' that Heidegger associates with the affective disposition of authentic Angst. But that leads us to the next important text.

II. 'What Is Metaphysics?' (1929)

On 24 July 1929, Heidegger, newly installed as the Chair of Philosophy at the University of Freiburg, delivered his inaugural lecture, titled 'What Is Metaphysics?' (published later the same year; hereafter WM). Some years later, in 1943, he appended a Postscript, and his remarks reveal that he was apparently stung by the public criticism in the intervening years of his emphasis on the importance of the mood of Angst in WM. He restates in his own words the complaints that he had 'isolated' one mood, the 'morbid' mood of Angst, and elevated it to the 'fundamental mood' (*Grundstimmung*). According to his critics, he notes, his line of thinking amounted to a negative and paralysing 'philosophy of anxiety.'[8]

Heidegger insisted in the Postscript that such criticism missed the mark, and he was right; but it is also true that it did not miss the mark altogether. In *Being and Time*, though his meaning was apparent that the Angst that is constitutive of Dasein as finite openness is not the same as the morbidity of neurotic anxiousness, he was not sufficiently explicit in distinguishing between the ontic and ontological dimensions of Angst. Moreover, his phenomenological analysis of Angst, especially in *Being and Time*, did betray an excessively 'negative' tenor. As we have noted, his focus was on how, in anxiety, Dasein experiences itself as primordially *unheimlich*, 'unsettled,' and *unheimisch*, 'not at home,' and he made a point of derisively dismissing all 'at home,' 'tranquillized,' and 'familiar' ways of being-in-the-world as inauthentic and as belonging to the fallen 'publicness' of the 'they.'

In his 1929 lecture 'What Is Metaphysics?' Heidegger focuses again on the uniquely disclosive mood of Angst. Yet even though his phenomenological description of Angst in WM is similar to his earlier description in *Being and Time*, there is a subtle but significant difference that I hope to make clear. In WM, he is interested in how Angst brings Dasein face to face with *das Nichts*, the Nothing, the No-thing that allows all forms of beings to appear.[9] He emphasizes that by the Nothing he does not mean the simple negation of all beings; rather, the Nothing is another name for Being itself, if only we are mindful that Being itself is what allows all beings to shine forth, to appear, to 'be.' Whereas other moods bring Dasein in relation to other beings or even to the totality of beings, it is principally the mood of Angst that brings Dasein face to face with the Nothing itself (Being itself).

As in *Being and Time*, Heidegger distinguishes between the affective dispositions of fear and Angst, emphasizing that whereas fear is always fear of something, anxiety is anxiety before no-thing. Accordingly, 'anxiety reveals the Nothing.' He also warns that we must not confuse Angst with 'the quite common anxiousness [*Ängstlichkeit*], ultimately reducible to fearfulness, which all too readily comes over us,'[10] and this remark provides additional textual support for my suggestion that we make an explicit distinction between 'ontic anxiousness' and 'ontological anxiety.'

In describing the affective disposition of Angst, he returns to the ground he covered in *Being and Time*. In anxiety, Dasein feels 'unsettled' (*unheimlich*). Beings, including Dasein itself, 'sink into indifference,' and 'the receding of beings as a whole that closes in on us in anxiety oppresses us.' Dasein is 'struck dumb' as it becomes aware of itself as radically finite openness to the Nothing. In this quiet, Dasein has the opportunity to take up resolutely the *Grundstimmung* of Angst and what it reveals. More typically, however, Dasein tries to 'shatter the empty stillness with mindless chatter.'[11]

The subtle but significant difference in this essay comes in his making greater note of the distinctive 'calm' of the affective disposition of Angst. More clearly than in Section 40 of *Being and Time*, he frees the mood of Angst from the turbulence of ontic anxiousness. He insists that no kind of buzzing 'confusion' is a feature of Angst. 'On the contrary,' he observes, 'Angst is suffused with a peculiar kind of calm [*Ruhe*].'[12] Soon after, he adds: 'In Angst there is a drawing back from ... which is surely not flight, but rather a stunned calm [*gebannte Ruhe*].'[13] And later, he makes this revealing statement: 'The Angst born of risk is not the opposite of joy, or even of quiet activity and calm enjoyment. It transcends such oppositions and lives in secret communion with the serene and gentle yearnings of creativity.'[14] His emphasis, then, is that the mood of Angst is one of serene beholding and creative 'calm.' In this phenomenological account, authentic Angst bears less resemblance to 'ontic anxiousness.' If they remain related, the thread linking them has become thinner.

This subtle difference suggests a subtle but important shift in Heidegger's thinking. As in *Being and Time*, in WM he identifies Angst as the defining mood of Dasein as being-in-the-world, and he continues to characterize the mood in terms of 'unsettledness' (*Unheimlichkeit*). Even so, in WM he offers a more meditative and serene version of this 'unsettledness.' In *Being and Time* he pressed the point (arguably too hard) that Dasein is constitutively 'unsettled' because it is so unremittingly finite as limited, lacking, and incomplete ('the absolute impossibility of Dasein' and 'the null basis of its null projection').[15] In WM, however, he seems more interested in making the point that Dasein is constitutively unsettled because it finds itself as the finite *between* of Being (the Nothing) and beings. Dasein alone among beings has this 'essence' of 'going-beyond-beings' to the Nothing (Being) or of being 'held out into the Nothing,' and therefore Dasein alone can experience itself as 'unsettled' precisely as this 'going-beyond.' Characterized in this way, Dasein's Angst is a somewhat different phenomenon, and Dasein's 'unsettledness' seems far less unsettling. In Heidegger's description, the mood of Angst is one of quiet and calm – not at all opposed to joy, as he says – which at the end of the lecture he even characterizes as 'wonder' (*Verwunderung*).

Yet it is fair to ask: Is this affective disposition so described still Angst? His account in WM suggests that how we find ourselves ontologically in Angst (calm) is markedly different from how we find ourselves as ontically anxious (trembling). The relatedness of the two may remain, but it is certainly more difficult to identify. In this lecture, he seems to be stretching the meaning of the term Angst to its limit; the word seems overburdened and barely able to capture his additional concerns in characterizing the defining affective disposition of Dasein's ex-sistence. As Heidegger's focus shifts in WM towards 'liberating' Dasein for the Nothing (Being), his discussion of Angst presents us with an important clue that he was perhaps *already* thinking beyond the phenomenon of Angst in seeking to name the mood that fundamentally defines Dasein's authentic existence. We should not be at all surprised, I think, that after the publication of WM in 1929, he never again accorded to the mood of Angst such a unique and privileged status.[16]

This observation is not meant to diminish the importance and value for both philosophy and psychology of Heidegger's analysis of Angst in *Being and Time* and in WM. Rather, it simply raises the question of whether his focus on the phenomenon of Angst was ever his ownmost matter for thought in the first place, especially when we consider that he marginalized the theme after 1929. We may reasonably propose that in his early thinking he inherited the theme of Angst principally from Kierkegaard, but also more generally from a tradition of German thinking that included a romanticism imbued with anti-bourgeois sentiment and a Nietzschean emphasis on the heroic and 'tragic.'[17] Heidegger's own analysis of the phenomenon of Angst is both original and compelling; nevertheless, his focus on this mood in his early thinking seems to have been largely determined by these multiple influences. This would help explain why even in the 1929 essay, we find him subtly metamorphosing the affective disposition of Angst into something else – a *Grundstimmung* not quite yet named but more in keeping with his own unfolding understanding of Dasein's cor-relation with Being.

III. Hölderlin Elucidations (1943) / Postscript to 'What Is Metaphysics?' (1943)

During the 1930s and early 1940s, one of Heidegger's major preoccupations was with Hölderlin's poetry.[18] In 1943 he composed beautiful elucidations on the poems 'Homecoming / To Kindred Ones' and 'Remembrance.'[19] In these two essays, Heidegger emphasizes how Being 'hails' or 'greets' Dasein, and using the language of the poems, he offers a host of positive words to characterize Being, including such names as the Gladsome, the Most Joyous, the Source, the Origin, and the Holy.[20]

Since it is Being that attunes or affectively disposes Dasein, it follows from these bright and positive characterizations of Being that Dasein is fundamentally disposed in hale and wholesome ways as well. Throughout these commentaries, he names a number of positive moods, such as serenity, gaiety, love, and especially *joy*, as constitutive of the poet's (Dasein's) authentic cor-respondence with Being. The major theme of his readings is Dasein's being 'at home' (*heimisch, zu Hauß*) in nearness to Being. Human beings are primordially 'at home' in nearness to Being as the Source of all beings; yet in the beginning, we are not aware of this as such. Only after 'valiantly forgetting the homeland' and 'wandering abroad' is the poet (in particular) called (by Being) to make the long journey 'home.' 'Homecoming' (*Heimkunft*) is the occasion for great joy, but there remains the task of learning to 'abide' and 'dwell' in nearness to Being in its mysterious revealing-concealing. The poet, for one, sustains such dwelling in nearness to the Origin through the poetic word, through 'remembrance' (*Andenken*).[21]

Certainly, we must first of all take note of how Heidegger's principal motif of Dasein's 'homecoming' and dwelling 'at home' is strikingly different from his basic view in *Being and Time* that all 'at home' modes of being belong to the 'they' and are steeped in inauthenticity. Though the Hölderlin commentaries are not strictly philosophical analyses, it is sufficiently clear that Heidegger's fundamental position in these essays is that Dasein's being 'at home' in nearness to Being is ontological or primordial (*ursprünglich*). This position is in sharp contrast with his earlier insistence in *Being and Time* that *'from an existential-ontological point of view, the "not-at-home" must be conceived as the more primordial phenomenon'* (Heidegger's italics).[22] These contrasting positions represent an intriguing aspect of his thinking that I have addressed in the previous chapter; yet in view of our present concern, it is enough to make the observation that as he unfolds this theme of Dasein's being primordially 'at home,' he also brings into view and highlights Dasein's primordially positive moods.[23]

In these two commentaries on Hölderlin, Heidegger illuminates a manifold of bright moods that are constitutive of Dasein's cor-respondence with Being.[24] He is not unmindful of darker moods, but these are not the moods principally thematized. There is, however, one mood that he identifies that appears to be neither 'positive' nor 'negative,' though it is closely related to the profound joy of 'homecoming.' In the commentary on the poem 'Remembrance,' Heidegger speaks of 'awe' (*die Scheu*) and suggests that this mood may be most definitive of the poet's and the thinker's (Dasein's) authentic comportment to Being.[25] As he describes it, awe is 'the fundamental mood [*Grundstimmung*] of the holidays for the slow paths' and it 'determines that one go to the origin.'[26] It is the fundamental mood of Dasein's 'remembering' that all beings (both bright and dark) unfold in Being – and that all moods (both bright and dark) are attunements to beings as they unfold in Being. As Dasein steps back from its involvement with beings, returns 'home,' and 'remembers' Being itself as the originating of all beings, Dasein finds itself in *awe*. In Heidegger's words:

> As this primordially firm holding oneself back [*Ansichhalten*] before what is awesome, awe has at the same time the most intimate affection for it ... Awe is that reserved, patient, astonished remembrance of that which abides near in a nearness that consists solely in keeping what is distant in its fullness distant, and thereby keeping it ready for its welling-up emergence from its source. This essential awe [*wesenhafte Scheu*] is the mood of a *thinking*, which has come home, of the origin.[27]

He brings this mood of awe to the forefront again in the Postscript (also written in 1943) to his 1929 'What Is Metaphysics?' In the two Hölderlin essays, Heidegger gave no attention to the mood of Angst, yet in the Postscript he returns to a discussion of this mood and reframes its significance. Responding to his critics, he insists that Angst must not be confused with the ontic concern with subjective 'feelings.' Angst is a distinctive affective disposition (understood ontologically) because it 'makes a claim on the human being in his essence so that he learns to experience Being in the Nothing.'[28] Moreover, it requires 'courage' on Dasein's part to respond to the negativity of this disposition and risk opening itself to 'the experience of Being.' The mood of Angst is a 'speechless' experience of stunned quiet in which Dasein comes to hear the 'voice' of Being – and this description recalls his emphasis on the 'calm' of the mood of Angst in WM.

However, in the Postscript he no longer privileges Angst as he had done in the 1929 lecture. The mood of awe (*Scheu*) – the same mood that he had highlighted in the commentary on 'Remembrance' – appears to have become for Heidegger the more fitting name for the disposition most constitutive of Dasein's holding itself open to Being in all its richness and ambiguity. In a key line in the Postcript, he states: 'For close by essential [ontological] anxiety, in the terror of the abyss, there dwells awe. Awe clears and embraces that place of being essentially human within which one abides at home in the abiding.'[29]

As William J. Richardson noted, Heidegger's phrase 'abides at home in the abiding' (*heimisch bleibt im Bleibenden*) 'sets the entire passage in the context of the Hölderlin analyses.'[30] Richardson also took note that 'once we learn to experience Being for itself, as the Hölderlin interpretations tried to do ... the fundamental disposition in There-being [Dasein] becomes less anxiety than awe.'[31] In fact, we need to take this observation one step further and say that once we learn from Heidegger that Dasein is primordially 'at home' in nearness to Being, we understand more clearly why, for Heidegger, Angst is no longer the pre-eminent and privileged mood. His heartfelt and reassuring words in the Postscript that Being bestows 'grace' and 'favour' upon Dasein and calls Dasein to assume 'the guardianship [*Wächterschaft*] of Being' make it apparent that the fundamental mood of Dasein's cor-relation with Being is no longer Angst. We learn from the Postscript that in the mood of *awe* Dasein is poised to listen and respond to Being in inward calm, in speechless reserve, in quiet thankfulness, in patient and gracious awaiting.

IV. Introduction to 'What Is Metaphysics?' (1949)

In 1949, Heidegger added an Introduction to his 1929 'What Is Metaphysics?' This Introduction bears its own title: 'The Way Back into the Ground of Metaphysics.'[32] Of interest to us is his treatment of the mood of Angst. Not surprisingly, this theme that had been so prominent in the 1929 lecture has all but disappeared in 1949. His reference to Angst is brief and cryptic, but Dreyfus and Rubin appear to be right in observing that Angst 'is now read [by Heidegger] as the experience of "the oblivion of being" uniquely characteristic of the modern age.' As they see it, he now 'interprets anxiety as a specific response to the rootlessness of the contemporary technological world.'[33]

According to Heidegger, it is the modern age in particular that is determined by the 'oblivion of Being' – or, perhaps better, the 'forgottenness of Being' (*die Seinsvergessenheit*). To be sure, metaphysical thinking, which only thinks beings, is forgetful of Being, but he also detects that in the modern age the human being is more and more 'abandoned' to beings. This leaves Dasein more and more 'forsaken,' cut off from its 'ground,' and deprived of the nourishing 'relation' (*Bezug*) to Being itself. His observation would be clear enough if it were not for his enigmatic claim that it is Being itself that has withdrawn and hidden itself from Dasein, and the philosophical difficulties with this language can be taken up another time. The important point for our present concern is that he links the mood of Angst especially to the modern preoccupation with beings and the accompanying estrangement from Being, the emerging-appearing of all beings. His interest appears to be in identifying Angst, *not* as the mood constitutive of Dasein, but rather as the mood constitutive of the modern age, which is marked so decisively by this estrangement from Being. Thus he asks: 'What more can thinking do than to endure in anxiety this dispensation [*Geschick*] of Being, so as first of all to face up to the forgottenness of Being?'[34]

He adds rhetorically, 'What does such anxiety, as a dispensation of Being, have to do with psychology or psychoanalysis?' His meaning appears to be that this anxiety is not simply ontic and addressable (and redressable) by psychology and psychoanalysis. Rather, Angst is a principal attunement of the modern age. Nevertheless, we must take careful notice that he does not say, as he once had, that Angst is the defining affective disposition of Dasein's ex-sistence. Quite to the contrary, his pointed suggestion here is that the Angst constitutive of the modern age must be resolutely confronted by Dasein precisely in order for Dasein to lessen its sting – and perhaps even to overcome it – by finding the way back to an originary thinking that recalls (*das andenkende Denken*) and restores the relationship of Being and human being.[35] And precisely this possibility of a transformed 'sojourn' (*Aufenthalt*) of human beings in the present age engaged Heidegger's thinking more and more into the 1950s and 1960s and right up to his death in 1976.

V. 'What Is That – Philosophy?' (1955)

One of Heidegger's more elegant – and overlooked – lectures is '*Was ist das – die Philosophie?*' published in 1956 as the text of the lecture he gave in 1955 at Cérisy-la-Salle, Normandy, France.[36] Since it is an important statement for our purposes, it is worth considering at some length. He considers that the Greek word *philosophos* was likely coined by Heraclitus. What does Heraclitus mean by 'loving' (*philein*) the *sophon,* the wise itself? As Heidegger understands Heraclitus' own words, the *sophon* means *Hen-Panta* or, as he translates this, 'One (is) all' (*Eines [ist] Alles*). *Panta,* the many ('all'), is to be understood as all beings. *Hen,* one, means 'the One, the unique, the all-uniting,' and is therefore the name for Being. *Hen* (Being) 'is' *Panta* (beings) in the sense that Being lets be and 'gathers together' beings. Being is this 'gathering-together'; Being is the primordial *Logos.*[37]

According to Heidegger, Heraclitus' words were in originary correspondence (*homologein*) with Being (*Logos*). This cor-respondence (or accordance) is a harmony, and 'this *harmonia* is the distinctive feature of *philein,* of "loving" in the Heraclitean sense.' The *philosophos,* then, is one who in harmony with Being says the words 'One (is) all,' which means 'all beings in Being.' Moreover, this utterance is accompanied by a fundamental mood or 'attunement' (*Gestimmtheit*), and Heidegger identifies this defining affective disposition of the one who is in authentic cor-respondence with Being as 'astonishment' (*das Erstaunen*). In his words:

> And yet, just this, that beings are gathered together in Being, that in the shining of Being, beings shine forth – this astonished the Greeks and first astonished them and them alone. Beings in Being [*Seiendes im Sein*]: this became the most astonishing thing for the Greeks.[38]

The affective disposition named *das Erstaunen* had been discussed by Heidegger in other contexts before, but among his published works, it is in this lecture, in the later years, that he thematizes this mood with particular attention and emphasis.[39] *Das Erstaunen* could be translated as 'wonder,' and this translation has the advantage of hearkening directly back to Plato's and Aristotle's word *thaumazein,* which has been traditionally translated as 'wonder.' Yet despite this advantage, the word 'wonder' may fail to convey the mood that Heidegger wishes to emphasize. Kluback and Wilde translated *das Erstaunen* as 'astonishment,' which seems to be a good choice. The Greeks who loved the *sophon* did not just 'wonder' in the pale intellectual sense that we might use this word today; their thoughtful cor-respondence was defined by *astonishment.* This word suggests the deep and abiding joy that comes with profound discovery, and this sense, too, seems in keeping with Heidegger's intention.

Indulging in a bit of myth making perhaps, he maintains that
Parmenides and Heraclitus did not yet need to 'yearn' for the *sophon*
because they were in fundamental harmony with the *sophon*, namely,
the emerging of beings in Being. The need to rescue and preserve and
protect 'this most astonishing thing' that 'One (is) all' from the super-
ficiality of sophistical thinking – that is what gave rise to the *striving*
for Being, namely *philosophia*, and this 'was first accomplished by Socrates and Plato.'[40] But despite falling away to some degree from the
more originary thinking of Parmenides and Heraclitus, this *philosophia*
of Socrates, Plato, and Aristotle remained near the origin and, therefore,
remained 'tuned' as astonishment.

Heidegger draws attention to how both Plato and Aristotle named
the defining *pathos* of the philosopher *thaumazein* – 'astonishment.' He
reads Plato (*Theatetus* 155d) to say: 'This is indeed the *pathos* of a philosopher, astonishment [*das Erstaunen* translating *to thaumazein*]; for
there is no other determining origin of philosophy than this.'[41] And he
reads Aristotle's well-known words (*Metaphysics* A 2, 982b12) to mean:
'Through astonishment human beings have reached in the present
time, as well as at the beginning, the determining path of philosophizing (that from which philosophizing first proceeds and that which altogether determines the path of philosophizing).'[42] As Heidegger sees
it, the Greek philosophers understood the *pathos* of astonishment (wonder) to be the *arche* (beginning) of philosophy not in the 'superficial'
sense of an efficient 'cause' that simply sets philosophizing into mo-
tion. Rather, astonishment is *arche* because it altogether 'governs' thinking and is never 'left behind.' In other words, *philosophia* begins – and
ends – in 'astonishment.'[43]

He also reminds us that the Greek word *pathos* 'is related to *paschein*,
to suffer, endure, undergo, carry out, to be borne along by, to be determined by.' Consequently, the Greek understanding of *pathos* is far
removed from the modern psychological understanding of inward
subjective feelings and emotions. *Pathos* is more originarily understood
as the way in which the human being is 'attuned' or 'disposed' by Being, and the *pathos* of 'astonishment is the disposition in which and for
which the Being of beings unfolds. Astonishment is the tuning [*Stim-
mung*] within which the Greek philosophers were granted the cor-respondence to the Being of beings.'[44]

In keeping with his understanding of the devolution of thinking
from the Greeks to the present, Heidegger admits that the 'tuning' of
thinking after the Greeks and into the modern period was different
and not principally the mood of 'astonishment' that defined the dawn

of Western thinking. He also laments that especially in the present age we appear to be at the mercy of various and random moods such as 'doubt and despair' and 'fear and anxiety [*Angst*] ... mixed with hope and confidence.'[45] Note that he gives no special status to Angst; it is simply one 'tuning' among others in the present age, all of which reveal that we are profoundly *out of tune* with Being – yet he proposes that this may be precisely how Being itself has attuned the contemporary world.

Nevertheless, despite his talk about our being affectively disposed by Being in different ways in different epochs, we gather from the tenor of his discussion that he deems and esteems the originary Greek correspondence with Being, with its accompanying affective disposition of astonishment, to be the more *essential, defining, and authentic* relation of the human being and Being. Also, at the end of the lecture, he speaks of poetry and pointedly refuses to allow the discussion to be artificially 'limited' to the question concerning philosophy. In fact, he goes further and concludes that 'our discussion does not set itself the task of unfolding a fixed program. But it would like to endeavor to prepare all [people] who are participating [in the discussion] for a gathering in which we are addressed by that which we call the Being of beings.'[46] So, following Heidegger's hints, we may say that not only the philosopher, but also the poet and indeed every human being who in whatever way beholds the simple truth and seeks to dwell in the simple truth of Being as the emerging-appearing-disappearing of beings – all find themselves in astonishment (wonder).

Furthermore, what is especially noteworthy is that his phenomenological description of the mood of astonishment is virtually *identical* to his description of awe (*die Scheu*), which we highlighted earlier in his commentary on Holderlin's poem 'Remembrance' from 1943. In particular, in both descriptions he employs the word *Ansichhalten*, a holding oneself back, a stepping back – a comportment that he also famously thematized as *Gelassenheit* in another address in the very same year as WP (1955)![47] In WP, he puts it this way:

In astonishment, we hold ourselves back (*être en arrêt*). We step back, as it were, from beings, [astonished] that they are rather than are not. And astonishment is not exhausted in this stepping back before the Being of beings; but as this stepping back and holding oneself back [*Ansichhalten*], it is at the same time enraptured by and, as it were, held fast by that from which it steps back.[48]

Thus, we discover that Heidegger's phenomenological descriptions of 'awe' and 'astonishment' (and even *Gelassenheit*) are essentially the same – and we may even recognize in these descriptions the 'stunned calm' of Angst that goes all the way back to WM (1929). Finally, then, to bring all of these observations together, we may characterize Dasein's situation in this way: *In calm and thoughtful reserve, we take account of our fragile, finite openness in joyful nearness to the astonishing unfolding of all beings (including ourselves) in Being; and we graciously accept and courageously take up the risk of holding ourselves open unto the Open. And by virtue of this gentle resolve, we think, we dwell, we create authentically.*

In sum, astonishment, awe, marvelling, wonder – any one of these words seems able to capture what the later Heidegger often suggests and hints is the defining mood of our authentic cor-respondence with Being. Of course, it is true – as he never fails to remind us in his later work – that the contemporary preoccupation with calculative and instrumental modes of thinking and existing has made this authentic cor-respondence with Being more difficult to achieve. Difficult, yes, but not impossible. Authentic thinking and dwelling – in astonishment – is *always* a possibility for Dasein.

Conclusion

From Angst to astonishment. In a phrase, this is one way of describing the development of Heidegger's thinking about the defining mood of authentic existence. His early emphasis on Angst was decisively marked by Kierkegaard's discussion of the theme, but also by Nietzsche's heroic romanticism and by other romantic, anti-bourgeois perspectives. But even if the problematic of Angst was more found than founded by Heidegger, he nonetheless worked out a distinctive and compelling account of the phenomenon of Angst that remains of value for philosophy and for psychology. As he moved past these early influences and gradually unfolded his ownmost matter for thought, his focus shifted away from Angst towards other moods, and the moods of awe (*die Scheu*) and astonishment (*das Erstaunen*) in particular. For the later Heidegger, we might say that Dasein's authentic cor-respondence with Being is affectively 'tuned' principally as astonishment, awe, marvelling, wonder.

Despite the formidable obstacles presented to us in our time – an age dominated by calculation and commodification (*das Gestell*) – authentic existing always remains a possibility – and a choice. Admittedly, the existential importance of *choosing* is often veiled in the later Heidegger's vigorous polemic against our 'wilful' modern age; yet surely his own life's work continues to give eloquent testimony to the freedom that is always a possibility for human beings. The choice to release ontic thinking to recall in astonishment that all beings – including ourselves – unfold in Being. The gentle resolve to think and dwell in wonder – the wonder spoken of long ago by the ancient Greeks – in nearness to the Source. Or in Heidegger's own poetic words, in nearness to:

> Everything that shimmers and blooms in the sky
> and thus under the sky and on the earth;
> everything that sounds and is fragrant, rises and comes –
> but also everything that goes and stumbles,
> moans and falls silent, pales and darkens.[49]

5 *Lichtung*: The Early Lighting

Nevertheless, [all doubts] are unable to touch the illuminating power of images, their originary and unavoidable presence.

On the Question of Being (1956)

Heidegger's notion of the clearing (*die Lichtung*) is rich in philosophical and existential possibilities, so it is not surprising that it has been an appealing idea to many different kinds of readers, including those who have sought to build a bridge of understanding to Chinese and Japanese thinking and meditative practice.[1] Indeed, towards the end of his life, Heidegger himself explicitly invited such an effort, stating in a 1968 foreword that an understanding of the proper character of what he called the clearing would 'perhaps make it possible to bring a transformed European thinking into a fruitful engagement with East Asian "thinking."'[2] He also did not shy away from suggesting the profound existential implications of his notion of the clearing and of such a dialogue with the East, adding that 'it could be of help in the effort to save the essence [*Wesen*] of the human being from the threat posed by an extremely technical reckoning and manipulating of human Dasein.'[3] For Heidegger, nothing less than a fundamentally transformed sojourn in the world for human beings lay in the offing of naming, thinking, and experiencing *die Lichtung*.

This existentially transforming possibility inherent in the phenomenon of the clearing is an important dimension of Heidegger's later discussion and is certainly worthy of further reflection; but I think that, first, we need greater clarity about the notion itself. Heidegger noted in the same 1968 foreword that 'this phenomenon was first named in *Being and Time* and since then thought through ever anew.'[4] But this only hints at the interesting story of the development of his thinking about *die Lichtung*. There are several aspects of the story that need clarifying, but for the present, I would like to focus on one fundamental but over-looked issue: the *development* in his thinking from early to late regarding the primary metaphor conveyed by the word itself. The textual analysis I propose takes us from *Being and Time* (1927; hereafter BT) through several representative texts of the middle period to the key statements of the 1960s – namely, two related texts, 'The End of Philosophy and the Task for Thinking' (1964; hereafter EPTT) and the little known but equally significant 'On the Question Concerning the Determination of the Matter for Thinking' (1965; hereafter QDMT). Also important are his comments from the *Zollikon Seminars* (1964; hereafter ZS) and from the 'Heraclitus Seminar' (1966–7; hereafter HS) with Eugen Fink. What we find is that in the early and middle years Heidegger elucidated *die Lichtung* in terms of the metaphor of 'lighting,' which, however, he ul-timately decisively abandoned in the later work of the 1960s – with interesting implications.

I. Appropriating the Traditional Metaphor of Light

It may be surprising to some that the notion of *die Lichtung* does not emerge as a leading theme in Heidegger's thinking until quite late. Spe-cifically, he became intensely concerned with thematizing *die Lichtung* in the period of a few years, roughly from 1963 to 1968. He accorded the notion prominence in his lecture 'The End of Philosophy and the Task for Thinking,' composed sometime in 1963–4 and first published in a French translation by Jean Beaufret and François Fédier in 1964.[5] He also highlighted this phenomenon for the seminar participants in a Zollikon seminar dated 6 July 1964.[6] A little over a year later, he gave another major address, similar in many respects to EPTT, in which he again featured the matter of *die Lichtung*. Titled *'Das Ende des Denkens in der Gestalt der Philosophie'* ('The End of Thinking in the Form of Phi-losophy'), this talk was given on 30 October 1965 in Amriswil on the occasion of a celebration for the Swiss psychiatrist Ludwig Binswanger. In a somewhat expanded form, the address was first published in Japan (translated into Japanese) in December 1968 with a new title *'Zur Frage nach der Bestimmung der Sache des Denkens'* ('On the Question Concern-ing the Determination of the Matter for Thinking'). The German text, with this same title, was not published until 1984, and a complete En-glish translation by Richard Capobianco and Marie Göbel has recently been published.[7] For the Japanese edition in 1968, Heidegger added a brief foreword, which I have previously cited. In the winter semester of 1966–7, about a year after his talk at Amriswil, he joined with Eugen Fink at the University of Freiburg to conduct a series of seminars on the fragments of Heraclitus; and especially in the closing session, Heidegger once more gave special attention to the notion of *die Lichtung*, stressing its importance for thinking.[8] It appears, then, that in this five-year period 1963–8, he was especially occupied with the task of working out and presenting his mature position on the meaning and significance of *die Lichtung*.

One of the fundamental features of his mature position of the 1960s – the account familiar to most readers of Heidegger – is that *die Lichtung*, thought metaphorically as a spatial clearing in the wood or forest, is emphatically not to be defined in terms of *lux*, that is, 'light' in the sense of 'luminosity' or 'brightness.' But what has been largely overlooked is that this is *not* how Heidegger thought about the matter early on in *Being and Time*.[9] Let us turn to the crucial passage in BT. Because the meaning of several key words is at issue, I will give it in both the German and English:

> Die ontisch bildliche Rede vom *lumen naturale* im Menschen meint nichts anderes als die existenzial-ontologische Struktur dieses Seienden, daß es *ist* in der Weise, sein Da zu sein. Es ist 'erleuchtet', besagt: an ihm selbst *als* In-der-Welt-sein gelichtet, nicht durch ein anderes Seiendes, sondern so, daß es selbst die Lichtung *ist*. Nur einem existenzial so gelichteten Seienden wird Vorhandenes im Licht zugänglich, im Dunkel verborgen. Das Dasein bringt sein Da von Hause aus mit, seiner entbehrend ist es nicht nur faktisch nicht, sondern überhaupt nicht das Seiende dieses Wesens. *Das Dasein ist seine Erschlossenheit.*[10]

> The ontically figurative talk about the *lumen naturale* in the human being means nothing other than the existential-ontological structure of this being, that it *is* in such a way as to be its there. It is 'illuminated' means that it is lighted in it itself *as* being-in-the-world, not by another being, but in such a way that it itself *is* the lighting. Only for a being that is lighted in this way existentially does that which is present-at-hand become accessible in the light, hidden in the dark. The Dasein brings its there along with it, and lacking this there, it is not only not factically what it essentially is, but simply not the being of this essence at all. *Dasein is its disclosedness.* (my translation)

This one passage is important for a number of different reasons, but let us focus on Heidegger's use of the metaphor of light in elucidating the proper character of Dasein. He begins with a reference to the traditional metaphysical understanding of the human intellect as a 'natural light' (*lumen naturale*). There is a long history to this metaphor in Western philosophical thinking, going back ultimately to Plato's image of the sun in the metaphor of the cave in Book VII of the *Republic*.[11] But the specific Latin expression Heidegger uses here belongs especially to the Romanized Christian tradition of thinking extending from the early Church Fathers (especially Augustine) to Aquinas and into the later Schools (and even to Descartes). Aquinas, following Aristotle, maintained that the activity of the human intellect was like a 'light' that shines upon things and renders them (actually) 'viewable,' that is, (actually) intelligible; this 'natural light' was created by the Divine or Uncreated Light but distinct from it and autonomous in its operation (a position that met with stiff opposition from the more Augustinian-minded Christian thinkers of the Middle Ages).[12] Heidegger was no doubt familiar with the rich intellectual history bound up with this term, but what matters most for us at present is that he specifically invokes this particular metaphor of the *lumen naturale* in speaking of Dasein.

The decisive observation is that Heidegger does *not* reject this metaphor of light in elucidating Dasein's activity of disclosing beings and world; quite to the contrary, he takes it up as his own. His complaint is not that the older metaphysical figurative characterization of the human intellect as the *lumen* is inaccurate or inappropriate, but only that it is *ontic*. In other words, in the metaphysical tradition, the *logos* or *ratio* of the human being had been understood as the principal characteristic of a self-sufficient, time-less, space-less, world-less soul substance (ancient, medieval) or subject (modern) that has the power to know 'things' or 'objects' that are merely present-at-hand. In Heidegger's view, the metaphor of the 'natural light' had been inextricably linked to this metaphysical understanding of the human being. Yet his point is that this is not a necessary connection, for it is possible to understand the metaphor in terms of 'the existential-ontological structure' of Dasein – that is, in terms of the constitutive disclosing activity of Dasein as the ek-sistent, temporally ek-static 'there.' Dasein primordially *is* this disclosing activity, he emphasizes, and not a 'something' that has this faculty, power, or property of disclosedness. Therefore, in (fundamental) ontological terms, Dasein simply *is die Lichtung* – figuratively, this 'lighting' – and not the ontic reified 'light' spoken of in the metaphysical tradition.

It is apparent, then, that Heidegger's concern in this passage is not to refuse or reject the metaphysical metaphor of light in speaking of Dasein, but rather to take it up in existential-ontological terms. He appropriates the trope of the *lumen naturale* in his own way, and the sense of the passage compels us to translate *die Lichtung* as 'the lighting' – and not as the spatial 'clearing' as other translations have it, including the standard one by Macquarrie and Robinson and Joan Stambaugh's as well.[13] It is not justified, I think, to read back into this passage Heidegger's much later position that *die Lichtung* must not be understood in terms of *lux*, light – no matter how explicit and insistent he became in his statements in the 1960s. In *Being and Time*, it is evident that his understanding of *die Lichtung* was indeed in terms of the metaphor of luminosity: Dasein is the *lumen* in the ontological sense that it is 'illuminated' (*erleuchtet*) in itself as being-in-the-world and, therefore, is itself, in its very being-as-disclosing, 'the lighting' (*die Lichtung*).

If there is any cause for doubt here, it would be his use of the past participle *gelichtet* and the related adjectival form *gelichteten*. These words are derived from the verb *lichten*, which can mean 'to brighten' or 'to thin out and clear' (see Appendix), and it is the latter sense that he emphatically favoured in the work of the 1960s. Nevertheless, in the context of this passage, it is apparent that he is using these words strictly in terms of *Licht*, 'light' in the sense of luminosity. In fact, we have additional textual evidence that I think confirms this reading. *Gesamtausgabe* (hereafter GA 2) includes selected marginal notes that Heidegger made in his copy of *Sein und Zeit* over the years (and impossible to date precisely). The note that he appended directly next to the word *gelichtet* reads: '*Aletheia – Offenheit – Lichtung, Licht, Leuchten.*' This is arguably the decisive clue that Heidegger understood *Lichtung* in this passage in terms of *lux*, for he relates *Lichtung* to *Licht* (light) and *Leuchten* (lightening, brightening, illuminating). In other words, the note makes transparent that his understanding of the relation of the words is decidedly in terms of luminosity: *gelichtet – Lichtung – Licht – Leuchten.*[14] In *Being and Time*, *die Lichtung* is the lightening in the sense of brightening, or, more simply, 'the lighting.'

Why is this important? By clarifying the primary figurative sense of *die Lichtung* in *Being and Time*, we establish that there was indeed an important shift in his reading of the word *Lichtung* from the early work to the later statements of the 1960s. It also tells us that we cannot simply read his later account of *Lichtung* back into the early and middle work and uniformly translate *die Lichtung* as the spatial 'clearing.' To do so would be to overlook and even cover over this development in his thought. Thus, as I have argued, the fitting translation of *die Lichtung* in *Being and Time* is 'the lighting.' This issue of the word's proper translation comes into play in other texts as well.

For example, consider the matter in one of Heidegger's most significant statements from the middle period, 'Letter on Humanism' (1947).[15] He makes several references to *die Lichtung*, this time principally in the form of *die Lichtung des Seins*, and he makes no qualifying remarks that would lead us to conclude that he is using *Lichtung* in a metaphorical sense different from the one he had used in BT. For this reason, it is perfectly understandable that Frank Capuzzi (in collaboration with J. Glenn Gray and David Farrell Krell) translated *die Lichtung des Seins* as 'the lighting of Being' in his translation of LH for the first edition of *Basic Writings* (1977).[16] Indeed, there is a clue in the text of LH that would seem to confirm this. Heidegger states that 'every departure from beings and every return to them already stands in the light of Being [*im Lichte des Seins*].'[17] His very next sentence reads: 'But metaphysics recognizes the *Lichtung* of Being either as the view of what is present in "appearance" (*idea*) or critically as what is seen as a result of categorial representation on the part of subjectivity.'

In this context, what else could *die Lichtung* mean but 'the lighting'? Capuzzi's choice seems right on target. Yet curiously, this translation was changed throughout LH for the revised edition of *Basic Writings* (1993).[18] The editor David Farrell Krell simply notes in his Preface that '"clearing" is now used for *Lichtung*' in the entire collection of writings, but no reason is given for this.[19] The unstated assumption seems to be that this revision is necessitated by Heidegger's later statements on *Lichtung* – and perhaps that is not unreasonable – yet it does not take into account the evidence that his reading of the word evolved over time from the visual metaphor of 'lighting' to the spatial metaphor of the 'expanse' or 'clearing' in the wood or forest. In LH, the translation 'the lighting' makes perfect sense, especially in view of *Being and Time*, so it is unclear why it was edited out of the text without further comment in *Basic Writings* (1993), which then became the text of record in *Pathmarks* (1998).[20]

A similar issue arises regarding Heidegger's 1949 Introduction to 'What Is Metaphysics' (I-WM), which also bears the title 'The Way Back into the Ground of Metaphysics.'[21] In this essay, published two years after LH, he employed the metaphor of light in elucidating his understanding of Being itself (*das Sein selbst*):

> Metaphysics thinks beings as beings. Wherever the question is asked what beings are, beings as such are in sight. Metaphysical representation owes this sight to the light of Being [*dem Licht des Seins*]. The light [*das Licht*], i.e., that which such thinking experiences as light, no longer comes within the range of metaphysical thinking; for metaphysics always represents beings only as beings. Within this perspective, metaphysical thinking does, of course, inquire about the being that is the source and originator of this light. But the light itself is considered sufficiently illuminated through its granting the transparency for every perspective upon beings.[22]

Metaphysics thinks beings in their beingness, and it owes this 'sight' to Being itself understood as the 'light' (*das Licht*), which is itself not another being but rather the enabling of all beings. We are reminded here of his effort in 'Plato's Doctrine of Truth' (1942), and even in much earlier elucidations of Plato, to read the image of the 'sun' in the *Republic*, Book VII, in terms of Being itself as the primordial 'light' that enables or allows all beings to shine forth (but that is not itself a being).[23] Of special interest in this passage from I-WM is a marginal note that Heidegger added (date undetermined) in his own copy of the first edition of *Wegmarken* (1949). Directly next to the word *Licht* in the phrase '*dem Licht des Seins*,' he wrote the word *Lichtung*.[24] But it is entirely uncertain what exactly he intended by this word. Did he make this note with *Being and Time* in mind, in which case *Lichtung* would have the figurative sense of 'lighting'? Or did he add the note with his much later perspective in mind, in which case he was rethinking and restating *Licht* in terms of *Lichtung* thematized as the spatial 'clearing' altogether apart from light? We cannot know for sure, though I am inclined to think that he had 'lighting' in mind here. In any case, in the edited English translation in *Pathmarks* the matter appears to be settled too easily: *Lichtung* is simply translated as 'Clearing.'[25] Maybe. But maybe not. What this shows, and this is my point, is that the translation of *Lichtung* in LH and in other early and middle texts requires more attention.

Still, in certain middle-period texts there can be no debate. The translation of *Lichtung* as 'lighting' in terms of luminosity is perfectly evident in Heidegger's discursus on Heraclitus (*Aletheia*), which was a Festschrift contribution published in 1954 but reflective of a line of thinking that went back to his lecture courses on Heraclitus in 1943 and 1944. The essay is framed by his clever wordplay on how Heraclitus, the 'dark one' (*der Dunkle*), is the thinker who thinks questioningly into the 'lighting' (*die Lichtung*) – that is, into the fundamental matter for thought, which Heidegger brings poetically to language as the unique 'light' or 'lighting' that in a finite manner allows to shine forth all beings in their beingness.[26] Heidegger is explicit from the outset that he understands the word *licht* in terms of luminosity: 'The word "light" [*licht*] means: illuminating, beaming, brightening. Lighting [*das Lichten*] grants the shining, frees up what shines for an appearance.'[27] This is the sense – and the metaphorical play – that he sustains throughout the reflection, leaving us with no doubt that *Lichtung* in this text conveys the core figurative image of 'lighting': 'But the golden gleam of the unapparent shining of the lighting [*Lichtung*] cannot be grasped because it is not itself something grasping; rather, it is the pure appropriating.'[28]

In some texts of the 1950s the precise figurative sense of the word is perhaps not as clear. So, for example, in his important lecture course *The Principle of Reason* (PR), given at Freiburg in 1955–6, he uses the term several times in Lecture Eleven, but he does not thematize the word itself.[29] As a result, we are left uncertain about whether he is continuing the imagery of 'lighting' or whether he is now playing more on the sense of the spatial 'clearing.' For instance, in the following sentence, we simply cannot tell: 'We are the ones bestowed by and with the *Lichtung* of Being in the dispensation of Being, and accordingly the same ones that Being touches in and by its withdrawal, the same ones to whom Being, as such a dispensation, refuses the *Lichtung* of its originating of essence.'[30] This uncertainty in the text is perfectly reflected in the published translation by Reginald Lilly, who, understandably, chooses not to choose. In the previous passage, and in each instance elsewhere in the text, he translates *die Lichtung* as 'the clearing and lighting'![31]

II. Stepping Back from the Light and into the Clearing

In the end, we cannot avoid citing Heidegger's own contribution to this difficulty of translation in the scholarship. In the early 1960s, he made his way to his mature understanding and thematization of the word *die Lichtung* in terms of the spatial metaphor of the clearing or opening in a wood or forest *distinct from light or brightness*; but it is precisely his *way* to this position that he did not clarify in his reflections. What we find in his statements of the 1960s is that he explicitly asserts that *Lichtung* cannot and must not be understood from 'lighting' – but without any mention that he himself had adopted the figurative sense of *lumen*, light, in *Being and Time* and elsewhere in his earlier work. Without overstating the case, I think that this development in his thinking is both striking and largely overlooked. Thus, in EPTT (1964), Heidegger works out the metaphor of the forest clearing and explicitly *rejects* the metaphor of light as luminosity:

> The substantive '*Lichtung*' goes back to the verb '*lichten*.' The adjective '*licht*' is the same word as 'light' [*leicht*]. To lighten something means to render it light, free and open, for example, to make the forest free of trees at one place. The free space thus originating is the clearing [*die Lichtung*]. *The lightening in the sense of being free and open has nothing in common, neither linguistically nor materially, with the adjective 'light' which means 'bright.'* (my italics)[32]

He states the matter in a similar way in the Zollikon seminar dated 6 July 1964:

> By the way, when the light is turned off, how is it then with the clearing [*Lichtung*]? 'Clearing' means 'to be open.' There is clearing also in darkness. Clearing has nothing to do with light [*Licht*] but comes from 'light' [*leicht*]. Light [*Licht*] has to do with perception. One can still bump into something in the dark. This does not require light, but a clearing. Light – bright; clearing [*Lichtung*] comes from light [*leicht*], to render free.[33]

A year later in his talk QDMT (1965), he again rules out light as illumination in thinking about *die Lichtung*:

> A forest clearing is what it is, not because of brightness and light, which can shine within it during the day. At night, too, the clearing [*Lichtung*] remains. The clearing means: At this place, the forest is passable.
>
> The lightening in the sense of brightness and the lightening of the clearing are different not only regarding the matter, but regarding the word as well. To lighten [*Lichten*] means: to render free, to free up, to let free. To lighten belongs to light [*leicht*]. To render something light, to lighten something means: to clear away obstacles to it, to bring it into the unobstructed, into the free. To raise [*lichten*] the anchor says as much: to free it from the encompassing ocean floor and lift it into the free of water and air.[34] (our translation)

And in the 1966–7 seminar on Heraclitus conducted with Eugen Fink, Heidegger reiterates this position – again, without a reconsideration of his earlier reading of the word or of his earlier appropriation of the metaphor of lighting in elucidating his core concern:

> Do clearing [*Lichtung*] and light [*Licht*] have anything at all to do with each other? Evidently not. Clearing means: to thin out, to raise anchor, to clear out. That does not mean that where the clearing clears, there is brightness. What is cleared [*das Gelichtete*] is the free, the open, and, at the same time, what is cleared is what conceals itself. We may not understand the clearing [*Lichtung*] from out of light [*Licht*]; rather, we must understand it from the Greeks.[35]

All of these texts attest to Heidegger's compelling mature elucidation of *die Lichtung* as a matter for thinking – even though we must make note that his oft repeated claim in these statements of the 1960s that the words *Lichtung* and *Licht* have nothing in common linguistically is most dubious (see the Appendix for a discussion of this point). Yet what is even more puzzling about these statements is that he does not address that he himself had once rendered *die Lichtung* in terms of *lux*, light. He does not acknowledge, let alone reflect upon, this interesting development in his own thinking, and consequently, we are left without an account from him regarding the path of thinking that took him from elucidating *Lichtung* in terms of *lumen* in *Being and Time* to his outright rejection of such imagery in the work of the 1960s. In other words, we are left to consider his *Denkweg* for ourselves.

What is it about *die Sache des Denkens*, the fundamental matter for thought, that led Heidegger to abandon the metaphor of light (and emphatically so)? One answer, I think, has to do with his deepening meditation over the years on what he understood to be the Greek experience of *aletheia*. Over time, he seems to have arrived at the conclusion that the metaphor of luminosity was simply too entangled with the long-standing Western onto-theological understanding of truth as *veritas* (the 'correct' correspondence of knower and known, subject and object) for it to serve the *Sache*. More to the point, it seems that it was not until the early 1960s that he decisively determined for himself that the metaphor of 'lighting' was ultimately inadequate precisely because it could not make manifest the *negatived* modes of presencing (concealment, absence, lack, withdrawal, refusal, distortion, errancy) that are intrinsic to *aletheia*. That is, in the 'light' of metaphysics, going all the way back to Plato, what principally appears are beings (*das Seiende*) in their beingness (*die Seiendheit*) and what stubbornly remains out of view is the negatived dimension of the presencing of beings, that is, the *lethe*-dimension of *a-letheia*. It is this consideration that appears to go to the heart of his ultimately decisive rejection – but not until the 1960s – of the metaphor of light. In the ruling metaphor of the Western onto-theological tradition, light dispels the darkness, but Heidegger's concern was to make manifest both 'light' and 'darkness,' presence and absence, truth and untruth. It seems, then, that over time he found his way to thematizing a *Grund*-metaphor that could convey this: in the spatial forest 'clearing' as discussed by the later Heidegger, *both* light and dark are present to us, the full experience of *aletheia*.

In the 'Heraclitus Seminar' (1966–7), he comes close to revealing something about his path of thinking regarding *die Lichtung*. He notes that his thinking had struggled to get free of the dominant metaphysical theme of 'truth' and its corresponding image of 'light'; yet disappointingly, he does not go so far as to acknowledge that his rendering of *die Lichtung* had apparently accordingly evolved over time from 'the lighting' to 'the clearing' – a clearing that must not be understood from *Licht*:

> *Aletheia* thought *as aletheia* has nothing to do with 'truth'; rather, it means unconcealment. What I said at the time in *Being and Time* about *aletheia* already goes in this direction. *Aletheia* as unconcealment had already occupied me, but in the meantime 'truth' shoved itself in between. *Aletheia* as unconcealment heads into the direction of that which is the clearing ... We may not understand the clearing from out of light [*Licht*]; rather, we must understand it from the Greeks. Light and fire can first find their place in the clearing. In the lecture, 'On the Essence of Truth,' where I speak of 'freedom,' I had the clearing in view, except that here also truth always walked behind. The dark is surely without light, but cleared. For us, it is a matter of experiencing unconcealment as clearing.[36]

He intimates that he was only *on the way* to his mature understanding of *die Lichtung* in the lecture 'On the Essence of Truth' (1930/1943) but that he had not yet arrived. Indeed, if we return to that text, we can better understand his meaning. In the first edition, Heidegger spoke repeatedly about 'the open' (*das Offene*), but he did not thematize *die Lichtung* in relation to the open. What is instructive comes in the first paragraph of Section 9 (*Anmerkung*/Note), which he added for the second edition in 1949. In this added paragraph, Heidegger specifically drew attention to *die Lichtung* in thinking about *aletheia* – but it is evident from the text that he was still thinking of *Lichtung* primarily in terms of the traditional trope of 'lighting.' He states: 'Because luminous sheltering [*lichtendes Bergen*] belongs to it, Beyng shines forth originarily in the light [*im Licht*] of concealing withdrawal.' And he immediately adds: '*Der Name dieser Lichtung ist aletheia.*'[37] Given the context, this line is most plausibly translated as 'The name of this lighting is *aletheia.*'[38] As we have noted before, his thinking about *die Lichtung* in these middle years – even with respect to *aletheia* – was still largely informed by the metaphor of light. He was still some years away from working out his final position of the 1960s, which radically and emphatically divorces the sense of light as luminosity from *Lichtung*. And I am suggesting that this development was compelled, at least in part, by the exigency he found in the experience of *aletheia* itself.

In the lecture EPTT (1964), we find that here, too, his mature understanding of *die Lichtung* as the spatial 'clearing' is intimately related to his ongoing meditation on *aletheia*. Returning to Parmenides' words, Heidegger elucidates the phenomenon of the clearing in terms of *aletheia*. The experience of the 'well-rounded' (*eukukleos*) clearing/*aletheia* is the experience of both the positive and negatived modes of presencing. As he puts this in terms of *die Lichtung*: 'Presence as lingering in the open always remains dependent upon the already prevailing clearing. What is absent, too, cannot be as such unless it is as presencing [*anwesend*] in the free of the clearing.'[39] Consequently, clearing/*aletheia* must be considered the 'primordial phenomenon' and the 'primordial matter' because it is more fundamental than metaphysical truth/*veritas*, which can see in its 'light' only the positive mode of presencing, that is, beings in their beingness (*eidos, idea, essentia,* essence). And he concludes that '*aletheia*, unconcealment in the sense of the clearing, may not be equated with truth. Rather, *aletheia*, unconcealment thought as clearing, first grants the possibility of truth.'[40]

This mature unfolding of the theme of *die Lichtung* strictly in terms of the spatial metaphor of the 'clearing' is original and evocative. Even so, there is also one easily overlooked passage in EPTT that brings us back to the issue of his relation to his own earlier reading of *die Lichtung* as 'the lighting' in *Being and Time*. At one point, he singles out for criticism the metaphor of the *lumen naturale* of the metaphysical tradition without any mention that he himself had taken up and taken over this very metaphor in *Being and Time*. He comments:

But philosophy knows nothing of the clearing. Philosophy certainly does speak about the light of reason, but does not attend to the clearing of Being. The *lumen naturale*, the light of reason, only brightens the open. It does indeed concern the clearing, but so little does it form it that it needs it in order to be able to illuminate what is present in the clearing. This is true not only of philosophy's *method*, but also and primarily of its *matter*, that is, of the presence of what-is-present [*Anwesenheit des Anwesenden*].[41]

As he sees it, the metaphor of *lux*, *lumen*, light, inherited from the onto-theological tradition, is limited to illuminating beings in their be-ingness (i.e., what-is-present in its presence) and, thus, ultimately fails to bring into view the fundamental matter for thought, namely, *aletheia*. Implicit here is that the failure (or at least inadequacy) of this tradi-tional metaphor of light is one of the features of the end of philoso-phy as metaphysics. The task for thinking moving forward is to think *aletheia as aletheia* (which even the Greeks could not quite do), and for this task, a fundamentally different metaphor, not a visual but a *spatial* metaphor, is needed: the clearing in the wood or forest. His unfolding of the matter is a tour de force, no doubt, but it represents his most mature view. He does not speak to the issue that in his earlier thinking, and specifically in *Being and Time*, he had worked out *Lichtung* precisely in the figurative terms of 'lighting.' In effect, then, in this very passage, he was revisiting and revising his own earlier view *without explicitly saying so*, for it was surely not by chance that he inserted a mention of the *lumen naturale* in this text – a text composed almost forty years after *Being and Time*.

Conclusion

What we have discovered is that there is more to the story of Heidegger's thinking about *die Lichtung* than is apparent from his own statements: in a phrase, the story reads *from* 'the lighting' *to* 'the clearing.' This de-velopment in his thinking concerning the core metaphor at work in this word is significant, I have argued, because it reflects his deepening appreciation over time of the implications of his insight into what the Greeks named *aletheia*. In *Being and Time*, he attempted to retrieve the traditional metaphor of the *lumen naturale*, 'natural light,' in existential-ontological terms; and in subsequent works after the 'turn' (*die Kehre*) in his thinking, he continued to employ the metaphor of lighting in elucidating his understanding of Being itself (*das Sein selbst*).[42] But in his statements of the 1960s we find a distinct and decided shift in perspective, albeit unacknowledged by Heidegger as such. It appears that by the 1960s he had come to the firm conclusion that the link between the metaphor of 'lighting' and the onto-theological understanding of truth/*veritas* could not be sufficiently undone for this metaphor to be of continued service for the 'task' of thinking in the present age. Earlier in his thinking he had attempted a 'grounding' of the traditional metaphor of light, but by the 1960s he had opted instead for a decisive 'step back' from this metaphor; and in stepping back from the 'light,' he found in *die Lichtung* only the open space of the forest 'clearing,' which he then founded as a *Grund*-metaphor for his thinking. At the end of philosophy in the form of onto-theology the task of thinking may be guided by the metaphor of the 'clearing' in which appears both light and dark, both what shines brightly in the day and what is covered and hidden in the darkness of night. In other words, the spatial image of the forest clearing – and no longer the traditional imagery of light and lighting – is more proper to the task of thinking insofar as it is mindful of the appearing of both presence and absence, truth and untruth, which properly characterizes *a-letheia* itself / Being itself in both its positive and negatived modes of manifestation.[43]

It appears that by the time Heidegger added a few words on *die Lichtung* in his 1968 foreword to the Japanese publication of QDMT, he had reached an impasse with the Western onto-theological tradition – including the Biblical tradition – which had been so decisively shaped by the metaphor of light. We might crystallize the difference this way: Thomas Aquinas, citing the Bible (*Ephesians* 5), affirmed for the tradition that 'all that is made manifest [truth/*veritas*] is light';[44] whereas Heidegger's lifelong meditation on *aletheia* led him to maintain – ever more radically and insistently – that all that is made manifest (*aletheia*) is not just light, but *both light and darkness* in the clearing. In the guiding visual metaphor of the tradition, light conquers darkness; in Heidegger's spatial metaphor of the clearing, light and darkness are let be.

But at the same time, he recognized the essential relatedness of his notion of the 'clearing' with 'East Asian' thinking and meditative practice, and he increasingly welcomed a 'fruitful engagement' and dialogue. He intimated that along this way, by turning to the East, his fundamental insight into *aletheia*/clearing – which perhaps could never be accommodated by the dominant Western philosophical, religious, and spiritual traditions – could possibly be clarified and amplified. He was hopeful but always somewhat cautious about such a project;[45] but about the 'matter itself' (*die Sache selbst*), whether this was brought to language in the West or the East, he was much more decisive: our thinking – and, moreover, our *experiencing* – the *Ur*-phenomenon that he named the 'clearing' has the power to transform us and liberate us for an authentic sojourn on the earth, under the sky, with others, between birth and death. Elucidating more fully how precisely this is so is one task that I will take up in the next chapter.

Appendix
A Note on the Word *die Lichtung*

There is no doubting the originality and resonance of Heidegger's mature elucidation of *die Lichtung* as a matter for thinking, but his repeated claim in his statements of the 1960s (see within the chapter) that the substantive *die Lichtung* has nothing in common linguistically with the word *das Licht* is problematical and deserves further attention by linguists. Several observations bear this out. In German, there is (1) the verb *lichten*, related to *das Licht*, which means 'to brighten' and 'to clear,' and there is also (2) the verb *lichten*, which is derived from *leichten*, meaning to unburden, to ease, or to lift, as we find in the common German expression *den Anker lichten*, to raise the anchor. In his statements of the 1960s – which are in sharp contrast to his reflections in his earlier work – Heidegger thematizes the verb (2) *lichten/leicht* and insists on deriving *Lichtung* from *lichten/leicht* exclusively, but it is dubious that *Lichtung* has no relation to (1) *lichten* and *das Licht* in the sense of brightness and luminosity, as he claims.

As evidence of this, we find in Grimm's *Deutches Wörterbuch* (Leipzig: S. Hirzel, 1854–1960), vol. 12, that there are two entries for *die Lichtung* at 893. The second entry derives *die Lichtung* from *lichten/leicht*, as Heidegger maintains in the 1960s, and has the sense of a 'lifting or raising,' as of an anchor. Nevertheless, the first entry states that *die Lichtung* is related to one sense of *das Licht* (II, 18a at 877; an opening in a house or door that lets light in) and to the verb *lichten*, which is related to *Licht*, sense 4, at 880 (to thin out a forest so that the light may stream in; a lightening and brightening). It certainly seems that his featured rendering of the word as the 'clearing' is indeed related linguistically to *lichten/Licht* and not to *lichten/leicht*! What is more, we also find in vol. 12 (at 879) the antiquated *feminine* form '*die Lichte*,' which according to the entry conveys both the sense of 'brightness' and the sense of 'clearing' or 'opening' as in a wood or forest.

Of course, I defer to linguists to decide the matter about the derivation of the word. But given the attention that Heidegger lavished upon words and their histories, it is likely that he was familiar with the Grimm's entries on *die Lichtung*. Why, then, was he so insistent on separating *Licht* from *Lichtung* in his series of statements in the 1960s? As I see it, he overstated the linguistic claim because of his polemical interest in decisively rejecting the traditional metaphysical metaphor of light (linked to *veritas*) in favour of his metaphor of the forest clearing (linked to *aletheia*). What is more, his overstatement probably reveals something of the unstated development in his own thinking, namely, that he was thereby emphatically separating *himself* from his own earlier view of the matter. We might refer to this as Heidegger's own 'clearing' regarding the proper metaphor to be thought.

6 Plato's Light and the Phenomenon of the Clearing

[Plato's] 'allegory' speaks of the sun as the image for the Idea of the Good.
'Plato's Doctrine of Truth' (1942)

In the previous chapter, I examined how Heidegger ultimately abandoned the traditional philosophical image of 'lighting' (*Licht, leuchten, lux, lumen*) in thinking about his notion of *die Lichtung*, which in recent scholarship is most commonly translated as the 'clearing.'[1] Presently, I want to come back to this subtle but important development in his thinking by carefully considering his several elucidations, from 1926 to 1940, of Plato's image of the 'sun' in Book VII of the *Republic*. I also want to shed some light on two other key issues, specifically (1) the relation of his notion of *die Lichtung* to the much discussed 'turn' (*die Kehre*) in his thinking, and (2) the basic features and existential significance of the phenomenon of the 'clearing' and the question of a correspondence with what Heidegger called 'East Asian' traditions of thinking.

I. Plato's Light and *die Lichtung*

As I argued previously, the primary figurative sense that Heidegger gives to his notion of *die Lichtung* in *Being and Time* is 'lighting,' so there is no need to restate the case here. What remains important to investigate, however, is the background in his thinking at the time that informs this sense of 'lighting,' and this leads us to his efforts to elucidate – and appropriate – Plato's light of the 'sun' (*helios*) in Book VII of the *Republic*. Most readers of Heidegger are familiar with his elucidation of Plato's allegory of the cave in his 1942 essay 'Plato's Doctrine of Truth,' but many may not be aware that this line of thinking goes much further back. As early as 1926, Heidegger was sketching a reading of the allegory, which he would return to several times in later years. Specifically, to put these key elucidations in chronological perspective:

- 1926 lecture course, summer semester, at the University of Marburg, 'The Basic Concepts of Ancient Philosophy.'[2]
- 1927 lecture course, summer semester, at the University of Marburg, 'The Basic Problems of Phenomenology.'[3]
- 1931–2 lecture course, winter semester, at the University of Freiburg, 'On the Essence of Truth' (On Plato's Cave Allegory and *Theaetetus*); not to be confused with the 1930 lecture 'On the Essence of Truth,' published in 1943.[4]
- 1933–4 lecture course, winter semester, at the University of Freiburg, 'On the Essence of Truth' (related to the earlier lecture course and not to the 1930 lecture).[5]
- 1940 essay 'Plato's Doctrine of Truth' (published in 1942).[6]

The broad lines of his reading of Plato's allegory are generally well known, so what I wish to focus on is his understanding of the character and role of light. Already in his 1926 lecture course, Heidegger roughly establishes his basic reading: Plato glimpses in his thinking that the Idea of the Good is 'beyond' (*epekeina*) beings and even being(ness) in the sense that it 'enables' or 'makes possible' all beings in their beingness (their full 'appearance' or 'look,' what Plato called the *eidos* or *idea* and what later came to be understood as the enduring presence or 'essence' of a thing, the core concern of metaphysics). For Heidegger, Plato's Idea of the Good is no 'it' at all, no something, no essence or value; rather, the Idea of the Good is to be understood as the (temporal) 'enabling' (*ermöglichend*) of all beings in their beingness. As he excitedly expresses his insight in the lecture course, the Idea of the Good is 'the most *originary possibility*! Originarily *enabling* everything.'[7] With respect to the imagery of the allegory, he correlates the Idea of the Good with the 'light itself,' the 'illumination' that makes possible 'anything at all to be seen.' This purely enabling 'light,' which he identified as the 'sun' according to Hermann Mörchen's student lecture notes, is not the light belonging to illumined entities, but rather the source of all light. This light, the light-source itself, makes possible all lighted beings.[8]

A year later in his 1927 summer·lecture course, he returned to a reading of the allegory in the context of a further unfolding of the themes of *Sein und Zeit* (published in 1927). Here again he observes that 'what we are in search of is the *epekeina tes ousias*.'[9] What is 'beyond being[ness]' is the Idea of the Good that makes possible or is 'the condition of the possibility' for all knowledge and truth about beings in their beingness.[10] This time around, he more explicitly works out the correspondence of the Idea of the Good with the image of the sun, which he identifies as the light-source for all visible light, the light-source that is seen only indirectly: 'For seeing with the eyes there is required not only eyes and not only the being that is seen but a third thing, [namely], *phos*, the light, or, more precisely, the sun, *helios*.'[11] Thus, as he had a year earlier, Heidegger appropriates Plato's metaphor of *light* in order to unfold his ownmost concern and the fundamental matter for thought, namely, the (temporal, finite and negatived) enabling/letting/giving of beings and their ontic truth. As he expresses this: 'The basic condition for the knowledge of beings as well as for the understanding of being[ness] is: standing in an illuminating light.'[12] And further: 'The understanding of being[ness] already moves in a *horizon* that is everywhere *illuminated, giving brightness*' (his emphasis).[13]

These texts from the 1927 lecture course provide the key to a more complete understanding of his notion of *die Lichtung* in *Being and Time*. As Heidegger observed many years later, it was in *Being and Time* that he first introduced the term *die Lichtung*, and I have discussed his effort in §28 to rethink and recast the early Christian and medieval metaphysical metaphor of the human *lumen naturale* (natural light) in fundamental ontological terms as Dasein's (always-already) disclosing activity (*legein* as *hermeneuein*) that enables all beings to be meaningfully in language.[14] Ontologically, Dasein is this 'lighting' itself, he maintains, and not, in the first place, an ontic entity that possesses the 'natural light' of reason.

This much is clear from a careful reading of the text in §28, yet it is to §69 that we need to turn in order to make a firmer connection with Heidegger's reading of Plato's allegory. In the opening part of §69, he restates the characterization of Dasein's ontologically disclosive character more explicitly in terms of temporality, observing (with emphasis) that '*ecstatic temporality lights [lichtet] the "there" primordially*.'[15] In other words, it is Dasein's temporally disclosive existence itself that makes possible all ontic truth about beings. Figuratively, he refers to this ontological structure of Dasein as a special kind of 'light' – that is, as the light that is the source for all that is seen in the light:

The light [*das Licht*] that constitutes this lightedness [*Gelichtetheit*] of Dasein is not something ontically present-at-hand as a power or source for a radiant brightness occurring in this being on occasion ... This lightedness first makes possible all illuminating or illumining, every perception, 'seeing,' or having of something. We understand *the light* [*das Licht*] of this lightedness only if we are not seeking some power implanted in us and present-at-hand. (my emphasis)[16]

Though he does not mention Plato's allegory explicitly in this passage, it is clearly in the background of his thinking. The 'light' that he speaks of that metaphorically characterizes Dasein's always-already temporally disclosive character (*logos*) is perfectly parallel to the 'sun' of the allegory, the light-source, that enables or makes possible all that is lighted and directly visible to the eye. Consequently, this part of §69 of *Being and Time* really cannot be fully understood until we refer it to Heidegger's reading of the role of light in his Plato elucidations of 1926 and 1927. In these texts, we find him appropriating Plato's metaphor of light in order to articulate his primary concern with that which *enables* the truth of all beings in their beingness – the *enabling*, which, on his reading, Plato had glimpsed as 'beyond being[ness].'

Heidegger first fully developed and unfolded his reading of the allegory in his 1931–2 winter lecture course 'On the Essence of Truth.' This lecture course is not to be confused with the widely known lecture of the same title that he first delivered in 1930 (and later published in 1943), nor with the lecture course, again of the same title, from the winter semester of 1933–4, which was largely a restatement of the themes of the earlier lecture course. His lengthy and painstakingly careful elucidation of the allegory takes up all of Part I of the 1931–2 lecture course. There are many remarkable insights and observations along the way, but let us keep our focus on his reading of the role of light, which, in fact, is central to the entire reading. Early on, he makes this important distinction:

Already here, and for the understanding of the whole allegory (of all following stages), it is necessary to make note of the difference between *pur*, fire (the light-source [*Lichtquelle*]), and *phos*, brightness (to which there corresponds in the Latin: *lux* and *lumen*).[17]

Though he does not remain perfectly consistent in employing these terms in precisely this way as he proceeds, he nonetheless maintains this fundamental distinction throughout. And it is a distinction with which we are already familiar. On his reading, when thinking about light in Plato's allegory we must distinguish between the light of visible things and the light-source, *die Lichtquelle*, which makes possible in the first place all that is lighted. It is the *light-source*, the 'fire' in this passage – but ultimately the 'sun' – that is of most interest to Heidegger.[18]

One interesting note about these lines is his passing claim that corresponding to the important distinction that he is making is the pair of Latin words *lux* and *lumen*. He makes a similar observation in a comparable place in his later lecture course of 1933–4, only to add shortly thereafter that a reference to *lumen* belongs to the history of 'Christian speculation.'[19] Since Heidegger says nothing more in these places about the intellectual history of these Latin words, we cannot say precisely what he has in mind, but I think we can reasonably assume that he was referring to the distinction between *lux* and *lumen* that had been made in the long Christian tradition of thinking about light. This tradition culminated in the medieval 'metaphysics of light' best represented by the small treatise *On Light* (*De Luce*) by the English bishop and theologian Robert Grosseteste (1175–1253).[20] In his treatise, Grosseteste employs the two Latin words *lux* and *lumen* to make a distinction regarding the substance of light, 'the first corporeal form,' which suffuses the entire created order. In the manner of more ancient Christian authors, he appears to reserve *lux* to designate light in its source, the primordial light substance, whereas *lumen* is used to refer to light as it is reflected or radiated.[21] That Heidegger would be interested in such a distinction is immediately apparent, for it nicely corresponds to his reading of Plato's imagery of light. In other words, both of these traditional accounts of light are useful to him in making manifest his own primary interest in distinguishing between what is lighted (beings in their beingness; the ontic truth of beings) and the light-source, that is, that which temporally enables/lets/gives/grants beings in their beingness. What is clear at this point in our discussion and worth emphasizing is how Heidegger, in his early work, was influenced and indeed even *inspired* by the traditional philosophical and theological discussions of light and how he made every effort to appropriate the metaphor of light to elucidate his ownmost matter for thinking.

But let us return to the text of the 1931–2 lecture course. In due course, Heidegger passes from a consideration of the 'fire' in the cave to the 'sun,' or as he refers to it, 'the *primordial* light' (*dem ursprüng-lichen Licht*).[22] The central importance of the theme of light in his thinking is evident in his extended meditation on the meaning of light in Sections 6 and 7. What he offers is a quite beautiful and subtle (perhaps overly subtle) existential phenomenology of brightness and light. The fundamental point he wishes to make is that, properly understood, both light and brightness have the character of 'letting-through' (*Durchlassen*). According to Heidegger, 'brightness' and 'bright' (*Helle, hell*) originally derive from the German word *hallen*, 'to echo or resound,' and thus originally belong to the realm of sound (a bright sound) and not to the visible. Even so, the meaning of 'brightness' was eventually carried over to refer to the visible as well (a bright and sunny day). This came to pass because the two phenomena, brightness and light, are essentially related and have in common the basic characteristic of 'penetrating,' 'going-through,' 'spreading-out,' 'letting-through.' He sums it up this way:

> Brightness is that *through which* we see. More precisely: Light is not only that which penetrates, but is itself the throughness – that which *lets-through*, namely, seeing and the view. Light is the transparent [*das Durchsichtige*], that is, the spreading out, opening, letting-through. The *essence* of light and brightness is being transparent. (his emphasis)[23]

For Heidegger, light (and brightness), properly understood, is a transparency that permits or makes possible all that may be seen in both the day and the night (such as the stars). Light frees up everything, and consequently, for us to comport ourselves and 'bind' ourselves to this primordial light, this light-source, is for us to achieve authentic freedom: 'Comportment to the *giving*-free (to the light) is itself a *becoming*-free. Authentic becoming-free is a projective *binding of oneself* [*ein entwerfendes Sich-binden*]' to that light in which everything is always-already made free.[24]

Thus, light, as it 'lights up,' most fundamentally 'frees up' and 'makes free' everything that appears in both the day and the night. Light is a making-free in the same way that the 'forest clearing,' *die Waldlichtung*, is a free and open space that gives passage through.[25] Of particular importance for our study is to note that here Heidegger elucidates the forest clearing in terms of the proper character of *light* – which, as we shall see shortly, he later rejected in his work of the 1960s. But here in this 1931–2 lecture course, and in his early and middle work generally, his thinking is that *Lichtung* and *Licht* must be thought together, that *die (Wald)lichtung* must be understood in terms of *das Licht* as that primordial phenomenon that gives / grants / lets through / opens up / frees up everything. *Die Lichtung* is a 'lighting' in this fundamental sense.

Returning to Plato's text, Heidegger observes that it is not surprising that Plato correlated the Ideas to light because just as light is a letting-through, the Ideas are a kind of letting-through – namely, a letting something be known as what it is in its full 'look' (*eidos*), presence, whatness, beingness. This aspect of Plato's thinking ultimately served as the foundation for the Western onto-theological tradition with its focus on the timeless and immutable 'essences' of particular things, the distinctively metaphysical rendering of the 'being of beings.'

Yet as Heidegger reads it, the allegory reveals to us that Plato's thinking did not come to rest at this point, no matter how powerfully compelling the Ideas were for him. In Sections 12 to 14, he comes back to Plato's insight into the 'beyond' of being(ness): the Idea of the Good and its symbol (*Sinnbild*) the sun.[26] For Plato, as for the ancient Greeks more generally, the 'good' (*agathon*) did not have in the first instance a moral significance; rather, 'good' meant sound, suitable, effective. What is 'good,' understood in its proper character, 'enables' and 'empowers' something to be what it is, and the Idea of the Good, as the 'highest' Idea, must be understood as 'the enabling' (*die Ermöchlichung*) and 'the empowering' (*die Ermächtigung*) of all the other Ideas, *indeed of all being(ness) and truth*. The Idea of the Good is the 'yoke' (*das Joch* as he understands Plato's *zugon*) that first enables, empowers (and grants, gives, frees up) subject and object, subjectivity and objectivity, all ontic knowledge and truth about beings in their being(ness). And how is this expressed metaphorically in the allegory? It is the sun (*helios*) that enables and empowers both seeing and being-seen:

> What is enabling must be *one and the same*, must be the ground for *both*, or, as Plato expresses it, the ability to see and the ability to be seen must both be *harnessed together under one yoke* (*zugon*). This yoke, which makes possible the reciprocal connectedness of each to the other, is *phos*, brightness [*die Helle*], light [*das Licht*]. (his emphasis)[27]

There can be no question that he chooses to elucidate his own fundamental concern – what *enables* the truth of beings and being(ness) – in terms of the metaphor of light that he appropriates from Plato. And we should make special note that in this passage he employs all three terms for luminosity interchangeably and without qualification: '*phos*, brightness, light.' It is evident, then, that his guiding metaphor for thinking about the fundamental matter for thought is the *light* that enables / lets through / opens up / frees up all beings and all truth about beings. As a consequence, I must take issue with commentators who, reading only Heidegger's statements from the 1960s, maintain that he never understood *Lichtung* from *Licht*. The textual evidence makes apparent that the metaphor of light played a central role in Heidegger's thinking in the early and middle periods.

This conclusion is certainly confirmed by his additional reading of Plato's allegory in the 1933–4 lecture course 'On the Essence of Truth,' which is largely a repetition and restatement of the extensive reading he presented in the 1931–2 lecture course. Since he unfolds the same themes in much the same way in 1933–4 as he had in 1931–2, I will forgo here a lengthy textual reading of the later lecture course; nevertheless, a few lines are worth highlighting. So, for example, in correlating the Idea of the Good with the sun, he states that 'the sun itself is the ground of all being[ness].'[28] And, as he had in the earlier lecture course, he identifies the sun as the enabling light: 'To visibility belongs the enabling power – brightness, light – and therefore the *sun*.'[29] Furthermore, the sun's light is the 'yoke' that holds together seeing and what is seen, and this primordial 'light' is 'the light-source = the sun (*phos, helios*).'[30] He uses a diagram, one more complete than in the earlier lecture course, to summarize his understanding of the correlation of the sun with the Idea of the Good (GA 36/37, 196):

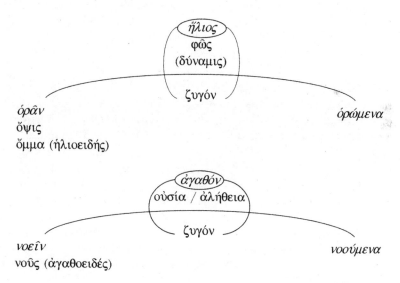

This same reading of Plato's 'sun' is carried through one more time in his well-known 1940 essay 'Plato's Doctrine of Truth' (published in 1942), albeit in a much less detailed manner. Here, the Idea of the Good is that which enables or grants all 'things' in their 'thingness,' and as before, he maintains that this is metaphorically expressed by the sun and its unique light:

> By its shining the sun bestows brightness upon everything that appears, and along with that brightness visibility and thus 'unhiddenness.' But not just that. At the same time its shining radiates warmth and by this glowing enables everything that 'comes to be' to go forth into the visibility of its stable duration. (509b)[31]

The textual case has been made, then, so at this point, let us move on. What remains to be discussed is the striking change in Heidegger's statements in the 1960s concerning this metaphor of light.

This development in his thinking I have addressed in detail in the previous chapter. Suffice it to say that in roughly the five-year period 1963–8, he moved the notion of *die Lichtung* to the forefront of his thinking and thematized the word in several texts and lectures. What is so striking is that in each case he was determined to strip away any suggestion of *Licht* from *Lichtung*. For the present effort, I want to focus on just one representative text – a text that will also serve us well in the next section of the present essay – his 1965/1968 address 'On the Question Concerning the Determination of the Matter for Thinking' (hereafter QDMT; complete translation by Capobianco and Göbel).[32]

Let us begin by observing that over the course of his lifetime of thinking, Heidegger brought forth a number of ways of naming *die Sache selbst*, the fundamental matter for thought, which in the context of our present discussion we might state briefly in this way: the temporal, finite and negatived, enabling / giving / granting / letting / freeing up / opening up of beings in their beingness. This is the *Ur*-phenomenon that he named *das Sein selbst*, Being itself (right to the very end of his life), but that he also named *Ereignis*, *Es gibt*, and *Lichtung*. As we have discussed, in his readings of Plato's allegory of the cave, Heidegger appropriated the metaphor of light in order to elucidate his primary concern, and these readings of 'light' inform the sense of *die Lichtung* in *Being and Time* and in other early and middle texts.[33] Yet when he returns to the phenomenon of *die Lichtung* in the 1960s, we find that he decidedly turns away from the 'light' as a guiding metaphor. Here is the relevant text from QDMT:

What this word [*die Lichtung*] gives us to think about may be made clear by an example, assuming that we consider it sufficiently. A forest clearing is what it is, not because of brightness and light [*der Helle und des Lichtes*], which can shine within it during the day. At night, too, the clearing [*die Lichtung*] remains. The clearing means: At this place, the forest is passable.

The lightening in the sense of brightness and the lightening of the clearing are different not only regarding the matter, but regarding the word as well. To lighten [*Lichten*] means: to render free, to free up [*freigeben*], to let free. To lighten belongs to light [*leicht*]. To render something light, to lighten something means: to clear away obstacles to it, to bring it into the unobstructed, into the free. To raise [*lichten*] the anchor says as much: to free it from the encompassing ocean floor and lift it into the free of water and air. (our translation)[34]

What Heidegger is emphasizing – that which opens up, frees up, lets free – he had elucidated in terms of *light and brightness* in his Plato readings. Yet here, as in other statements from the 1960s, he altogether rejects reading *Lichtung* in terms of *Licht* – a striking development in his thinking that he does not directly acknowledge or discuss anywhere in the later work as far as I can tell.

Indeed, his resolve to divorce *Licht* from *Lichtung* is so complete that he claims here (and elsewhere) that the word *Lichtung* has no linguistic relation at all to *Licht* – a claim that, as I have discussed previously, is highly dubious.[35] It seems that at some point in his thinking (late 1950s or early 1960s perhaps), he became aware of the linguistic relation between *Lichtung* and *leicht*, 'light' in the sense of 'easy,' 'effortless,' 'unburdened,' 'free.' After this point, he adopted this derivation and this sense of *Lichtung* to the complete exclusion (and outright rejection) of the word's other linguistic connection to *Licht* – a connection which he had always previously maintained.[36]

Presumably, Heidegger *could* have embraced both linguistic derivations and both families of meaning in elucidating the phenomenon of *die Lichtung* in his statements of the 1960s – but he did not. He opted instead to reject entirely any linguistic relation to light as luminosity. Why? The answer is no doubt subtle and complex, and in the previous chapter, I framed a response in terms of his deepening meditation on *aletheia*. But put more concisely, it appears that by the 1960s he had concluded that the metaphor of light was simply too much a part of the Western onto-theological tradition of thinking for it to be successfully appropriated to serve *die Sache selbst* in what he had come to call 'another' thinking. Apparently, in the end, this visual metaphor of light that so essentially belonged to the Greeks, the people of the eye above all others, had to be abandoned in favour of a different metaphor for a different kind of thinking, a *spatial* metaphor: the open, the region, the expanse, the *clearing*. In other words, we might say that by the 1960s Heidegger had decided to step back – and step away altogether – from the brilliance of Plato's light.

II.   *Die Lichtung* and *Die Kehre*

Much – too much, probably – has been written on the matter of whether there was a significant 'turn' (*die Kehre*) in Heidegger's thinking in the 1930s and whether, if in fact there was, it is properly named *die Kehre*. The debate has engaged many a commentator ever since William J. Richardson introduced the heuristic 'Heidegger I' and 'Heidegger II' in his masterful book in 1963.[37] I do not wish to enter into this long-standing debate as such, a debate that has seen some superb scholarship come to light; yet I cannot help but note that as late as 1969, Heidegger himself referred to *die Kehre* in a manner that corresponded very closely to how Richardson had carefully laid it out in his study. According to the protocol of the seminar in Le Thor on 6 September 1969, Heidegger commented:

> The thinking that proceeds from *Being and Time*, in that it gives up the word 'meaning of Being' in favor of 'truth of Being,' henceforth emphasizes the openness of Being itself, rather than the openness of Dasein in regard to this openness of Being.
>
> That signifies 'the turn' ['*die Kehre*'], in which thinking always more decidedly turns to Being as Being.[38]

Texts such as this one will certainly keep the debate spirited, but my concern at present is the more limited one of identifying *precisely this kind of Kehre* in his thinking regarding the phenomenon of *die Lichtung*. According to Thomas Sheehan, whose carefully constructed new 'paradigm' for Heidegger research has been both provocative and influential, Heidegger never wavered in maintaining that Dasein is the clearing as such:

> The most extraordinary thing about all of Heidegger's thought, both early and late, is his unwavering insistence that *human being is* that 'open' and thus *is* 'the thing itself' [*die Sache selbst*]. From the beginning to the end of his career, he never got beyond that point. (Sheehan's emphasis)[39]

Few commentators read Heidegger as insightfully as Sheehan, but this position, at least as articulated here, seems especially dubious. We certainly can agree with him that the *early* Heidegger understood *die Lichtung* principally in terms of Dasein's ekstatic-projective-disclosive character. The key text for this is §28 of *Being and Time*, where he states that Dasein 'is itself *die Lichtung*.'[40] In other words, it is entirely reasonable to maintain that the early Heidegger understood the opening/enabling/giving of beings – the 'lighting' – in terms of Dasein as thrown-*projection*. But surely this is not Heidegger's later view as well. In his 1947 'Letter on Humanism,' he returned to this matter of *Lichtung* and emphasized that the primary and proper locus of the enabling/giving is Dasein as *thrown*-projection. In fact, the shift in his emphasis from Dasein as 'projective' to Dasein as 'thrown' was so pronounced that he even reversed (without explicitly saying so) his earlier articulation of the proper character of *Lichtung*: in the 'Letter' he states unequivocally, 'But *die Lichtung* itself is *Being*' (my emphasis).[41]

Yet even if such texts are still not enough to indicate a significant turn in Heidegger's thinking regarding *die Lichtung* after *Being and Time*, the case is surely strengthened by his own words on the matter. Rarely did Heidegger explicitly acknowledge changes or developments in his thinking, but on this issue of the proper understanding of *die Lichtung*, he did indeed offer something like an Augustinian 'retraction.' The lines are to be found in the address QDMT, which I cited in the last section, and here I provide the full context for consideration (and now translate *die Lichtung* as the spatial 'clearing' in accordance with the development in his thinking regarding the word):

> Thus, it may be appropriate at this time to indicate, at least broadly, the clearing [*die Lichtung*] as the distinctive matter for another thinking. This is called for because four decades ago the hermeneutic analytic of Dasein spoke about the clearing with the aim of unfolding the question of Being in *Being and Time*. Later, 'Daseinsanalysis,' which aimed at a clarification of the foundations of psychiatry, entered into a dialogue with the analytic of Dasein and its positioning.
>
> Yet it required a decades-long walk along those forest paths that lead only so far [*Holzwege*] to realize that the sentence in *Being and Time:* 'The Dasein of the human being is itself the clearing' (§28), perhaps surmised the matter for thinking but in no way considered the matter adequately, that is, in no way posed the matter as a question that arrived at the matter.
>
> The Dasein is the clearing for presence as such, and yet Dasein is, at the same time, certainly not the clearing insofar as the clearing is Dasein

in the first place, that is, insofar as the clearing grants Dasein as such. The analytic of Dasein does not yet attain to what is proper to the clearing, and by no means attains to the region to which the clearing, in turn, belongs. (our translation)[42]

This passage is remarkable because it is one of the few places in Heidegger's corpus where he revises a specific line from an earlier work. He attests to a fundamental development in his thinking (which is fully in accordance with the term *Kehre* as he employed it at Le Thor in 1969) concerning what is 'proper to the clearing.' Specifically, he observes that what *Being and Time* could not say is that, *in the first place*, 'the clearing grants Dasein as such.' From his later perspective, Dasein is indeed the clearing in one sense, but it is not the clearing properly speaking, not the clearing as such. Here, I think, we have the most compelling textual evidence that counters Sheehan's claim that 'from the beginning to the end of his career' Heidegger maintained that the human being is *die Lichtung* itself, and thus 'the thing itself' (*die Sache selbst*) for thought.

Thus, Dasein is by no means the whole of the clearing; rather, it *belongs* to the clearing. This much may be settled, but there is another intriguing issue raised by the text. Heidegger suggests that the clearing itself *belongs* to the 'region' (*Bereich*). How exactly does he understand this relation between the 'clearing' and this 'region'? There is no obvious answer provided by the address as a whole, so to attempt to answer this question would take us down another path of thinking that is better left for another time. Nevertheless, I will offer a suggestion in the next section.

III. Basic Features and Existential Significance of the Phenomenon of the Clearing

As we have noted, by the 1960s Heidegger had fully purged his understanding of *die Lichtung* of any relation to *Licht*, so the translation of *Lichtung* as 'clearing' in his statements of the 1960s is much more in line with his explicit intentions. Even so, we should keep in mind that the German word *Lichtung* in the sense of 'clearing' does have a linguistic relation to *Licht/lichten* in the sense of 'lighting' and 'brightening,' so Heidegger's featured rendering of *Lichtung* as the 'clearing' in a wood or forest still retained a connection to *Licht* despite his repeated disavowals. Strictly speaking, exclusively deriving *Lichtung* from *lichten/ leicht* would limit the sense to 'easing,' 'freeing up,' 'lifting,' or 'raising' as in the common German expression, *den Anker lichten* (raising the anchor).[43] Be this as it may, I do not wish to belabour the point.

Instead, let us turn our attention more closely to the phenomenon of the 'clearing.' As we have discussed, for the later Heidegger, *Lichtung* names the phenomenon that includes Dasein but is by no means limited to Dasein. What we have not yet fully investigated is how he considered the experience of the 'clearing' as radically existentially transforming. His view on this is perhaps most succinctly stated in a foreword he wrote in 1968 on the occasion of the publication in Japan of his address QDMT (translated into Japanese by K. Tsujimura). Since the foreword is brief, I provide the full text:

> We ask: What is, and what is the determination of, the matter for thinking in the present age? The matter – this means that by which thinking is claimed. Through this claim, thinking, for its part, is first of all attuned to what it has to think.
>
> When we try to experience this determination, that is, to listen to the voice of this claim, we will catch sight of something that I call the 'clearing.' This phenomenon was first named in *Being and Time* and since then thought through ever anew.
>
> Through the thinking of the clearing and through its sufficient characterization, we arrive at a region [*Bereich*] that perhaps makes it possible to bring a transformed European thinking into a fruitful engagement with East Asian 'thinking.' It could help in the effort to save the essencing [*Wesen*] of the human being from the threat posed by an extremely technical calculating and manipulating of human Dasein. (my translation)[44]

First, here again we find a reference to the 'clearing' in relation to 'region.' The same basic question presents itself that we posed at the end of the last section: How precisely does Heidegger understand this relation? Are these both names for the same phenomenon? Or does the 'clearing' belong to the 'region,' which is an even more fundamental phenomenon than the clearing? A complete answer would require that we examine other texts, and in particular, investigate more fully what he has to say about 'regioning' (*die Gegnet*) in the dialogue 'Conversation on a Country Path Concerning Thinking'; but again, this would take us too far afield in the present discussion.

Still, we may recall that in his lecture 'The End of Philosophy and the Task for Thinking,' which is a close companion text of QDMT, Heidegger calls the 'clearing' the 'primordial matter' (*Ur-sache*) and, using a word from Goethe, the 'primordial phenomenon' (*Urphänomen*).[45] This is a strong indication that Heidegger employs both *Lichtung* and *Bereich* in this passage to characterize the one, simple, and fundamental phenomenon that he also names elsewhere *Ereignis* and *Es gibt* and, of course, *Sein selbst* (Being itself), namely: the temporal, finite and negatived, giving or letting of beings in their beingness. Indeed, let us not forget his important remark in the 1969 seminar in Le Thor: 'It is a matter here of understanding that the deepest meaning of Being is *letting*.'[46] Therefore, we may provisionally conclude that it is reasonable to understand Heidegger to mean in this foreword that 'clearing' and 'region' both name the one fundamental phenomenon; in other words, by stepping back from calculative reckoning, thinking is able to 'arrive' at the 'region' that he has called the 'clearing.' If there is a difference-in-identity here, it appears to be that Heidegger tends to reserve the name *Lichtung* for the distinctive cor-relation of Dasein and Being itself.

Another issue that the foreword raises concerns the precise relation of his notion of the clearing to 'East Asian' ideas and practices. Heidegger clearly thought that there was some fundamental affinity to be explored, and he pointedly invited further discussion. He himself always remained rather cautious about making any specific connections between his own thinking and Eastern traditions of thinking, but an abundance of scholarship – both in the East and in the West – has attempted to draw out more complete correspondences. Reinhard May, in his influential study, linked the notion of the 'clearing' with the Chinese written character for 'nothing,' *wu*, and its significance; and Zen teachers and scholars have related it to the Buddhist notion of 'emptiness.'[47] All such efforts are valuable and important, but I think that before we can make any meaningful assessments about these proposed connections, we need to bring into sharper relief the basic features of the phenomenon of the 'clearing' as we can discern them in Heidegger's work.

So far, in an effort to bring together his multiple indications regarding the proper character of the 'clearing,' I have employed an extended phrase, which I would extrapolate in this way: the temporal-spatial, finite and negatived, enabling/giving/granting/letting/opening/freeing of beings, including Dasein, who correspondingly lets beings be in language. Let us consider each of these aspects in Heidegger's own words:

The clearing is a temporal phenomenon

Time temporalizes. It liberates unto the free of the onefold of the ekstatic of having-beeness, future, and present. In the temporalizing of time, clearing plays.[48]

The clearing is a spatial phenomenon

Space spatializes. It makes room. Space frees up, namely, nearness and farness, narrowness and width, places and distances. In the spatializing of space, clearing plays.[49]

The clearing is a finite and negatived phenomenon

The finitude of thinking rests not solely and not primarily in the limitation of human ability, but rather in the finitude of the matter for thinking. To experience this finitude is much more difficult than hastily positing an absolute.[50]

Furthermore, we must consider that how the clearing clears must be thought in terms of *a-letheia:* what is unhidden, remains also hidden; what is opened up, remains also closed off; what is freed, remains also bound; what is granted, remains also whithheld; what is given, remains also withdrawn. So, as Heidegger states this:

Clearing is never mere clearing, but is always the clearing of concealment. In the proper sense, the clearing of *concealment* means that the inaccessible shows and manifests itself as such – as the inaccessible ... What manifests itself as the inaccessible is the mystery [*Geheimnis*].[51]

The clearing grants Dasein in the first place, but Dasein clears the clearing in language

This clearing ... this free dimension, is not the creation of the human being; it is not the human being. On the contrary, it is that which is assigned to him, since it is addressed to him: it is that which is dispensed to him.[52]

And in another place:

The human being is the guardian of the clearing, of *Ereignis*. He is not the clearing himself, not the entire clearing, nor is he identical with the whole of the clearing as such. But as the one ecstatically 'standing out' into the clearing, he himself is essentially cleared, and thus cleared himself in a distinguished way. Therefore, he is related to, belongs to, and is appropriated by the clearing. Da-sein's being-needed as the shepherd of the clearing [through language] is a distinguished manner of belonging to the clearing.[53]

Gathering together and thinking through these basic features of the 'clearing' is an important task in itself; but in doing so, we also realize that there are as many *challenges* as there are possibilities in any attempt to relate the clearing to key ideas in the 'East Asian' traditions. If Heidegger's position is that the clearing is an irreducibly temporal-spatial phenomenon, can a proper correspondence be drawn with traditional notions in the Chinese and Japanese philosophical and spiritual traditions? Also, does Heidegger's insistence on the finite and negatived character of the clearing pose a significant difficulty? Even Koichi Tsujimura, perhaps the foremost proponent of relating Heidegger's thinking to Zen, admitted that

> while Zen Buddhism has not yet arrived at clarifying *in a thinking way* the field of truth, or more precisely, of un-truth with respect to its essential features, Heidegger's thinking unceasingly attempts to bring to light the essential features of *Aletheia* (un-concealment).[54]

Furthermore, if, in accordance with Heidegger's fundamental phenomenological approach, Dasein must be considered an irreducible component of the clearing (albeit certainly not the whole of the clearing), can this view be accommodated by the major East Asian traditions? This matter is further complicated by the consideration that Dasein is structurally an ontic/ontological unity, and therefore Dasein's ontic features are constitutive (whether 'authentic' or 'inauthentic') and cannot be *entirely* disengaged, released, or stepped back from. Is this position reconcilable with Eastern perspectives? The answers to all of these questions are not immediately apparent, and much more careful and patient thinking is required. Given such difficult questions, it is perfectly understandable that though Heidegger welcomed a dialogue with 'East Asian' thinking, he was, for his own part, quite careful not to say or claim too much. There is more thinking to be done along this promising path.

Finally, let us reflect on his words in the foreword, echoed in many places in his later work, that our getting in view the phenomenon of the 'clearing' is decisive in 'the effort to save the essencing of the human being.' Dasein's attunement or step back or 'releasement' (*Gelassenheit*) to the clearing grants a measure of freedom from technicity, the calculating and commodifying 'enframing' (*Gestell*) that dominates our contemporary world. This much is abundantly evident from Heidegger's own writings, but the existential implications of such releasement to the clearing are surely more far-reaching, even if he addressed some of these possibilities only indirectly, or perhaps not at all, in his own thinking. It remains for us to continue to think through these implications and to draw out understandings that touch upon every aspect of our human sojourn. So, in this spirit, and with a glance towards the East, we may also consider that:

Releasement to the clearing ...

lets be and accepts the arriving and departing of all beings upon the earth and beneath the sky – including ourselves.

lets be and accepts the arriving and departing of the divinities.

undoes the binding power of thoughts, images, phantasies, feelings, emotions, and desires – and frees up their flow.

loosens the hold of egoistic demand, insistence, control, and mastery.

tempers the ought, the must, the should.

dissipates anger and enables acceptance of what comes to pass.

slows down and unclutters the time-space (*Zeit-Raum*) of our existence, enabling us to dwell and also give leeway (*Spielraum*) to all beings.

reveals the co-abiding and co-belonging of all Daseins and of all beings within the open.

brings forth compassion and humility and gentleness before the multiple forms and degrees of absencing and distortion intrinsic to presencing.

glimpses what has been refused and repressed by ideologies and dogmatisms, and thereby sets it free.

frees and opens us for the *Ereignis* (event as advent) of new social and cultural forms.

opens the way for us to see past prevailing economic and political systems – systems of all kinds – and to put into question their implicit or
explicit claims to permanence.

makes room for the becoming of art.

is attuned by a calm and quiet wonder before the unceasing ebb and
flow of all that is.

Concluding Thought

In the final session of his lecture course *The Principle of Reason* in 1955–6,
Heidegger, reflecting on Heraclitus' Fragment 52, likened Being to a
child's play (*Spiel*). Being, understood originarily and fundamentally, is
simply the 'play' of presencing, of emerging, a play without 'why.' 'It
remains simply play,' he observes, 'but this "simply" is everything, the
one, the only.'[55] Similarly, we may say that Being is the 'clearing' that
simply clears. We are cleared in the clearing. And in releasing ourselves
to the clearing, we see through to the utter simplicity of our existence.

7 Building: Centring, Decentring, Recentring

Human beings dwell when they are able to concretize the world in buildings and things.

Christian Norberg-Schulz, *Genius Loci*

Heidegger's remarks on 'building' are few, but they have been exceptionally influential. Over the decades, a whole new field – phenomenology of architecture – has emerged based largely upon the central notions of his seminal statement 'Building Dwelling Thinking' (1952).[1] In a series of remarkable books, including *Meaning in Western Architecture*, *Genius Loci*, and *The Concept of Dwelling*, the Norwegian architectural scholar Christian Norberg-Schulz worked out a detailed and comprehensive phenomenological approach to architecture.[2] In addition, many others have elaborated Heidegger's insights and extended them to discuss a wide variety of architectural, landscape, environmental, and design issues.[3]

These authors have been principally inspired by the Heidegger of 'Building Dwelling Thinking' who speaks of 'dwelling' (*das Wohnen*) as the basic feature of Dasein's being. Human beings dwell upon the earth and beneath the sky as mortals in the presence of the divinities. As these authors have developed this theme, their thinking about architecture and design has emphasized 'gathering,' 'presence,' and 'centring' as the most fundamental existential meanings. Architecture enables us to find our place or regain our lost place in the world, to gain or regain 'an existential foothold.' As Norberg-Schulz puts it: 'Human identity presupposes the identity of place ... The basic act of architecture is therefore to understand the "vocation" of the place.'[4]

On the other hand, another group of authors have found in Heidegger's thinking suggestions for a very different understanding of the nature and role of architecture.[5] Jacques Derrida and architects such as Bernard Tschumi and Peter Eisenman were more inspired by the Heidegger who, in *Being and Time*, identified *Angst* as the 'fundamental affective disposition' (*die Grundbefindlichkeit*) that leads Dasein beyond the tranquillizing modes of existence of the 'they–self' towards an authentic confrontation with our radically negatived finitude. This is also the Heidegger who reminds us in several different places of our *not*-at-homeness (*das Unzuhause*), of our unsettledness (*die Unheimlichkeit*), of the irreducibility of the *lethe* (concealment) dimension of *aletheia* (unconcealment), of *die Irre*, 'errancy,' that is, the multiple k-nottedness of Being itself.[6]

For these authors, this thread in Heidegger's work leads to an understanding of architecture as 'decentring.' Building is conceived as a 'de-constructive,' 'decentring' activity that not only reminds us of our uncertain, unfounded place – indeed our very placelessness – but also actively criticizes and refuses the tranquillizing architectural forms that are generally accepted and expected. To this end, Derrida and others use Heidegger against Heidegger. That is, the dis-placing, de-centring, ab-senting themes in Heidegger's work trump the language of conserving, protecting, sheltering, sparing, gathering, guarding, and so forth, which he puts into play in 'Building Dwelling Thinking' and elsewhere, especially in his later work.

In this generally 'postmodern' view, then, architecture is a 'dis-locating,' 'un-settling' activity. Jeffrey Kipnis, a champion of the deconstructivist approach, summarizes it this way:

> The concerns of deconstruction are twofold: first, to destabilize the meaning of apparently stable works and, secondly, to produce self-destabilizing works ... Such works resist, defer, and destabilize meaning by lending themselves to many frames while not allowing any particular frame to gain a foothold from which to narrow and confine the work to one particular meaning.[7]

Thus, Heidegger's thinking has been the source, whether directly or indirectly, for two very different theoretical approaches to 'building.' Let us, however, return to each view and complicate things somewhat.

I. Gathering the Fourfold

Stonehill College is in North Easton, Massachusetts, and North Easton is the home of five H.H. Richardson buildings, which together constitute the H.H. Richardson National Historic Landmark District. One of these remarkable Richardson buildings is the Gate Lodge, built in the 1880s, on the northern part of a large estate called the Langwater Estate. F.L. Olmsted collaborated with Richardson on the landscaping of the Gate Lodge, and Olmsted did additional landscaping on the grounds. Another Richardson building nearby is the dramatic Oakes Ames Memorial Hall (1881), which was landscaped by Olmsted in an equally dramatic manner.[8]

In 'Building Dwelling Thinking,' Heidegger speaks about the 'simple oneness' of the presencing of earth, sky, mortals, and divinities, which he calls *das Geviert*, the fourfold. For those working in the phenomenology of architecture in the spirit of Heidegger's essay, Richardson's Gate Lodge and Memorial Hall are perfect examples of 'building' as 'dwelling' as 'gathering' the fourfold. To use Norberg-Schulz's language, we may put it this way: both Richardson and Olmsted were deeply attuned to the *genius loci* or the 'spirit of the place' of North Easton in New England.

The place, the landscape, is essentially 'romantic.' As Norberg-Schulz describes this, the earth

> is rarely continuous, but is subdivided and has a varied relief; rocks and depressions, groves and glades; bushes and tufts create a rich 'microstructure' [on the ground]. [The sky is not] experienced as a total hemisphere, but is narrowed in between the contours of trees and rocks, and is ... continuously modified by clouds. The sun is relatively low and creates a varied play of spots of light and shadow, with clouds and vegetation acting as enriching 'filters.' Water is ever present as a dynamic element, both as running streams and quiet, reflecting ponds. [The atmosphere is] constantly changing.[9]

In sum, a romantic landscape, according to Norberg-Schulz, is neither one homogeneous place (like the desert), which he calls a 'cosmic' landscape, nor a harmony of places (like the gently rolling hills of Virginia), which he calls a 'classical' landscape; rather, a romantic landscape, such as the densely wooded areas of New England, is defined by an indefinite multitude of individual places. Therefore, for us to dwell, to gain an existential foothold in such a romantic place, our activity of building needs to be in tune with the 'spirit of the place.' Understood in its proper character, building is a 'gathering' of the fourfold of earth, sky, mortals, and divinities that corresponds to the way these emerge, appear, unfold in *physis*, which, for Heidegger, is an ancient Greek name for Being itself. In this case, Richardson's buildings and Olmsted's landscaping gather and 'concretize' the meanings of this place in New England and 'root' us mortals and 'centre' us in this place in a powerful and enduring way.

If we consider the Gate Lodge and Memorial Hall, we can appreciate the correspondence. For instance, we may take note of how the eye is forced to move dynamically from part to part of each building and does not come to rest on a view of the whole. This dynamic massing of the buildings responds to the romantic natural place where individual places dominate and no view of the whole can be attained. Similarly, the intricacy of the facades and the multiple stony textures and colours gather the rich variety of features of the romantic earth and sky. The deeply recessed windows and openings recall the deep and mysterious protective places of the woods. The powerful horizontality of the Gate Lodge and the dramatic verticality of Memorial Hall call forth the distinctive relationship of mortals to the expressive earth and sky. The numerous stone carvings and reliefs of flora and fauna let shine forth the multitude of 'divinities' (sprites, dryads, nymphs, fairies, gnomes, and so forth) who 'appear' in the romantic landscape and who enchant and bedevil the mortals who dwell.

II. Recentring

In this phenomenological view, Richardson's architecture 'centres' us and grants us an existential foothold. Nevertheless, the kind of 'centring' understood here needs to be clarified. Modernist architecture with its aspiration to create universal, clean, pure, ordered, and rational forms and spaces represents a centring, too, but of a very different sort. The typical modernist building may be said to represent the triumph of the scientistic/technological self and, thus, to affirm the mastering conscious subject as 'centre.' Of course, this kind of centring – that is, the centrality of conscious mastering – is precisely what Heidegger so strenuously objected to and criticized, as have those who have followed him in elaborating an architectural and environmental phenomenology.

Consequently, 'dwelling' and 'building' as spoken of by Heidegger and Norberg-Schulz and others is certainly not a 'centring' of the modernist sort, but rather what we might call a decentred centring or *recentring*. That is, Dasein becomes capable of dwelling only insofar as it is able to step back from the illusion of the mastery of the conscious subject (decentring) and sustain a relation and openness (recentring) to Being as *physis* as dynamic and powerful emerging-appearing. It is in the 'space' of this openness to Being that Dasein is recentred and dwells and becomes capable of the kind of building that creates buildings like Richardson's Gate Lodge. From this perspective, decentring is also recentring, and the recentred self dwells as gathering and keeping the fourfold in things, such as buildings. And certainly this recentred self has as little to do with the centred self of scientistic/technological discourse as Richardson's Gate Lodge has to do with the modernist glass-and-steel box. Indeed, the observations of Norberg-Schulz and of others in the field invite us to reflect more thoughtfully on 'dwelling' and 'building'; nonetheless, there is also a problematical aspect of their phenomenological studies. These authors generally have not taken seriously enough the implications of Heidegger's understanding of 'mortals' in his elaboration of the fourfold.

III. Mortals

In 'Building Dwelling Thinking,' Heidegger observes that human beings 'are called mortals because they can die. To die means to be capable of death *as* death. Only human beings die, and indeed ever so, as long as they remain on earth, under the sky, before the divinities.'[10] The force of these words may not be immediately apparent. Dasein dwells as openness to Being as the emerging-abiding-passing away of beings; therefore, dwelling is also dying. *Dwelling is finite; dwelling is 'thrown'; dwelling is risky; dwelling is courageously accepting radical finitude.*

It is this dimension of dwelling that is often neglected by many authors committed to the phenomenological approach. Their reflections on dwelling gravitate towards the religious and mystical; their studies of place tend to emphasize access to healing and wholeness. Their message is a consoling and reassuring one that the contingency, brokenness, and privations of existence may be ultimately transcended in our being-in-the-world. Yet Heidegger's point appears to be precisely that there is no overcoming our radically negatived finitude. Dwelling is always at risk. And authentic thinking – and building – should attest to this.

For example, H.H. Richardson's architecture puts us in our place, to be sure, but this place is not simply safe, secure, and assured. It is the place that corresponds to Dasein's resolute, dynamic, risky, mortal openness to Being as powerful emerging-appearing. This is the insight that seems to be lost in many of the phenomenological and anthropological studies in the field. These authors use the language bequeathed by Heidegger but tend to overlook this aspect of his thinking. Consequently, they infuse the notion of 'dwelling' with an overly mythical and mystical significance. They suggest that the (recentred) self who dwells gains access to the infinite, to plenitude, to abiding peace. What is missing in their thinking is a fuller recognition and understanding of what it means to say that *mortals* dwell.

IV. Resisting Place

On the other hand, *radicalizing* what Heidegger means by mortals is the hallmark of Derrida's thinking and of deconstructivist or 'postmodern' thinking generally. Dasein decentred becomes Dasein set adrift in an infinite sea of meanings. Dasein decentred is not recentred, but rather dispersed into the flux of signifiers. Dasein has no identity, no 'place' to dwell, and therefore, architecture is called on to be a radically 'dis-placing' activity, reminding us always that we have *no* existential foothold.

Such dis-placement is transparent in the work of architects such as Peter Eisenman, Bernard Tschumi, Zaha Hadid, and Coop Himmelblau. For example, David Goldblatt highlights Eisenman's Guardiola House and Wexner Center at Ohio State University as superior examples of deconstructivist 'non-architecture.' Goldblatt admits that these buildings appear 'fragmented, if not tortured and shaky' and 'fractured and looking incomplete'; yet in his view they nevertheless successfully dis-place or dis-locate the traditional 'architectural self,' which apparently includes the self that dwells in the Heideggerian sense.[11] In the deconstructivist view generally, Heidegger's notion of building as dwelling as gathering the fourfold still harbours and perpetuates the illusion of identity, meaning, presence, centre. And architecture, no less than the other arts, is called upon to shatter this illusion. As Derrida himself put this in an interview:

> For this point of view [deconstruction], I think that the architectural experience (let's call it that, rather than talking about 'buildings' as such) ... what they offer is precisely the chance of experiencing the possibility

of these inventions of a different architecture, one that wouldn't be, so to speak, 'Heideggerian.'[12]

Deconstructivist architecture is very explicit about radically displacing and dispersing the self; but in a more implicit way, much of 'postmodern' architecture, as it evolved as a particular style, accomplished the same goal.[13] One hallmark of the postmodern style – the self-conscious, ironic, and playful use of past architectural iconic elements – serves to remind us that our place is unfounded, that identity slips into other identities, and that meanings are gathered arbitrarily or merely as formal exercises in 'contextualism.' A good illustration is Robert Venturi's Sainsbury Wing of the National Gallery in London. The wing makes ample references to the place but refuses to make a *commitment* to the place. Though sedate in appearance, the facade of Venturi's addition carries over the architectural elements of the original building in such a self-consciously clever way that it appears almost to mock the noble old building on Trafalgar Square. Such postmodern buildings resist, in their own quieter way, what Heidegger calls dwelling.

Oddly enough, then, both deconstructivist and postmodern architecture end up sharing with modernist architecture something in common, namely, an avoidance of the richness of place. Modernist architecture leaps beyond place with its mathematizing and universalizing ideal, and deconstructivist architecture (in particular) energetically resists place as illusory and inauthentic. In effect, for all of the differences in theory and style, modernist buildings and deconstructivist buildings such as Eisenman's Wexner Center, Himmelblau's Vienna rooftop office, Tschumi's Lerner Hall at Columbia University, and Koolhaas's Seattle Public Library all may be said to share a *place-lessness*. They are structures of any place and, therefore, of no place.

Concluding Reflection

A strong and even vehement resistance to identity, meaning, and place still holds sway in contemporary postmodern thinking about building and design. The often articulated claim of these approaches is that such resistance holds open the space for us to affirm the sheer superfluity of life (and of meaning) or to confront and recognize the fragility, brokenness, and pain of mortal being. Ironically, though, when we consider many recent works of architecture and design inspired by such postmodern theories, we are often left with the impression that life has been flattened and faded and the travail of mortals trivialized. Unlike a building such as Richardson's Gate Lodge, many of these postmodern built forms have no presence and power; they do not speak of either life or death.

Contemporary postmodern thinking about architecture – and about literature and the arts more generally – remains dominated by the metaphor of the dispersion of meaning over an infinite surface and very much opposed to Heidegger's metaphor of the inexhaustible gathering of meaning in a defined place.[14] The contemporary determination to keep meaning and identity fluid and 'undecidable' is championed as a liberating and empowering exercise, but by refusing to break the surface of meanings, the result is oftentimes simply superficial. Is it possible that the richest and most profound questions about meaning and identity can be framed only once meaning and identity have been gathered, forged, put into place? Might Heidegger be right in saying that only if we have the courage to dwell can we truly build? If so, then it is worth hearing and considering once again his words that we must ever learn to dwell, to think for the sake of dwelling, and to build from out of the experience of dwelling.

8 Limit and Transgression

For evil, as the Pythagoreans say, is a form of the Infinite, and good a form of the Finite.

Aristotle, *Nicomachean Ethics*, Book II, vi.

Let us pick up a thread from the discussion in chapter 3 and develop another line of thinking regarding Heidegger's early reading of *Antigone* in *Introduction to Metaphysics* (1935). Both Heidegger and the celebrated French psychoanalyst Jacques Lacan, each in his own distinctive way, offered readings of Sophocles' *Antigone* that compel us to come to terms with our finitude, a familiar theme in existential philosophy and psychology, and one that was originally sounded in ancient Greek and Roman thinking. Of interest, though, is that both of their interpretations are uneasy with a traditional understanding that the ancient Greek notion for limit and measure, *sophrosyne*, is at the core of the message about human existence. In fact, Heidegger (in his early reading) and Lacan are almost contemptful of this perspective and favour a much more heroic rendering of Antigone's tragic situation.[1]

For both thinkers, the important theme in *Antigone* is not that prudential wisdom is 'the best of all of our wealth,' as Tiresias declaims, but that heroism is required to sunder convention in order to create authentically or pursue to the bitter end one's desire or life's project. If in a more classical reading of *Antigone*, it is an abiding respect for limit and measure, *sophrosyne*, that makes possible something like a happy human life, then for Heidegger and Lacan it is precisely the transgression of conventional limits in the name of one's project that appears to be the condition of the possibility of living an 'authentic' or 'heroic' – if not happy – life.

Yet, again, it is not quite as neat as this because a more fundamental notion of limit *is* central to the work of both thinkers. Both Heidegger and Lacan are, broadly speaking, philosophers of *finitude*. For Heidegger, the existential condition of the possibility of authenticity is the resolute acceptance of the multiple dimensions of our radically negatived finitude. For Lacan, the structural condition of the possibility of becoming a subject of desire is the mediation of the infinite *jouissance* of the imaginary by the finitude of the symbolic order. Thus, from this perspective, both thinkers reaffirm an ancient Greek emphasis on limit in their rejection of all philosophies, psychologies, and theologies that propose to transcend or overcome finitude and to permit access to the fullness, completeness, and plenitude of being.

Even so, it remains that their readings of *Antigone* share an enthusiasm for the transgression of convention and custom as a necessary condition of authentic selfhood and creativity. Yet while their emphasis on transgression certainly puts a more modern romantic twist on the ancient Greek message about finitude, the message itself is not fundamentally altered. Both Heidegger's 'ethics of authenticity' and Lacan's 'ethics of desire' reject any ethics of conformity and pose a serious challenge to a certain strain of Greek thinking represented particularly by Aristotle's ethics of the *phronimos*. Nevertheless, neither Heidegger nor Lacan intends by the transgression of limit *an overcoming of our finitude*.

I

Introduction to Metaphysics (1935) is a profoundly original and seminal philosophical work, but we should not overlook how the early Heidegger's way of characterizing Dasein and the relationship between Dasein and Being was influenced by German romantic thinking – and Nietzsche may be justifiably included in this tradition of thinking. The Heidegger of the 1930s, in his own way, carries forward Nietzsche's ethics of the *Übermensch* and his disdain for the ancient Greek tradition of *sophrosyne*, a contempt that we encounter in several of his writings and especially in *The Birth of Tragedy*.[2]

From our perspective today, Heidegger's early rendering of Dasein's engagement with Being in *Introduction to Metaphysics* is unmistakably coloured by the romance of the hero, and that is nowhere more apparent than in his reading of Sophocles' *Antigone*.[3] Commenting on the well-known choral lines 332 to 375, Heidegger understands Sophocles to be naming the human being (Dasein) as the 'strangest' or 'uncanniest' or 'most unsettled' being of all (*das Unheimlichste,* as he reads Sophocles' word *deinotaton*) who is 'estranged' from all that is familiar. *Sein,* Being, is the Overpowering (*das Überwältigende*), and Dasein is enjoined to stand out into the *polemos,* into the raging of *Sein,* which compels 'awe' and 'terror.' Solitary and disoriented, Dasein must 'contend' with the Overpowering with its own 'power' and even 'violence' in order to 'create' and 'stand out.' The 'violent one,' he solemnly declares, 'knows no kindness and conciliation (in the usual sense); he cannot be mollified or appeased by success or prestige. In all of this the violent, creative one sees only the semblance of fulfillment, and this he despises.'

To this end, Dasein's contending with the Overpowering may very well result in disaster. Dasein is always faced with the possibility of 'ruin' (*der Verderb*), and this does not occur 'only at the end, when a single act of power fails, when the violent one makes a false move; no, this ruin is fundamental, it governs and waits in the conflict between violence and the Overpowering.' Even so, the essential or inherent disaster of Dasein's daring departure into Being only affirms Dasein's 'greatness.'

For Heidegger, very much in a Nietzschean vein, Dasein must 'depart from its customary, familiar limits' and 'transgress the limit of the familiar' (*die Grenze des Heimischen überschreitet*) in order to exist authentically. Dasein's authentic selfhood and the originality and power of its creations depend on a heroic transgression of the customary and conventional and on the resolute acceptance of the extreme consequences. In a typical passage:

> The *violent one,* the creative one, who sets forth into the un-said, who breaks into the un-thought, compels the unhappened to happen and makes the unseen appear – this violent one stands at all times in daring (*tolma,* line 371). In daring to master Being, he must risk the assault of un-beings, *me kalon;* he must risk dispersion, instability, disorder, mischief. The higher the summit of historical Dasein, the deeper will be the abyss, the more abrupt the fall into the unhistorical, which merely thrashes around in issueless and placeless confusion.[4]

In authenticity, Dasein must 'contend' with the Overpowering with 'power' and 'violence' in order 'to manifest Being in the work as a being.' Dasein is structured by a 'need' or 'want' or even 'affliction' (*Not*) – compelled by Being itself – which 'drives him beyond himself to venture forth toward Being,' and even though this *Not* creates the possibility of downfall and ruin, it is at the same time the source of Dasein's originality, creativity, and authenticity – indeed, the condition of the possibility of 'true historical greatness,' as was achieved by the ancient Greeks.

Consequently, for Heidegger, Sophocles' words and the figure of Antigone call our attention to the tragic greatness of being human. Antigone exemplifies authentic Dasein; she is one who, as 'the strangest of all' refuses 'the usual bustle and activity,' 'breaks through and breaks up' the customary and familiar, stands out and stands alone, and, finally, is rejected by the city for her awesome heroic strangeness.[5] In keeping with his heroic reading of the drama, it is altogether fitting that Heidegger understands the chorus's anxiety about such 'estrangement' from the community of men and women (apolis, line 370) not as a thoughtful warning against recklessness or overreaching (tolma, line 371), but as 'a direct and complete confirmation of the strangeness and uncanniness of human being.'

This early Heidegger, like Nietzsche, is suspicious and even disdainful of the ancient Greek ethos of sophrosyne and phronesis and reads the Greek tragedy to work out an ethics of the hero that is at odds with an ethics of the phronimos. In his commentary on the Antigone text, Heidegger conspicuously passes over the passages which would suggest that not just Creon, but Antigone, too, is flawed by excess and lacks the measure, balance, and perspective – the life-wisdom – that is ingredient to living a complete or happy life.

For example, he overlooks Haemon's words to his father – important words that appear to apply as much to Antigone's unassailable certainty and unrelenting insistence as to Creon's intransigence:

> The kind of man who always thinks that he is right,
>   that his opinions, his pronouncements,
>   are the final word,
>   is usually exposed as hollow as they come.
> But a wise man is flexible, has much to learn
>   without a loss of dignity.
> See the trees in floodtime, how they bend
>   along the torrent's course,
>   and how their twigs and branches do not snap,
>   but stubborn trees are torn up roots and all.
> In sailing, too, when fresh weather blows,
>   a skipper who will not slacken sail, turns turtle,
>   finishes his voyage beam-ends up.[6]

And lost, too, in his commentary are the incisive – and perhaps decisive – words of Tiresias to Creon:

Tiresias: Creon! Creon!
          Is no one left who takes to heart that –
Creon: Come, let's have the platitude!
Tiresias: That wise deliberation [*euboulia*] is the best of all our wealth.[7]

Heidegger, like Nietzsche, does not consider that Sophocles' ultimate word may be that *both Creon and Antigone* are marked by an excess that precipitates the tragedy. Creon's and Antigone's awful insistence, their inflexibility, their blindness to proper measure in things human, their arrogant venturing past the fearful *Atè*, is what invites tragedy – and perhaps defines tragedy. Especially since Nietzsche, we are accustomed to reading the Greek tragedies *against* the philosophers. Yet from another perspective (in need of being recalled), the message of the tragedies is very much in harmony with the message of the ancient Greek philosophical tradition: measure, wisdom, *sophrosyne, phronesis* is 'the best of all our wealth.' As the chorus intones at the end of *Antigone*: 'Where wisdom [*to phronein*] is, there happiness [*eudaimonias*] will crown.'[8]

Heidegger's reading of *Antigone* in IM favours an ethics of heroic transgression over an ethics of wise measure and moderation. Even so, his thinking rejoins a particular ancient Greek tradition of thinking in affirming that there is one limit that cannot be transgressed: finitude. *Sein* and its Dasein are radically finite, and Dasein's authentic existence depends on resolutely accepting this. For Heidegger, Dasein has no access to the plenitude of infinite being or to the fullness of untrammelled meaning; Dasein cannot overcome its radically negatived finitude. There are multiple dimensions to Dasein's finitude and multiple places in Heidegger's work that make this clear. In *Introduction to Metaphysics*, he puts it in these stark terms:

All violence shatters against *one* thing. That is death. It is an end beyond all consummation, a limit beyond all limits. Here there is no breaking-out or breaking-through, no capture or subjugation. But this strange and alien thing that banishes us once and for all from everything in which we are at home is no particular event that must be named among others because it, too, ultimately happens. It is not only when it comes to die, but always and essentially that the human being is subject to death. Insofar as human beings *are*, they stand in relation to the inevitability of death.[9]

II

Lacan, like Freud, had a penchant for irony, scepticism, and suspicion, so it is fair to say that Lacan did not share the same kind of enthusiasm for heroic striving that appears in Heidegger's thinking of the 1930s. Nevertheless, if we consider his commentary on *Antigone* in his series of seminars in 1959–60, *The Ethics of Psychoanalysis*, we find a striking similarity with both Nietzsche's and Heidegger's readings of the Greek tragedies. As Lacan reads the unfolding drama, Antigone 'fascinates'; she is the image of 'beauty,' 'shining radiance,' and 'unbearable splendor,' all because she, unlike most, is *heroic* in remaining true to her desire to the bitter, tragic end. 'Antigone,' he declares, 'reveals to us the line of sight that defines desire.'[10]

Like Heidegger's ethics of authenticity, Lacan's ethics of desire has many of the features of an ethics of heroic transgression. In his final seminar for the year dated 6 July 1960, Lacan states, with typical rhetorical relish, that what Freud and psychoanalysis has uncovered is the centrality of desire:

> And it is because we know better than those who went before how to recognize the nature of desire, which is at the heart of this experience [of human action], that a reconsideration of ethics is possible, that a form of ethical judgment is possible, of a kind that gives this question the force of a Last Judgment: Have you acted in conformity with the desire that is in you?[11]

From Lacan's psychoanalytical point of view, then, 'the only thing of which one can be guilty ... is to have compromised one's desire.'[12] As he sees it, some experience of 'betrayal' is usually at the heart of an individual's abandoning his or her desire. Such betrayals will inevitably happen, but what matters for Lacan is the response. The response of the 'common man,'[13] he warns us, is to retreat to 'the common path,' to 'the service of goods,' by which he appears to mean that the average man or woman – in response to betrayal, resistance, or rejection – renounces his or her own desire(d) projects and compromises by conforming to ('servicing') the ideal, generalized, sanctioned, and sanitized 'goods' established and sustained by society and culture. As he puts it, it is as if the 'common man' says, in effect, '"Well, if that's how things are, we should abandon our position; neither of us is worth that much, and especially me, so we should just return to the common path."'[14]

Nevertheless, there is a high price to be paid for such conformity. No matter how respected and admired the 'common' individual may be, he or she may inevitably feel guilty, for 'in the last analysis what a subject really feels guilty about when he manifests guilt always has to do with ... the extent to which he has compromised his desire.'[15] For the 'common' man or woman who has sacrificed his or her root desire, there remains, despite whatever success and acclaim in the order of the city, an emptiness, an aridity, and an accompanying sense of loss and guilt.

But to pursue one's desire *despite* betrayal and the tumult of life is the response of the 'hero' (*héros*), according to Lacan. The 'hero' is 'betrayed with impunity' and follows the 'risky' path of unconditionally refusing to turn away from his or her own desire. Antigone is a hero of this ethics of desire. She refuses to compromise her desire for anyone and certainly not for any such Aristotelian 'common' good. In Lacan's strong words, she 'trembles before nothing, and especially not before the good of the other.'

Opposed to this heroic ethics of desire are those 'traditional' philosophical ethical perspectives that are founded on 'the order of powers' and that legitimize the 'tidied-up, ideal' hierarchy of 'goods' established by society.[16] Aristotle's ethics, in particular, comes in for sharp criticism from Lacan for 'cleaning up' desire so that the service of the cultural, social, economic, political, and religious goods of the city – the goods of the 'master' – can be carried out. Aristotle wants nothing to do with the 'array and disarray' of desire; instead, he offers a 'middle way' that is the way of the 'common' individual along the 'common path.' In Lacan's (overstated) criticism of Aristotle's ethical thinking, the *phronimos* appears to be none other than the 'common' man whose desire has been deadened by conformity to the prevailing order of goods.

Like Nietzsche and Heidegger, then, Lacan is mostly dismissive of the ancient Greek ethos informed by *sophrosyne* and *phronesis*. In his view, this is an ethos of compromise, and the Aristotelian promise of *eudaimonia* can only be had at the price of abandoning or conforming one's own desire. For Lacan, Aristotelian 'happiness' and the modern 'bourgeois dream' share a common failing: both deny the tragic dimension of existence – as well as the tragic heroism required to claim one's desire and live boldly and authentically or, like Antigone, with 'splendor.'

And this returns us to Lacan's reading of *Antigone*. He, too, offers a commentary on the choral lines beginning at 332, and while his reading is different from Heidegger's in certain particulars, it shares with Heidegger's early reading a disdain for what Lacan calls a 'humanist' perspective. 'As for us [today],' he states, 'we consider ourselves to be at the end of the vein of humanist thought.'[17] Like Heidegger, he understands the chorus's words to attest to the essential tragic strangeness of being human and to the common man's fascination with – and ultimate rejection of – the individual, such as Antigone, who heroically 'violates the limits of *Atè* through her desire.'[18] As with Nietzsche and Heidegger, he gleans from Greek tragedy an ethics of heroic transgression of the limits of the customary and conventional. For Lacan, Antigone heroically pursues her desire beyond the limit established by the law of the *polis* and stands splendidly and beautifully alone in doing so. Charles Sheperdson, commenting on Lacan's reading, puts it this way:

> The crucial feature of her action lies ... in the supreme indifference she displays, her disregard for any consequences in the world of the living – a hardness she reveals in the opening lines of the play, as though her choice had already been made in advance ... It is this supreme waywardness and detachment that cuts the hero off from the community, leading her to act in haughty solitude and indifference, but at the same time in a manner that turns out to have incalculable effects, so that her act still reaches the world of the living, to whom it was not addressed.[19]

Lacan's reading is remarkably in sync with Heidegger's high praise in *Introduction to Metaphysics* for all 'creators,' like Antigone, who through their striving become '*apolis*, without city and place, lonely, strange, and alien ... without statute and limit, without structure and order, because they themselves *as* creators must first create all of this.'[20]

For Lacan, Antigone's transgression of the law of the land, her crossing over the fearful boundary that the ancient Greeks marked with the word *atè*, makes her a hero of desire in much the same way that, for Heidegger, Antigone's 'breaking up and breaking through' the prevailing order makes her a herald of authentic selfhood and creativity.

III

Heidegger and Lacan, each in his own way, extract from Sophocles' *Antigone* an ethics of heroic overcoming that is much in keeping with Nietzsche's reading of the Greek tragedies. Nevertheless, these readings, as compelling as they may be, seem difficult to reconcile with the overriding ancient Greek concerns with society and friendship, measure and proportion, balance and harmony, prudential judgment and wisdom. No doubt these readings do illumine the tragedy in interesting and valuable ways, but they also conceal and cover over a core message of the ancient Greeks long known, long honoured, and long valued – a message not of heroic striving, solitude, and impassioned agony, but of wise discernment and judgment in the midst of a vibrant and often tumultuous communal life. Not Faust and Zarathustra, but Odysseus and Tiresias.

Even so, we must keep in mind that in another respect both Heidegger and Lacan remain very close to the classical legacy in insisting on *finitude*. The ethics of authenticity and the ethics of desire may celebrate an ethics of transgression, but in the end, this is not a transgression of finitude, not a transcendence of our radically finite existence.

Central to both Lacan's and Heidegger's thinking is the emphasis on limit *qua finitude*. For Lacan, as he reads Freud on the dynamics of the Oedipal complex, the imaginary fusion of the child with the mother – with its accompanying *jouissance* of plenitude – is ruptured by the 'no' of the father. The No of the father, the Name-of-the-Father – the prohibition against incest – differentiates the child from the mother and leaves the child structured by a 'lack' or 'want-to-be,' which defines human desire. For Lacan, the incest taboo is not just any law but the Law of laws that represents the structural condition of the possibility of being a subject of desire. In effect, the law against incest institutes the being of the self.

In Lacanian terms, the subject of desire that emerges is subject to the Law or symbolically 'castrated.' That is, the subject is structurally barred from the attainment of the Other as infinite *jouissance* and consigned to channel its 'want-to-be' or desire through projects governed by the symbolic order or the 'law of language.' Thus, symbolic castration is the measure of our finitude. The human being is structured by the Limit of limits, which denies access to infinite being and its *jouissance* (*das Ding*). There is no overcoming this Limit (without loss of the self). No overcoming this 'tragic' fact of existence, as he prefers to call it in *The Ethics of Psychoanalysis*.

Herein, in Lacan's view, lies Antigone's nobility: she chooses and embraces this 'death,' this radical finitude, and sees with the utmost clarity that 'life can only be approached, can only be lived or thought about, from the place of that limit where her life is already lost ... But from that place she can see it and live it in the form of something already lost.'[21] For Lacan, then, as for Nietzsche and Heidegger, the very condition of the possibility of living authentically is resolutely accepting and taking up *this* limit defined as our finitude.

For this reason, Lacan (following Freud) sharply criticized all philosophies, psychologies, and theologies, all popular cultural and religious ideals and practices, which compromise our finitude by holding out the promise of overcoming the 'lack of being' and recovering the lost (imaginary) plenitude. His often fierce opposition to religion turned on just this issue, for in his view, at the very core of religion is the promise – whether to be fulfilled in this world or in the next – to 'recuperate' the 'pound of flesh' that *must* be sacrificed in symbolic castration and in facing up to the brokenness of existence (the Real).[22] For Lacan, religion cannot bear our finitude without flinching.

IV

In summary, both the early Heidegger and Lacan cultivate an ethics of heroic transgression in their readings of Sophocles' *Antigone;* but in a more fundamental sense, they propound a philosophy/psychology of limit. Their reflections on the human condition defined by radical finitude link them not only to the major figures of existentialist thinking, but also to classical authors such as Homer, Epicurus, and Lucretius. In fact, not surprisingly, Homer may be our first and best teacher on such existential matters. In Book 6 of the *Iliad*, we find a striking image attesting to the necessity, attendant anxiety, and even terror of what Lacan, following Freud, called (symbolic) castration – the mark of our finitude:

> In the same breath, shining Hector reached down
> for his son – but the boy recoiled,
> cringing against his nurse's full breast,
> screaming out at the sight of his own father,
> terrified by the flashing bronze, the horse hair crest,
> the great ridge of the helmet nodding, bristling terror –
> so it struck his eyes.

Yet in the very following lines, Homer keeps us in touch with another dimension – the tender and loving and joyful dimension – of the work of the Name-of-the-Father – and of our mortal existence:

   And his loving father laughed,
his mother laughed as well, and glorious Hector,
quickly lifting the helmet from his head,
set it down on the ground, fiery in the sunlight,
and raising his son he kissed him and tossed him in his arms, ...[23]

Homer ever reminds us that our proper home, our proper dwelling, lies *between* tragedy and bliss and that we can face up to our strange and exasperating predicament with both heroism *and* prudence, strength *and* sweetness, resoluteness *and* gentleness, resistance *and* acceptance.

Afterword

As Heidegger observed more than once, if we attend more carefully to the expression 'to bring to language,' then we realize that it has the deeper meaning of

> to raise what was formerly unspoken, what was never before said, into word for the first time, and through saying, to let appear what until now has been concealed. If we thoughtfully consider the character of saying in this regard, this becomes evident: Language shelters within itself the treasure of everything that is essential.[1]

The 'founding' early Greek thinker Parmenides uttered the word *to eon*, Being, and thereby brought to language what is most essential. In uttering again that ancient word, Heidegger, as he understood it, was bringing to language the very Same as Parmenides – but also what was liminal and left unsaid as such in this originary word of Western thinking. And thus, for Heidegger, *to eon*, Being, names the unitary and unifying (*hen, das Eine*), temporal-spatial (*Ereignis, Lichtung, Gegnet*), finite and negatived (*a-letheia*), appearing/emerging/arising (*physis*) of beings in their beingness. This is the Simple (*das Einfache*) – which nonetheless required of Heidegger a lifetime of thinking and saying so that only now, after Heidegger, may we marvel with appreciation: how wondrously simple indeed!

The Simple – Being itself – is the temporal-spatial flow of all beings: the coming and going, appearing and disappearing, arriving and departing of beings; the emerging and lingering and passing away of all that is. And we – Dasein – are carried along this flow, temporally stretched out in our own peculiar way between birth and death. Being itself is *phainesthai*, the temporal shining-forth of beings – is this not Heidegger's great thought? And our being, we see more clearly, is not *in* time, but *is* temporal. Even our stillness is a moving stillness.

But among the beings who abide upon the earth and beneath the sky, it appears that only we, who 'have the word,' are able to bring this fundamental phenomenon of the temporal flow of all beings into language and into thought. We are the beings who are *mindful* of our mortality. And there's the existential rub. For the early Heidegger, this knowing indelibly marks our existence with Angst, but as his thinking unfolds, Angst gives way in importance to awe, to quiet astonishment, to the calm of releasement (*Gelassenheit*). To release ourselves to the inexhaustibly rich and ultimately mysterious temporal-spatial presencing of beings is to find ourselves not primarily anxious – though ontological anxiety remains – but, moreover, to find ourselves astonished and joyful and thankful that we exist *at all*. This is, in Heidegger's later reflections, thinking as thanking and dwelling as the humble ones. In other words: for the very shining-forth of our own existence and of all beings that accompany us on our sojourn, simply for this, we are thankful and humbly celebrate.

Notes

Foreword

1 Martin Heidegger, 'Preface' to William J. Richardson, *Heidegger: Through Phenomenology to Thought* (The Hague: Nijhoff, 1963), x.
2 Martin Heidegger, 'Time and Being,' in *On Time and Being*, trans. Joan Stambaugh (New York: Harper and Row, 1972), 1–24.

1. The Fate of Being

1 Kenneth Maly, 'Reading and Thinking: Heidegger and the Hinting Greeks,' in *Reading Heidegger: Commemorations*, ed. John Sallis (Bloomington: Indiana University Press, 1993), 221–40.
2 See especially Thomas Sheehan, 'A Paradigm Shift in Heidegger Research,' *Continental Philosophy Review* 34 (2001): 183–202. See also 'Being, Openedness, and Unlimited Technology: Ten Theses on Heidegger,' *Revista Portuguesa de Filosofia* 59, no. 4 (2003): 1253–9.
3 *Four Seminars*, trans. Andrew Mitchell and François Raffoul (Bloomington: Indiana University Press, 2003). For the German text, see *Seminare, Gesamtausgabe, Band* 15 (Frankfurt am Main: Vittorio Klostermann, 1986), 267–421. For all references, I give in parentheses the English volume's page number followed after a colon by the corresponding German volume's page number; thus, for example, (English:German). I have sometimes modified the English translations of Heidegger's texts that I cite in this essay. Also, all italicized words in the texts cited throughout are Heidegger's unless otherwise indicated. But note that in some instances where Heidegger has used italics for emphasis, I have found it necessary to underline the italicized German word in order to convey his emphasis.

4   Sheehan, 'A Paradigm Shift,' 189.
5   William J. Richardson, *Heidegger: Through Phenomenology to Thought* (The Hague: Martinus Nijhoff, 1963).
6   See the very helpful 'Translators' Foreword' (vii–xvii) and 'German Translator's Afterword' (85–92) in *Four Seminars*. Even so, the English translators (Mitchell and Raffoul) also appear to overstate the case for the importance of *Ereignis* in relation to Being without fully investigating the matter; see x–xi of the Foreword.
7   For his thematization of *der Unter-Schied*, see especially 'Language' (1950) in *Poetry, Language, Thought*, trans. Albert Hofstadter (New York: Harper and Row, 1971). For *der Austrag*, see especially 'The Onto-theo-logical Constitution of Metaphysics' (1957) in *Identity and Difference*, trans. Joan Stambaugh (Chicago: University of Chicago Press, 2002).
8   *Being and Time*, trans. John Macquarrie and Edward Robinson (New York: Harper and Row, 1962), 26; *Sein und Zeit*, *Gesamtausgabe*, *Band* 2 (Frankfurt am Main: Vittorio Klostermann, 1977), 8.
9   'On the Essence of Ground,' trans. William McNeill, in *Pathmarks*, ed. William McNeill (Cambridge: Cambridge University Press, 1998), 105. 'Vom Wesen des Grundes,' in *Wegmarken*, 3rd ed. (Frankfurt am Main: Vittorio Klostermann, 1996), 134. All page numbers are identical to *Gesamtausgabe*, *Band* 9, *Wegmarken* (Frankfurt am Main: Vittorio Klostermann, 1976). Though Heidegger's sentence is awkward, it is clear, I think, that he is correlating 'ontic' truth with the focus on *'beings in* their Being' and 'ontological' truth with the *'Being of* beings.' For this reason, McNeill's translation in *Pathmarks* is somewhat misleading; his translation reads: 'Ontic and ontological truth each concern, in different ways, *beings in* their being, and *being of* beings.'
10   *Introduction to Metaphysics*, trans. Gregory Fried and Richard Polt (New Haven: Yale University Press, 2000), 34. *Einfürung in die Metaphysik*, *Gesamtausgabe*, *Band* 40 (Frankfurt am Main: Vittorio Klostermann, 1983), 34.
11   *Hölderlin's Hymn 'The Ister,'* trans. William McNeill and Julia Davis (Bloomington: Indiana University Press, 1996), 110–14; *Hölderlins Hymne 'Der Ister,' Gesamtausgabe*, *Band* 53 (Frankfurt am Main: Vittorio Klostermann, 1984), 137–43.
12   *Parmenides*, trans. André Schuwer and Richard Rojcewicz (Bloomington: Indiana University Press, 1992), 88f; *Parmenides*, *Gesamtausgabe*, *Band* 54 (Frankfurt am Main: Vittorio Klostermann, 1982), 130f. Hereafter cited as P.
13   *What Is Called Thinking?*, trans. J. Glenn Gray (New York: Harper and Row, 1968), 110; *Was Heißt Denken?*, *Gesamtausgabe*, *Band* 8 (Frankfurt am Main: Vittorio Klostermann, 2002), 113. Hereafter cited as WT.

14 Yet in his essay published in 1956, *On the Question of Being*, Heidegger uses the phrase in several places in a manner that suggests that it does capture his own long-standing concern, for example: 'Everywhere the surpassing that returns to beings, the *"transcendens* pure and simple" (*Being and Time*, §7), is "the Being" of beings.' Trans. William McNeill in *Pathmarks*, 312. 'Zur Seinsfrage,' *Wegmarken*, 3rd ed. (Frankfurt am Main: Vittorio Klostermann, 1996), 413. Also, GA 9, 413.

15 Heidegger explained several times before in his published work how we are to understand 'the *epoché* of Being'; so, for example, in 'Anaximander's Saying' he states: 'We may call this luminous keeping to itself of the truth of its essencing the *epoché* of Being. However, this word, borrowed from the Stoic philosophers, does not have the Husserlian sense of the methodical bracketing by the thetic act of consciousness in objectifying. The *epoché* of Being belongs to Being itself ... From the *epoché* of Being comes the epochal essencing of its dispensation, in which world history properly consists.' *Early Greek Thinking*, trans. David Farrell Krell and Frank A. Capuzzi (San Francisco: Harper and Row, 1984), 26–7 (modified). 'Der Spruch des Anaximander' in *Holzwege* (Frankfurt am Main: Vittorio Klostermann, 1980), 333.

16 Heidegger's notoriously cryptic 1962 lecture 'Time and Being' gives special attention to the notion of *das Ereignis*; yet even in this lecture, he pointedly states that understood in the right way: 'the sole purpose of this lecture has been to bring into view Being itself as appropriating event [*das Sein selbst als das Ereignis*].' *On Time and Being*, trans. Joan Stambaugh (Chicago: University of Chicago Press, 1972), 21; *Zur Sache des Denkens* (Tübingen: Max Niemeyer Verlag, 2000), 22. I prefer to translate this key word *Ereignis* as 'appropriating event' rather than as 'appropriation' or 'event of appropriation' (too static) or as 'enowning' (too idiosyncratic). For a fuller discussion of the relation between *Ereignis* and Being itself, see chapter 2.

17 The Being (*Sein/Seyn*) of beings (*Seiende*) in their beingness (*Seiendheit*) may also be stated as the presencing itself (*das Anwesen selbst; anwesen selbst*) of what is present (*Anwesende*) in its sheer presence (*Anwesenheit*). Cf. GA 7, 232: 'In the thinking of Heraclitus, the Being (presencing) of beings [*das Sein (Anwesen) des Seienden*] appears as *Logos*, as the Laying that gathers. But this lightning-flash of Being remains forgotten.' And consider the comment 'From a Dialogue on Language' in GA 12, 116: 'What mattered then [in the effort in *Being and Time*], and still matters, is to bring forth into view the Being of beings; certainly not any longer in the manner of metaphysics, but such that Being itself [*Sein selbst*] comes to shine forth. Being itself – this

says: presencing [*Anwesen*] of what is present [*des Anwesenden*].' (My modification of the published English translation, which misses the mark, by Peter D. Hertz in *On the Way to Language* [New York: Harper and Row, 1971], 30.)

18 Note that Heidegger's own text uses the words *anwesen* and *anwesend* throughout. However, in the protocol text, these words are capitalized as *Anwesen* and *Anwesend*. In WT, Heidegger had used both *anwesen* and *das Anwesen* to translate *emmenai* (*einai*) (WT, 233f:237f). Might Heidegger's choice of *anwesen* instead of *das Anwesen* in this text reflect his even greater emphasis on the dynamic character of presencing (which must not be confused with sheer 'presence')? Might this be a clue that for the Heidegger of these late seminars, *Seyn* may be more suitably named with the infinitive form *anwesen* or *anwesen selbst*?

19 Though the word form is a bit awkward, I translate *anwesend* as 'presenc(ing)' in order to convey the suggested subtle emphasis on *what is present* in presencing and also to distinguish *anwesend* from the other part of Heidegger's paratactical formulation – that is, *anwesen* (presencing) or *anwesen selbst* (presencing itself). I suppose that 'present' for *anwesend* is another possibility, but the translators' choice of 'presencing' is simply too confusing in this context. Note also that Kenneth Maly offers 'emergent: emerging' as a solution; see his 'Reading and Thinking.'

20 Maly, 'Reading and Thinking,' 235. In what I understand to be a thoughtful response to my argument in the present essay (which was originally published in 2005), Maly offers a revision of his earlier reading in his recent book *Heidegger's Possibility* (Toronto: University of Toronto Press, 2008). On page 168, he writes: 'I once interpreted certain Heidegger-texts to be saying that he no longer used the word *being* to name the matter for thinking, the "question" for all his thinking. In hindsight, my reading and observation was short-sighted.' This is a most admirable admission – and entirely in keeping with Maly's lifelong commitment to the path of thinking with all of its twists and turns.

21 The protocol reads: 'das weder das Seiende noch lediglich das Sein ist' (79:397).

22 We might consider Heidegger's translation of the word '*bloß*' – in another text and in another context – which lends indirect support to my reading. In his 1961 lecture on 'Kant's Thesis About Being,' Heidegger singles out the word *bloß* in his reading of Kant's statement that being 'ist bloß die Position eines Dinges' (339:448). According to Heidegger, 'The "*bloß*" [in Kant's statement] does not limit, but rather assigns being [*das Sein*] to a domain where alone it can be characterized in its purity. "*Bloß*" means here:

purely [*rein*]' (342:452). As Heidegger unfolds Kant's position, being is purely a positing 'by thinking as an act of understanding,' and this defines Kant's determination of 'the being[ness] of beings as the objectiveness of the object of experience [Sein des Seienden als der Gegenständlichkeit des Gegenstandes der Erfahrung]' (350:462). Thus, Kant's thesis about 'Sein als bloß die Position' (360:476) is yet another articulation of the *metaphysical beingness of beings*. As Heidegger puts it: 'The age-old prevailing meaning of being (perduring presence) [*ständige Anwesenheit*] ... is preserved in Kant's critical interpretation of being as the objectness [Heidegger uses *Gegenständigkeit* here] of the object of experience' (351:464). The originary and unifying meaning of Being that is implicit but unquestioned in Kant's 'thesis' remains the further task of thinking (360–63:476–80). All page references (English:German) are to *Pathmarks* and to *Wegmarken*/GA 9, previously cited.

23 Heidegger's concluding translation of Parmenides' line is somewhat mistranslated by Mitchell and Raffoul. Properly rendered, Heidegger's translation reads: 'The presenc(ing): presencing itself thoroughly determines and attunes the encircling unconcealment appropriately disclosing it [the presenc(ing): presencing itself]' (97:407). Perhaps now we can discern, though admittedly with some difficulty, the import of Heidegger's reading of Parmenides: Being itself understood as *presenc(ing): presencing itself* must also be thought as *aletheia* as the encircling unconcealment. In other words, to put this paratactically, Being itself: *aletheia*: the Same. In support of this reading, I call attention to two remarkably similar statements from Heidegger going back to 1946: (1) from 'Anaximander's Saying' – 'Unconcealment itself is presencing [*Anwesen*]. Both are the same, but not identical'; and (2) from 'Wherefore Poets?' – 'The sphericality is to be thought from out of the essence of originary Being in the sense of unconcealing presencing [*Anwesens*].' Both texts collected in *Holzwege* (Frankfurt am Main: Vittorio Klostermann, 1980), 365 and 297 respectively.

2. *Ereignis*: (Only) Another Name for Being Itself

1 Martin Heidegger, *Beiträge zur Philosophie (Vom Ereignis)*, *Gesamtausgabe*, *Band* 65 (Frankfurt am Main: Vittorio Klostermann, 1989/1994). Hereafter GA 65. In translation: *Contributions to Philosophy (from Enowning)*, trans. Parvis Emad and Kenneth Maly (Bloomington: Indiana University Press, 1999). Hereafter CP.

2 The story of Heidegger's recurring dream and his arrival at the word *Ereignis* is discussed in William J. Richardson's 'Heidegger Among the

Doctors' in *Reading Heidegger: Commemorations*, ed. John Sallis (Blooming-ton: Indiana University Press, 1993), 49–63.

3 Precisely this strong claim is made in the recent work of Thomas Sheehan, who states in one place: 'I argue that Heidegger's focal topic was not 'be-ing' (the givenness or availability of entities for human engagement) but rather what *brings about* being, namely, *Ereignis* – the opening of a clearing in which entities can appear as this or that.' '*Kehre* and *Ereignis*: A Pro-legomenon to Heidegger's *Introduction to Metaphysics*,' in *A Companion to Heidegger's Introduction to Metaphysics*, ed. Gregory Fried and Richard Polt (New Haven: Yale University Press, 2001), 5. Other readers of Heidegger, especially those who read him through Derrida and other postmodern au-thors, also overplay *Ereignis* in relation to *Sein/Seyn* but largely because of a profound aversion to the very word 'being.' As will become clear in the course of the present essay, my disagreement with Sheehan's position lies in this: on my reading, Heidegger maintained that it is precisely *Being* un-derstood in an originary and fundamental way – Being itself (as *Ereignis*) – that 'brings about' (or originates, enables, gives, lets) beings in their beingness.

4 For more on retaining the convention of writing Heidegger's proper con-cern as Being (with a capital B), see chapter 1.

5 On the name of Being and its variants, see chapter 1.

6 See especially the extensive work on the early Heidegger by Theodore Kisiel and John van Buren; see also the essay by Richard Polt, '*Ereignis*,' in *A Companion to Heidegger*, ed. Hubert L. Dreyfus and Mark A. Wrathall (Oxford: Blackwell, 2005), 375–91, and his *The Emergency of Being: On Heidegger's Contributions to Philosophy* (Ithaca: Cornell University Press, 2006). As will become clear further along in the present essay, my reading is that Heidegger *tempers* his understanding of *Ereignis* from the *Beiträge*-related writings to the later work. The eruptive event-fulness and moment-ousness of *Ereignis* in the early work gives way to the 'gentle' temporal course of beings coming into their own and coming into relation with one another. In other words: in the late writings, *Ereignis* as the primordial *Logos!*

7 Martin Heidegger, *Seminare, Gesamtausgabe, Band* 15 (Frankfurt am Main: Vittorio Klostermann, 1986), 267–421; the reference is to the seminar in Zähringen, 6 September 1973, 377. In translation: *Four Seminars*, trans. Andrew Mitchell and François Raffoul (Bloomington: Indiana University Press, 2003), 67.

8 Martin Heidegger, *Reden und andere Zeugnisse eines Lebensweges, Gesamtaus-gabe, Band* 16 (Frankfurt am Main: Vittorio Klostermann, 2000), 747. For a complete translation of the letter, see the Appendix of chapter 1.

9 Martin Heidegger, 'Das Wesen der Sprache' (1957–8), in *Unterwegs zur Sprache, Gesamtausgabe, Band* 12 (Frankfurt am Main: Vittorio Klostermann, 1985), 190.

10 For a different, and quite thoughtful, reflection on the issue of translating such key words, see Gail Stenstad, '*Auseinandersetzung* in the Thinking of Be-ing,' *Existentia* 10 (2000): 8.

11 Additional page references in GA 65/CP: 7/6, 8/6, 11/9, 15–16/12, 21/16, 23/18, 24/18, 26/19, 29/21, 31/22, 228/161, 230/162, 238/169, 239/169, 248/175, 250/176, 252/178, 254/179, 256/180, 260/183, 263/185, 268/189, 274/193, 294/208, 299/211, 338/237, 345/242, 413/291, 460/324, 484/341, 494/348.

12 Martin Heidegger, *Besinnung, Gesamtausgabe, Band* 66 (Frankfurt am Main: Vittorio Klostermann, 1997). Hereafter GA 66.

13 Additional page references in GA 66: 88, 314.

14 Martin Heidegger, *Metaphysik und Nihilismus, Gesamtausgabe, Band* 67 (Frankfurt am Main: Vittorio Klostermann, 1999). Hereafter GA 67.

15 Additional page references in GA 67: 31, 34, 39, 51, 63, 64.

16 Martin Heidegger, *Die Geschichte des Seyns, Gesamtausgabe, Band* 69 (Frankfurt am Main: Vittorio Klostermann, 1998). Hereafter GA 69.

17 Additional page references in GA 69: 25, 61, 108, 116, 123, 131, 143, 146, 171.

18 Martin Heidegger, *Über den Anfang, Gesamtausgabe, Band* 70 (Frankfurt am Main: Vittorio Klostermann, 2005). Hereafter GA 70.

19 I have previously speculated that the word *die Anfängnis* might be a Heideggerian neologism, but on further research, this view cannot be maintained. Though the word does not appear in the Grimm's *Deutsches Wörterbuch*, it is nevertheless to be found in the dictionary of Early New High German, which covers the period from (roughly) 1350 to 1650. See *Frühneuhochdeutsches Wörterbuch*, ed. von Ulrich Goebel (Berlin: de Gruyter, 1989), 1094.

20 Additional page references in GA 70: 11, 21, 51, 118, 119, 129, 175.

21 Martin Heidegger, 'Der Weg zur Sprache,' in *Unterwegs zur Sprache, Gesamtausgabe, Band* 12 (Frankfurt am Main: Vittorio Klostermann, 1985). Hereafter GA 12. See especially page 248.

22 See, for example, GA 65, 288–9 / CP, 202–3.

23 Martin Heidegger, 'The Principle of Identity,' in *Identity and Difference* (English–German edition), trans. Joan Stambaugh (Chicago: University of Chicago Press, 1969), 36/101.

24 GA 12. Translated by Peter D. Hertz in *On the Way to Language* (New York: Harper and Row, 1971). Hereafter OWL. A more reliable translation, however, is by David Farrell Krell in the second edition of *Martin Heidegger:*

Basic Writings (New York: HarperCollins, 1993), 397–426. Nonetheless, there is one particular difficulty that I highlight in what follows in the present essay.

25 *Das Anwesen* is certainly one of the most important words in Heidegger's thinking, yet it is one of the most misconstrued by more recent commentators, who have tended to conflate *Anwesen* and *Anwesenheit*. As a name for *die Sache selbst, Anwesen* is used by Heidegger to convey the *full presencing of Being itself* in both its positive and negative modes of appearing, as we find, for instance, in his several meditations (especially in the 1940s) on the Greek fragments of Parmenides and Heraclitus. It is this fundamental sense that is intended when Heidegger maintains along with Parmenides that 'anything outside of presencing [*Anwesen*], anything besides the *eon*, is impossible' (*Moira [Parmenides VIII, 34–41]* in *Early Greek Thinking*, trans. David Farrell Krell and Frank A. Capuzzi [San Francisco: Harper and Row, 1984], 96). Nevertheless, at other times – and especially in the later work, as in this passage under consideration from OWL – he uses *Anwesen* with an emphasis on the positive and perduring mode of appearing (the proper metaphysical concern), and, thus, the word becomes tantamount to *Anwesenheit* – sheer *presence* – which is how I translate *Anwesen* here. In these latter cases, the translation 'presenc(ing)' is another option that might better capture the nuance, but the word form may simply be too awkward. See also the discussion in chapter 1, note 17.

26 The German edition only (GA 12, 249n.c) provides an unpublished marginal note that Heidegger added at the end of his footnote; it reads: 'dies zeigen: von dem lichtendem ... Er-eignen her – insofern Lichtung [Aletheia] Anwesenheit als solche gewährt. Die Nahnis.' Heidegger's meaning appears to be that *Ereignis*/Being may *also* be understood as *Lichtung/Aletheia* insofar as *Lichtung/Aletheia* 'grants presence as such.' Therefore, this little note leads us to a more complete understanding of his perspective: *Ereignis*/Being/*Lichtung/Aletheia* are all to be thought as that which originates (gives, grants, lets) beings (*das Seiende, das Anwesende*) in their beingness (*die Seiendheit, die Anwesenheit*). For a fuller discussion of the place of *die Lichtung* in his thinking, see the two chapters that follow.

27 Martin Heidegger, *Zur Sache des Denkens* (Tübingen: Max Niemeyer Verlag, 1969/2000). Hereafter SD. *On Time and Being*, trans. Joan Stambaugh (Chicago: University of Chicago Press, 1972/2002). Hereafter TB, but I have modified the translations.

28 Introduction to *The End of Philosophy*, trans. Joan Stambaugh (Chicago: University of Chicago Press, 1973), xiii.

29 SD, 25; TB, 24.

30 I am thinking in particular of Heidegger's formulation '*Sein: Nichts: Selbes*' in the Seminar in Le Thor, 11 September 1969. See GA 15, 363; *Four Seminars*, 58.

3. The Turn towards Home

1 The *variations* or *development* in Heidegger's thinking on this issue over time have gone unthematized in the literature. Nevertheless, several commentators certainly have recognized the importance of the theme of 'home/not-at-home.' See in particular William McNeill's article '*Heimat*: Heidegger on the Threshold' in *Heidegger Toward the Turn: Essays on the Work of the 1930s*, ed. James Risser (Albany: SUNY Press, 1999), 319–49. Two other fine essays are Fabio Ciaramelli, 'The Loss of Origin and Heidegger's Question of *Unheimlichkeit*,' *Epoché* 2, no. 1 (1994): 13–33; and David Farrell Krell, '*Das Unheimliche*: Architectural Sections of Heidegger and Freud,' *Research in Phenomenology* 22 (1992): 43–61. Also, for a full discussion of Heidegger's vocabulary of Being, beingness, and beings, see chapter 1.

2 *Prolegomena zur Geschichte des Zeitbegriffs, Gesamtausgabe, Band* 20 (Frankfurt am Main: Vittorio Klostermann, 1979). Translated by Theodore Kisiel as *History of the Concept of Time* (Bloomington: Indiana University Press, 1985), xv. Hereafter GA 20. All references to Heidegger's work throughout this essay will be given as 'GA' followed by the number of the volume and the page number in the German volume 'slash' the page number in the selected English translation, that is, German/English. I have modified many of the translations cited in this essay. Unless otherwise noted, all italicized words or phrases in cited texts are Heidegger's.

3 See chapter 4 for further discussion of this point.

4 Hubert Dreyfus also opts for 'unsettledness' in his *Being-in-the-World* (Cambridge, MA: MIT Press, 1991). So does Clare Pearson Geiman in 'Heidegger's *Antigones*,' in *A Companion to Heidegger's Introduction to Metaphysics*, ed. Richard Polt and Gregory Fried (New Haven: Yale University Press, 2001), 161–82.

5 GA 20 400/289.

6 GA 20 400/289.

7 GA 20 402/290.

8 GA 20 405–6/293.

9 *Sein und Zeit, Gesamtausgabe, Band* 2 (Frankfurt am Main: Vittorio Klostermann, 1977). Hereafter GA 2. Translated by John Macquarrie and Edward

Robinson as *Being and Time* (New York: Harper and Row, 1962). Section 40, GA 2 244–53/228–35.

10 GA 2 247/230; 248/231; 249/232.

11 GA 2 249/232.

12 GA 2 252/234.

13 GA 2 250/232. The double ellipsis appears only in the German text.

14 GA 2 250/233.

15 GA 2 251/233.

16 GA 2 251/234.

17 GA 2 252/234.

18 *Einführung in die Metaphysik, Gesamtausgabe, Band* 40 (Frankfurt am Main: Vittorio Klostermann, 1983). Hereafter GA 40. There are two fine translations, and I have freely consulted both in the translations that follow: Ralph Manheim (New Haven: Yale University Press, 1959); and Gregory Fried and Richard Polt (New Haven: Yale University Press, 2000). All page numbers that follow are to the Fried and Polt edition.

19 GA 40 160/161. In translating *unheimisch*, I will use 'unhomely' and 'not at home' interchangeably.

20 GA 40 172/174.

21 GA 40 167/168.

22 GA 40 163/164.

23 GA 40 167/169.

24 GA 40 165/167.

25 *Sophocles, Loeb Classical Library*, vol. 21, trans. Hugh Lloyd-Jones (Cambridge, MA: Harvard University Press, 1994), 36–7.

26 GA 40 157/158.

27 GA 40 173/175–6.

28 GA 40 173/176.

29 *Hölderlins Hymne 'Der Ister,' Gesamtausgabe, Band* 53 (Frankfurt am Main: Vittorio Klostermann, 1993). Hereafter GA 53. Translated by William McNeill and Julia Davis as *Hölderlin's Hymn 'The Ister'* (Bloomington: Indiana University Press, 1996).

30 See GA 4, *Erläuterungen zu Hölderlins Dichtung;* and GA 52, *Hölderlins Hymne 'Andenken.'* For a further discussion, see chapter 4.

31 See GA 39, *Hölderlins Hymnen 'Germanien' und 'Der Rhein.'* See also William McNeill's comments in '*Heimat*: Heidegger on the Threshold,' 329–32.

32 Geiman in her insightful article, 'Heidegger's *Antigones*,' also recognizes the important differences in Heidegger's two readings of Sophocles' *Antigone*, though her principal concern is different from that of the present essay.

33 GA 53 10/10.
34 GA 53 63/51.
35 GA 53 78/64.
36 GA 53 84/69.
37 GA 53 87/71.
38 GA 53 92/75.
39 GA 53 93/76.
40 GA 53 104/84.
41 GA 53 129/103.
42 GA 53 128/103.
43 GA 53 129/104.
44 GA 53 129/104.
45 GA 53 130/105.
46 GA 53 134/107.
47 GA 53 137/110.
48 GA 53 137/110.
49 GA 53 141/113.
50 GA 53 143/114.
51 GA 53 150/120.
52 GA 53, especially Section 20.
53 GA 53 151/121.
54 GA 53 202/164.
55 GA 53 60/49.
56 'Gelassenheit' in *Reden und andere Zeugnisse eines Lebensweges, Gesamtaus-gabe, Band* 16 (Frankfurt am Main: Vittorio Klostermann, 2000). Hereafter GA 16. Translated by John M. Anderson and E. Hans Freund as 'Memorial Address' in *Discourse on Thinking* (New York: Harper and Row, 1966).
57 GA 16 518/45. Note that in his *On the Question of Being*, composed in the same year as 'Gelassenheit' (1955), Heidegger (quoting from Nietzsche's *The Will to Power*) refers again to this 'most unsettling of all visitors' (*dieses unheimlichsten aller Gäste*). In this context, Heidegger is referring to the modern 'movement of nihilism' and adds that 'it is called the 'most unsettling" [*unheimlichste*] because, as the unconditional will to will, it wills homelessness [*Heimatlosigkeit*] as such.' See 'Zur Seinsfrage' in *Weg-marken, Gesamtausgabe, Band* 9 (Frankfurt am Main: Vittorio Klostermann, 1976/2004), 387. Translated by William McNeill as 'On the Question of Be-ing,' in *Pathmarks*, ed. William McNeill (Cambridge: Cambridge University Press, 1998), 292.
58 GA 16 521/48.
59 GA 16 522/48–9.

60 GA 16 525/52.
61 GA 16 527/54.
62 GA 16 528/55.
63 '700 Jahre Messkirch,' in *Reden und andere Zeugnisse eines Lebensweges,*
    Gesamtausgabe, Band 16 (Frankfurt am Main: Vittorio Klostermann, 2000).
    Hereafter GA 16. Translated by Thomas J. Sheehan as 'Messkirch's Seventh
    Centennial,' *Listening: Journal of Religion and Culture* 8, nos. 1–3 (1973):
    41–57.
64 GA 16 575/45.
65 GA 16 580/53.
66 GA 16 581/55.
67 GA 16 582/55.
68 GA 53 167/134.
69 GA 53 201/163.
70 GA 16 582/55.

4. From Angst to Astonishment

1 In what follows, I do not italicize the German words Angst and Dasein
   since they appear so often and also have become commonplace in the literature. Also note that I often modify the English translations cited throughout the essay.
2 All references are to *Being and Time,* trans. John Macquarrie and Edward
   Robinson (New York: Harper and Row, 1962). Hereafter BT. *Gesamtausgabe,*
   Band 2, *Sein und Zeit* (Frankfurt am Main: Vittorio Klostermann, 1977).
   Hereafter GA 2. Section 29: BT, 172–9; GA 2, 178–86.
3 BT, 179; GA 2, 186. Heidegger's emphasis.
4 'Reading Heidegger's "What is Metaphysics?"' trans. Thomas Sheehan,
   The New Yearbook for Phenomenology and Phenomenological Philosophy I
   (2001): 181–201.
       Sheehan's translation is of the first edition of this lecture, published in
   1929. Hereafter cited as WM, Sheehan. All German references to WM and
   to the later Postscript (1943) and Introduction (1949) are to *Gesamtausgabe,*
   Band 9, *Wegmarken* (Frankfurt am Main: Vittorio Klostermann, 1976/2004).
   Hereafter GA 9. In English, all three texts are available in the complete
   translation of *Wegmarken* titled *Pathmarks,* ed. William McNeill (Cambridge: Cambridge University Press, 1998).
5 BT, 230–1; GA 2, 247.
6 BT, 232; GA 2, 250. Heidegger's emphasis. The double ellipsis appears only
   in the German text.

7 BT, 234; GA 2, 252. Heidegger's emphasis. Heidegger speaks of '"eigent-liche" Angst,' and Macquarrie and Robinson, with some justification, trans-late *eigentliche* as 'real.' Even so, 'authentic' seems to be the better choice. The apparent sense of Heidegger's discussion is that 'authentic' anxiety is ontological/*existenzial* (and rarely confronted) and distinguishable from 'inauthentic' ontic/*existenziell* manifestations that are more commonly ex-perienced. A difficulty with his discussion of the *Angstphänomen* in this section is that he implicitly conflates the neutral structural distinction ontic/ontological with the qualitative existential distinction inauthentic/ authentic. Such a correlation may – or may not – be justified; in any case, he does not explicitly address this matter or sort the issues out.

8 A more recent translation of the Postscript to WM is by William McNeill in *Pathmarks*, 231–8. Hereafter cited as Postscript, McNeill. The reference is to page 232 (GA 9, 305). An earlier translation of the Postscript (and of WM) is available in *Existence and Being*, ed. Werner Brock (Chicago: Henry Reg-nery, 1949/1967), 325–61. The translation is by R.F.C. Hull and Allan Crick. Hereafter cited as WM, Hull and Crick.

9 In addition to WM, Sheehan, and WM, Hull and Crick, another translation is by David Farrell Krell in *Martin Heidegger: Basic Writings* (San Francisco: HarperCollins, 1977), 95–112. Hereafter WM, Krell.

10 GA 9, 111. WM, Krell, 102.

11 GA 9, 112. WM, Sheehan, 191.

12 GA 9, 111. WM, Sheehan, 191.

13 GA 9, 114. Sheehan translates 'gebannte Ruhe' as 'the calmness of won-der,' 192; Krell as 'bewildered calm,' 105; and Hull and Crick as 'spell-bound peace,' 338. I prefer 'stunned calm.' The ellipsis in the sentence is Heidegger's.

14 GA 9, 118. WM, Sheehan, 195.

15 BT, Sections 50 and 58, 294 and 333 respectively. GA 2, 333 and 381.

16 Even in his 1935 *Introduction to Metaphysics*, which heightens the tension between Dasein and Being, he no longer thematizes the mood of Angst, referring to it indirectly or only in passing. Translated by Ralph Manheim (New Haven: Yale University Press, 1959); see especially 149. Note that Manheim translates 'die wahre Angst' as 'true fear.' In a more recent trans-lation, Gregory Fried and Richard Polt choose 'true anxiety' (New Haven: Yale University Press, 2000), 159.

I also propose that my reading of the subtle transformation in Heidegger's account of Angst in WM is strengthened by way of reference to the lecture course he had given only a short time *earlier* at Freiburg (winter semester 1928–9) titled 'Introduction to Philosophy' (*Einleitung in die Philosophie, Gesamtausgabe, Band* 27 [Frankfurt am Main: Vittorio Klostermann, 1996]; untranslated). In this brilliant restatement and development of certain themes sounded in *Being and Time*, Heidegger suggests that the mood that most fittingly characterizes Dasein's fundamental ontological activity of the letting-be (*Seinlassen*) of beings is 'equanimity' (*Gleichgültigkeit*) (102). As I see it, the 'equanimity' that he speaks of here nicely parallels the 'calm' that he brings more to the fore in his discussion of Angst in WM. I thank Fred Dallmayr for calling attention to the overall importance of this lecture course in his remarks at the 2009 Heidegger Circle meeting.

17 The romantic emphasis on strife and heroic striving is also at work in Heidegger's thinking into the 1930s, especially in his *Introduction to Metaphysics* (1935) and in his lecture course 'On Schelling's Treatise on the Essence of Human Freedom' (1936). See also chapter 8 in the present volume.

18 Though not a complete accounting: Heidegger gave a lecture course on Hölderlin's poems 'Der Rhein' and 'Germanien' in 1934–5 at Freiburg. He composed the essay 'Hölderlin and the Essence of Poetry' in 1936 and the commentary 'As When On a Holiday ...' in 1939. In the summer of 1942 at Freiburg, he gave a lecture course on Hölderlin's 'Der Ister.'

19 *Gesamtausgabe, Band* 4, *Erläuterungen zu Hölderlins Dichtung* (Frankfurt am Main: Vittorio Klostermann, 1981). Hereafter GA 4. For a complete translation of the volume, see *Elucidations of Hölderlin's Poetry*, trans. Keith Hoeller (New York: Humanity Books, 2000). See also Douglas Scott's translation of Heidegger's elucidation of Holderlin's poem 'Homecoming' under the title 'Remembrance of the Poet' in *Existence and Being*, 233–69.

20 GA 4, 16–19. Heidegger uses the Old German word *das Heitere* (also in the form of *die Heitere*), a beautiful word that conveys both the sense of a 'bright' day and a 'bright' mood or disposition. Accordingly, translating the word is most difficult, but I follow William J. Richardson, who employs the translation 'the Gladsome' in his *Heidegger: Through Phenomenology to Thought* (The Hague: Martinus Nijhoff, 1963/1974), 443–4. Scott offers 'the Serene,' 251, and Hoeller chooses 'gaiety,' 37. The overall sense is that the Source and Origin (Being itself), characterized as *das/die Heitere*, is the primordial light and brightness that fundamentally attunes Dasein in a light and bright manner.

21 GA 4, 143f. 'Remembrance,' Hoeller, see especially 165f.

22 BT, 234; GA 2, 252.

23 For an extended discussion of the interplay of the themes at-home / not-at-home in Heidegger's thought, see chapter 3.

24 See also Heidegger's related discussion of Hölderlin's poem 'Remem-

brance' in *Gesamtausgabe, Band 52, Hölderlins Hymne 'Andenken'* (Frankfurt am Main: Vittorio Klostermann, 1992).

25 GA 4, 131–2. 'Remembrance,' Hoeller, 153. Hoeller translates this key word *die Scheu* as 'shyness.' I think that 'awe' better captures the resonance of the word (as Heidegger uses it). Richardson, Hull and Crick, and McNeill also translate *die Scheu* as 'awe.'

26 GA 4, 132. 'Remembrance,' Hoeller, 153.

27 GA 4, 131. 'Remembrance,' Hoeller, 153.

28 GA 9, 307. Postscript, McNeill, 234. See also WM, Hull and Crick, 354–5.

29 GA 9, 307. Postscript, McNeill, 234. WM, Hull and Crick, 355.

30 Richardson, 474n4.

31 Richardson, 474.

32 Trans. Walter Kaufmann in *Pathmarks*, 277–90. Hereafter cited as Intro WM, Kaufmann. But note that Kaufmann's original translation has been modified by William McNeill as it appears in *Pathmarks*. The original translation is found in *Existentialism from Dostoevsky to Sartre*, ed. Walter Kaufmann (New York: Meridian, 1989), 265–79.

33 'Kierkegaard, Division II, and Later Heidegger,' in Hubert L. Dreyfus, *Being-in-the-World* (Cambridge, MA: MIT Press, 1991), 336–7.

34 GA 9, 371. Intro WM, Kaufmann, 281–2. Kaufmann originally translated Angst as 'dread,' but McNeill revised the translation to read 'anxiety.'

35 GA 9, 369. Intro WM, Kaufmann, 280.

36 My thanks to Thomas Sheehan for pointing out the particular relevance of this lecture. *What Is Philosophy?* (German–English Edition), trans. William Kluback and Jean T. Wilde (New Haven: College and University Press, 1958). Hereafter WP. Also note that for the following citations to WP, I have often significantly modified Kluback and Wilde's translations.

37 WP, 46–9. For a more detailed discussion of this theme, see Heidegger's essay '*Logos* (Heraclitus, Fragment B 50)' in *Early Greek Thinking*, trans. David Farrel Krell and Frank A. Capuzzi (San Francisco: Harper and Row, 1975), 59–78. *Gesamtausgabe, Band 7, Vorträge und Aufsätze* (Frankfurt am Main: Vittorio Klostermann, 2000), 213–34.

38 WP, 49.

39 Heidegger's discussion of attunement and of *das Erstaunen* in WP is similar in several respects to Sections 36 to 38 of the text, unpublished in his lifetime, of his lecture course 'Basic Questions of Philosophy,' given at the University of Freiburg in the winter semester 1937–38. In the lecture course, he used the spelling *das Er-staunen*. But also note that in the available English translation of the lecture course, *das Er-staunen* is always translated as 'wonder' and not as 'astonishment.' *Gesamtausgabe, Band 45,*

Grundfragen der Philosophie: *Ausgewählte 'Probleme' der 'Logik'* (Frankfurt am Main: Vittorio Klostermann, 1992), 153–81. Translated by Richard Rojcewicz and André Schuwer as *Basic Questions of Philosophy*: *Selected 'Problems' of 'Logic'* (Bloomington: Indiana University Press, 1994), 133–56.

40 WP, 50–3.

41 WP, 79.

42 WP, 81.

43 Heidegger underscores this point by stating: 'The *pathos* of astonishment thus does not stand simply at the beginning of philosophy, as, for example, hand washing precedes the surgeon's operation. Astonishment sustains and entirely governs philosophy' (WP, 81). He further suggests that thinkers after the ancient Greeks lost sight of the 'fullest' meaning of the Greek word *arche* (usually translated as 'beginning') and consequently understood both Plato and Aristotle on the role of wonder in a 'superficial' and utterly 'un-Greek' (*ungriechisch*) manner. Heidegger's reading of Aristotle's words in *Metaphysics* A2, 982b12–983a23 may be debatable, but it is reasonable to ask along with Heidegger whether over the centuries commentators did indeed miss something essentially 'Greek.' Thus, for example, though Thomas Aquinas's commentary on the same lines in the *Metaphysics* may be arguably more faithful to the letter of Aristotle's text, we are surely left uncertain whether the spirit has been honoured in Thomas's all too matter-of-fact observation: 'Therefore, since philosophical investigation began with wonder [*admiratione*], it must end in or arrive at the contrary of this ... because when men have already learned the causes of these things, they do not wonder [*non mirantur*] ... Hence, the goal of this science [metaphysics], to which we should advance, will be that in knowing the causes of things, we do not wonder [*non admiremur*] about their effects.' *Commentary on the Metaphysics of Aristotle*, vol. 1, trans. John P. Rowan (Chicago: Henry Regnery, 1961), 27. Latin text: *Metaphysicorum Aristotelis Expositio (Liber Primus)*, ed. Cathala and Spiazzi (Rome: Marietti, 1950), 20.

44 WP, 85.

45 WP, 91.

46 WP, 95–7.

47 Heidegger delivered the lecture WP in August 1955. Just a couple of months later in October 1955 in Messkirch, he gave the talk that has been titled 'Gelassenheit' (also known as 'Memorial Address' in English translation in *Discourse on Thinking*, trans. John M. Anderson and E. Hans Freund [New York: Harper and Row, 1966]).

48 WP, 85.

49 Heidegger, '... Poetically Man Dwells ...,' trans. Albert Hofstadter in *Poetry, Language, Thought* (New York: Harper and Row, 1971), 225. *Gesamtausgabe, Band 7, Vorträge und Aufsätze* (Frankfurt am Main: Vittorio Klostermann, 2000), 204. I have taken the liberty of reformatting the lines.

5. *Lichtung*: The Early Lighting

1 See, for example, Reinhard May, *Heidegger's Hidden Sources: East Asian Influences on His Work*, trans. with a complementary essay by Graham Parkes (London and New York: Routledge, 1996). See also *Heidegger and Asian Thought*, ed. Graham Parkes (Honolulu: University of Hawaii Press, 1987).

2 Martin Heidegger, *Gesamtausgabe, Band 16, Reden und andere Zeugnisse eines Lebensweges* (Frankfurt am Main: Vittorio Klostermann, 2000), 695. Hereafter GA 16. In Germany, this foreword was originally published in the volume *Japan und Heidegger*, ed. Harmut Buchner (Sigmaringen: Jan Thorbecke Verlag, 1989), 230–1. I include a complete translation of this foreword in the next chapter. Note also that in most cases wherever an English translation is available, I will include the reference corresponding to the German text; however, I have often modified the cited translations.

3 GA 16, 695.

4 Ibid.

5 Martin Heidegger, 'Das Ende der Philosophie und die Aufgabe des Denkens' in *Zur Sache des Denkens* (Tübingen: Max Niemeyer Verlag, 1969/2000). Hereafter SD. Joan Stambaugh's translation, modified by David Farrell Krell, in *Martin Heidegger: Basic Writings*, ed. David Farrell Krell (San Francisco: HarperCollins, 1993).

6 Martin Heidegger, *Zollikoner Seminare* (Frankfurt am Main: Vittorio Klostermann, 1987), 10–20. Hereafter ZS. *Zollikon Seminars*, trans. Franz Mayr and Richard Askay (Evanston: Northwestern University Press, 2001), 8–17.

7 *Zur Frage nach der Bestimmung der Sache des Denkens*, ed. Hermann Heidegger (St Gallen: Erker-Verlag, 1984). Later published in 2000 in GA 16, 620–37. The text has been hitherto untranslated into English, but a complete translation by Richard Capobianco and Marie Göbel of the Erker-Verlag edition has recently been published in *Epoché: A Journal for the History of Philosophy*, Spring 2010.

8 Martin Heidegger, *Heraklit* in *Gesamtausgabe, Band 15, Seminare* (Frankfurt am Main: Vittorio Klostermann, 1986), 11–263. Hereafter GA 15. *Heraclitus Seminar*, trans. Charles H. Seibert (Evanston: Northwestern University Press, 1993). Hereafter HS.

9 The most prominent exception among commentators is William J. Richardson, who took notice of this in his book *Heidegger: Through Phenomenology
to Thought* (The Hague: Martinus Nijhoff, 1963/1974), 59.

10 Martin Heidegger, *Gesamtausgabe, Band* 2, *Sein und Zeit* (Frankfurt am
Main: Vittorio Klostermann, 1977), 177. Hereafter GA 2. *Being and Time*,
trans. John Macquarrie and Edward Robinson (New York: Harper and
Row, 1962), 171.

11 See also Aristotle, *De Anima*, III, 5 (430a15): 'And in fact intellect as we
have described it is what it is by virtue of becoming all things, while there
is another [intellect] which is what it is by virtue of making all things: this
is a sort of state like light; for in a sense light makes potential colors into
actual colors.'

12 For Aquinas's position, see, for example, *Summa Theologiae*, I, q. 12, a. 5
and a. 13; I, q. 79, a. 4. The Augustinian tradition, relying more heavily on
the Platonic tradition, insisted that human understanding depended upon
God, the Intelligible Light, to know what is true. See, for example, Augustine, *City of God*, VIII, 7: 'And the light of our understanding, by which all
things are learned by us, they [the Platonists] affirmed to be that selfsame
God by whom all things were made.'

13 *Being and Time*, 171. Joan Stambaugh follows suit in her translation *Being
and Time* (Albany: SUNY Press, 1996), 125.

14 Stambaugh, who includes the marginal notes of GA 2, appears to completely miss the significance of this note by translating Heidegger's se-
quence of words 'Lichtung, Licht, Leuchten' as 'clearing, light, shining,'
125. Also consider that Heidegger used 'gelichtet' in the very same sense
of 'lighted or 'illumined' a few years later in a 1930 lecture course: 'Auch
hier steht das Problem in der Helle des natürlichen alltäglichen Seinsver-
ständnisses, ohne daß das Licht selbst gelichtet wäre.' Martin Heidegger,
*Vom Wesen der menschlichen Freiheit: Einleitung in die Philosophie, Gesamtaus-
gabe, Band* 31 (Frankfurt am Main: Vittorio Klostermann, 1994), 93.

15 Martin Heidegger, *Brief über den Humanismus* in *Gesamtausgabe, Band* 9,
Wegmarken (Frankfurt am Main: Vittorio Klostermann, 2002). Hereafter
GA 9.

16 *Martin Heidegger: Basic Writings*, ed. David Farrell Krell (San Francisco:
HarperCollins, 1977).

17 GA 9, 331. *Basic Writings* (1977), 211. Heidegger uses the somewhat more
poetic variant *das Lichte* in this line, but of course, the two words *Licht* and
Lichte have the same meaning of 'light' in the sense of 'brightness.' Yet if he
had wanted to suggest something more here, then he might have chosen
– but did not – the antiquated *feminine* form *'die Lichte,'* which according

to the Brothers Grimm in their *Deutches Wörterbuch* (Leipzig: S. Hirzel, 1854ff.), vol. 12, at 879, conveyed both the sense of 'brightness' and the sense of a 'clearing' or 'expanse' as in a forest.

18 Contrast the same lines in *Martin Heidegger: Basic Writings*, ed. David Farrell Krell (San Francisco: HarperCollins, 1993), 234–5.

19 *Basic Writings* (1993), ix.

20 'Letter on Humanism' in *Pathmarks*, ed. William McNeill (Cambridge: Cambridge University Press, 1998), 239–76.

21 Martin Heidegger, *Einleitung zu 'Was ist Metaphysik?'* in GA 9, 365–83. Introduction to 'What Is Metaphysics?' in *Pathmarks*, 277–90.

22 GA 9, 365. *Pathmarks*, 277.

23 Composed by Heidegger in 1940, but the line of thinking goes back much earlier. Martin Heidegger, 'Platons Lehre von der Wahrheit' in GA 9, 203–38. 'Plato's Doctrine of Truth' in *Pathmarks*, 155–82, especially 175. Cf. his reference to Plato and 'the guiding idea of light' in relation to *die Lichtung* in the 1936–8 GA 65, *Beiträge zur Philosophie (Vom Ereignis)* (Frankfurt am Main: Vittorio Klostermann, 1994), §214, 338–40. Consider also his even earlier elucidation of the role of light in Plato's thinking in the 1927 lecture course *Die Grundprobleme der Phänomenologie*, GA 24, 401–5 – for example, his statement: 'The basic condition for the knowledge of beings as well as for the understanding of being[ness] is: standing in an illuminating light [*das Stehen in einem erhellenden Licht*],' 402. And in the 1926 summer semester lecture course *Die Grundbegriffe der antiken Philosophie*, GA 22, especially 98-106 and 252–8; so, for example, on page 256 he observes (according to the Mörchen transcription), 'Also the seeing and comprehending of the being of a being requires a light, and this light whereby being[ness] as such is illuminated is the *agathon*, the Idea of the "Good."' I examine more fully Heidegger's series of elucidations of Plato's 'light' in the following chapter.

24 GA 9, 365.

25 *Pathmarks*, 277.

26 Martin Heidegger, *Aletheia (Heraklit, Fragment 16)* in *Gesamtausgabe, Band 7, Vorträge und Aufsätze* (Frankfurt am Main: Vittorio Klostermann, 2000), 265 and 288. Hereafter GA 7. But note that the English translation of the text in *Early Greek Thinking*, trans. David Farrell Krell and Frank A. Capuzzi (San Francisco: Harper and Row, 1984) misses Heidegger's important wordplay by translating *der Dunkle* as 'the Obscure.' For his earlier rendering of *Lichtung* in terms of (a special kind of) luminosity, see his lecture courses on Parmenides (1942–3) in GA 54, especially Section 8, and on Heraclitus (1943 and 1944) in GA 55, especially 142–77 and 327.

27 GA 7, 266.

28 GA 7, 288.

29 Martin Heidegger, *Gesamtausgabe, Band 10, Der Satz vom Grund* (Frankfurt am Main: Vittorio Klostermann, 1997), see especially 125–30. Hereafter GA 10. *The Principle of Reason*, trans. Reginald Lilly (Bloomington: Indiana University Press, 1991). Hereafter PR.

30 GA 10, 127–8. PR, 86.

31 See especially PR, 84–6.

32 SD, 72. *Basic Writings* (1993), 441–2.

33 ZS, 16. ZS (translation), 13. The published English translation errs in one line in this passage. Heidegger says that 'clearing [*Lichtung*] comes from light [*leicht*],' but the translation has 'Light' for *Lichtung*; p. 13, line 25.

34 GA 16, 630.

35 GA 15, 262. HS, 161.

36 GA 15, 262. HS, 161–2. And consider that Heidegger's insistence in the 1966–7 'Heraclitus Seminar' that *die Lichtung* must not be understood from 'light' in the sense of luminosity is in sharp contrast to how he unfolded the term in his lecture courses on Heraclitus in 1943 and 1944 (GA 55) and in his subsequent essay on Heraclitus and *aletheia* published in 1954 (GA 7 and *Early Greek Thinking*, cited above).

37 GA 9, 201.

38 Note that the translation of *Lichtung* is 'clearing' in *Basic Writings* (1993), 138, and in *Pathmarks*, 154. But the translation was changed from 'lighting' as it appeared in *Basic Writings* (1977), 140.

39 SD, 74. *Basic Writings* (1993), 443–4.

40 SD, 76. *Basic Writings* (1993), 446.

41 SD, 73. *Basic Writings* (1993), 443.

42 See the following chapter for a discussion of how his thinking about *die Lichtung* is intimately related to the 'turn' (*die Kehre*) in his thinking after *Being and Time*.

43 Thus, for the Heidegger after the 'turn' in his thinking, *die Lichtung* is another name for the originary and fundamental meaning of Being, properly named by him over the course of his thinking, Beyng (*das Seyn*), Being itself (*das Sein selbst*), Being as such (*das Sein als solches*), Being as Being (*das Sein als Sein*). See also the next chapter.

44 *Summa Theologiae*, I, q. 106, a. 1. In the *Respondeo*, Aquinas states: 'To prove this, it should be maintained that light, according to which it pertains to the intellect, is nothing other than a certain manifestation of truth [*veritatis*], according to which it is said in Ephes. V: *all that is made manifest is light* [*omne quod manifestatur, lumen est*].'

45 For a comprehensive summary of Heidegger's attitude, see Lin Ma and
    Jaap van Brakel, 'Heidegger's Comportment Toward East–West Dialogue,'
    Philosophy East and West, 56, no. 4 (2006): 519–66. In the next chapter, I sug-
    gest one reason why Heidegger may have been so (understandably) reluc-
    tant to take up in any depth or detail what he generally called 'East Asian'
    thinking.

6. Plato's Light and the Phenomenon of the Clearing

1 The vicissitudes of translating this key word in the Heidegger scholarship
    were examined in the previous chapter.
2 References throughout the chapter will be to the German texts followed by
    the available English translation. Please note, however, that I have often
    modified the published translations. Martin Heidegger, *Die Grundbegriffe
    der antiken Philosophie, Gesamtausgabe, Band* 22 (Frankfurt am Main: Vittorio
    Klostermann, 1993). Hereafter GA 22. Translated by Richard Rojcewicz
    as *Basic Concepts of Ancient Philosophy* (Bloomington: Indiana University
    Press, 2008). Hereafter BCAP.
3 Martin Heidegger, *Die Grundprobleme der Phänomenologie, Gesamtausgabe,
    Band* 24 (Frankfurt am Main: Vittorio Klostermann, 1975/1997). Hereafter
    GA 24. Translated by Albert Hofstadter as *The Basic Problems of Phenomenol-
    ogy* (Bloomington: Indiana University Press, 1988). Hereafter BPP.
4 Martin Heidegger, *Vom Wesen der Wahrheit (Zu Platons Höhlengleichnis
    und Theätet), Part* I, *Gesamtausgabe, Band* 34 (Frankfurt am Main: Vittorio
    Klostermann, 1988/1997). Hereafter GA 34. Translated by Ted Sadler as
    The Essence of Truth (New York: Continuum, 2002). Hereafter ET(1). On the
    whole, Sadler's translation is admirable and commendable, but there are
    occasional problems, and I have made modifications.
5 Martin Heidegger, *Sein und Wahrheit (2. Vom Wesen der Wahrheit), Gesamt-
    ausgabe, Band* 36/37 (Frankfurt am Main: Vittorio Klostermann, 2001).
    Hereafter GA 36/37. Translations are my own; a complete translation is
    being prepared for publication by Gregory Fried and Richard Polt.
6 Martin Heidegger, 'Platons Lehre von der Wahrheit,' in *Wegmarken, Gesamt-
    ausgabe, Band* 9 (Frankfurt am Main: Vittorio Klostermann, 1976/2004).
    Hereafter GA 9. English translation: 'Plato's Doctrine of Truth,' in *Path-
    marks*, trans. Thomas Sheehan, ed. William McNeill (Cambridge: Cam-
    bridge University Press, 1998.) Hereafter *Pathmarks*.
7 GA 22, 106; BCAP, 87 (Heidegger's emphasis).
8 Heidegger's own lecture course manuscript does not discuss in any detail
    the role of the sun (as in the later readings); but according to Hermann

Mörchen's student lecture notes, it appears that Heidegger did explicitly identify this purely enabling light as the sun and that he had worked out a correspondence with the Idea of the Good: 'This light, which makes possible the visibility of what can be perceived by the senses, is the "sun," *ho helios* ... The seeing and grasping of the being[ness] of a being also requires a light, and this light, whereby being[ness] as such is illuminated, is the *agathon*, the Idea of the "Good."' GA 22, 256; BCAP, 197.

9 GA 24, 404; BPP, 285.
10 GA 24, 404; BPP, 285.
11 GA 24, 401; BPP, 283.
12 GA 24, 402; BPP, 284.
13 GA 24, 402; BPP, 284.
14 See chapter 5.
15 Martin Heidegger, *Sein und Zeit*, *Gesamtausgabe*, *Band* 2 (Frankfurt am Main: Vittorio Klostermann, 1977), 464. Hereafter GA 2. Translated by John Macquarrie and Edward Robinson as *Being and Time* (New York: Harper and Row, 1962), 402. Hereafter BT.
16 GA 2, 464; BT, 401–2.
17 GA 34, 26; ET(1), 21.
18 Heidegger also refers to the sun as 'the *primordial* light' that is 'the light-*giving*' (das Licht-*gebende*). GA 34, 41–3.
19 GA 36/37, 153–4.
20 Robert Grosseteste, *On Light*, trans. Clare C. Riedl (Milwaukee: Marquette University Press, 2000). In a later reference (1954) to this Christian tradition of thinking, Heidegger observes: 'The same holds true of the Augustinian and medieval theories of light, which, not to mention their Platonic provenance, can find their space of play only in the region of *aletheia* that already prevails in the dispensation of the twofold.' *Moira (Parmenides, VIII, 34–41)* in *Vorträge und Aufsätze*, *Gesamtausgabe*, *Band* 7 (Frankfurt am Main: Vittorio Klostermann, 2000), 257. Hereafter GA 7.
21 See Riedl's Introduction to Grosseteste, *On Light*, 5.
22 GA 34, 41; ET(1), 32.
23 GA 34, 55; ET(1), 41.
24 GA 34, 58–9; ET(1), 44 (Heidegger's emphasis).
25 GA 34, 59; ET(1), 44.
26 GA 34, 96; ET(1), 70.
27 GA 34, 101–2; ET(1), 73–4.
28 GA 36/37, 145.
29 GA 36/37, 197 (Heidegger's emphasis).
30 GA 36/37, 197. One notable observation that Heidegger makes in this part

of his elucidation (199) that does not appear in the 1931–2 lecture course text reads: 'The Good is *beyond* being[ness], *epekeina tes ousias* (VI, 509b9), thus = Nothing (*formally* said). That means that if we inquire about the Good as we usually inquire about something that is good, then we will not find it; we will always plunge into the Nothing. The Good is never at all to be found under the guise of a being or of being[ness]. It requires that we question in another manner.' Even so, I think that it is very likely that he also had this correspondence in mind in the 1931–2 lecture course since the Nothing (*das Nichts*) had been a prominent theme in his 1929 inaugural lecture at the University of Freiburg, 'What Is Metaphysics?'

31 GA 9, 229; *Pathmarks*, 175. We should also note that in the same year that he composed his essay on 'Plato's Doctrine of Truth,' 1940, Heidegger also offered a lecture course on Nietzsche's *The Will to Power* with the title 'European Nihilism.' In Section 29 of the lecture course, he gives a brief account of his reading of Plato's Idea of the Good, again emphasizing Plato's own words that the Good must be understood to be 'beyond even beingness,' which Heidegger renders in the German as 'jenseits noch der Seiendheit.' Note that here he specifically uses the word *Seiendheit* in this formulation. See GA 48, 301.

32 Martin Heidegger, 'Zur Frage nach der Bestimmung der Sache des Denkens,' in *Reden und andere Zeugnisse eines Lebensweges, Gesamtausgabe, Band* 16 (Frankfurt am Main: Vittorio Klostermann, 2000), 620–33. Hereafter GA 16. Originally published in German in 1984 by Erker-Verlag, St. Gallen. Complete translation by Richard Capobianco and Marie Göbel, 'On the Question Concerning the Determination of the Matter for Thinking,' in *Epoché: A Journal for the History of Philosophy*, Spring 2010. Hereafter cited as QDMT.

33 I have cited other middle texts in chapter 5, but here I would again specifically mention his important essay on Heraclitus and *aletheia* published in 1954 (but which thematically goes back to his lecture courses on Heraclitus in 1943 and 1944; cf. GA 55). Throughout this text, Heidegger thinks through *die Lichtung* in terms of *das Licht*, understood in the same fundamental sense that he had worked it out in his Plato readings. Thus, he says, for example, 'Das Wort "licht" bedeutet: leuchtend, strahlend, hellend. Das Lichten gewährt das Scheinen, gibt Scheinendes in ein Erscheinen frei.' ('The word "light" means: illuminating, beaming, brightening. Lighting grants the shining, frees up what shines for an appearance.') *Aletheia* (*Heraklit, Fragment 16*) in GA 7, 266. Also consider Heidegger's observation from the early 1950s that ordinary (and metaphysical) seeing, though familiar with luminosity, nevertheless 'does not pay attention to the still

light [*stillen Licht*] of the lighting [*Lichtung*] that issues from the unfolding of the twofold.' We recognize here the distinction that he had made in the Plato readings between light seen directly and the light-source itself that is seen only indirectly – that is, the sun, or in this line, 'the still light.' *Moira (Parmenides, VIII, 34–41)*, GA 7, 259.

34 GA 16, 629–30.

35 See the Appendix to chapter 5.

36 The differences in his statements on the linguistic provenance of the German word *licht* (related to *Lichtung*) are striking, and as far as I can tell, he gave no account for these differences. In his 1954 *Aletheia (Heraklit, Fragment 16)*, 266, he states: 'Das Wort "licht" bedeutet: leuchtend, strahlend, hellend.' ('The word "light" means: illuminating, beaming, brightening.') But altogether different is his derivation of the very same word in his 1964 lecture 'The End of Philosophy and the Task of Thinking': 'Das Adjektivum "licht" ist dasselbe Wort wie "leicht" ... Das Lichte im Sinne des Freien und Offenen hat weder sprachlich noch in der Sache etwas mit dem Adjektivum "licht" gemeinsam, das "hell" bedeutet.' I render: 'The adjective "light" [*licht*] is the same word as "light" [*leicht*, as in free and easy] ... The light in the sense of the free and the open has nothing in common either linguistically or substantively with the adjective "light" in the sense of "bright."' 'Das Ende der Philosophie und die Aufgabe des Denkens,' in *Zur Sache des Denkens* (Tübingen: Max Niemeyer Verlag, 1969/2000), 72. Translated by Stambaugh and Krell as 'The End of Philosophy and the Task of Thinking,' in *Martin Heidegger: Basic Writings*, ed. David Farrell Krell (San Francisco: HarperCollins, 1993), 441–2.

37 William J. Richardson, *Heidegger: Through Phenomenology to Thought* (The Hague: Nijhoff, 1963).

38 Martin Heidegger, *Vier Seminare*, in *Seminare, Gesamtausgabe, Band 15* (Frankfurt am Main: Vittorio Klostermann, 1986), 345. Translated by Andrew Mitchell and François Raffoul as *Four Seminars* (Bloomington: Indiana University Press, 2003), 47.

39 Thomas Sheehan, 'A Paradigm Shift in Heidegger Research,' *Continental Philosophy Review* 34 (2001): 193.

40 GA 2, 177; BT, 171.

41 'Die Lichtung selber aber ist das Sein.' *Brief über den 'Humanismus'* in GA 9, 332; *Pathmarks*, 211.

42 GA 16, 631.

43 See the Appendix to chapter 5.

44 GA 16, 695. In this foreword, as in QDMT, Heidegger uses the word *der Bereich*, which is often translated as 'realm' or 'domain.' Yet these words seem too abstract to do justice to the metaphorical sense of a place or an

area that Heidegger suggests (especially in QDMT), and thus I prefer 'region.'

45 *Zur Sache des Denkens*, 72; *Basic Writings*, 442.

46 GA 15, 363; *Four Seminars*, 59 (Heidegger's emphasis). Related here is how Heidegger explicitly thinks *Seyn* and *Lichtung* (in terms of luminosity!) as the Same in a philosophical 'musing' that has been recently published in GA 81, *Gedachtes* (Frankfurt am Main: Vittorio Klostermann, 2007), 76. In a note to one of his poems, he reflects on the primordial meaning of *Freyheit* or 'freedom' as a preserving (*schonen*), caring for (*hüten*), or sparing (*sparen*) something in its 'essence,' and in the key line he observes: 'Die "Heit" (altgerm. Wort) ist die Heitere, die leuchtend-erglühende Lichtung – die 'Heite' des Freyens, die Freyheit, ist das Seyn.' I translate: 'The "bright" (Old German word) is the bright and gladsome, the luminous-glowing lightening – the "bright and gladsome" of sparing [freeing], sparedness [freedom], is Beyng.' The note, undated, is probably from the early 1940s and related to Heidegger's elucidation of Hölderlin's poem 'Homecoming' (1943), where we find Heidegger featuring this word *das/ die Heitere* and the metaphor of light in thinking *die Sache*. See also chapter 4n20.

47 For a basic orientation to the issues, see Reinhard May, *Heidegger's Hidden Sources: East Asian Influences on His Work*, trans. and with a complementary essay by Graham Parkes (New York: Routledge, 1996).

48 GA 16, 630–1; QDMT, our translation.

49 GA 16, 630; QDMT, our translation. But note that immediately thereafter Heidegger opens a line of questioning regarding 'the onefold of space and time' that includes this enigmatic question: 'But does this clearing exist for itself, above and beside space and time?' He simply leaves these questions as questions in the address. On the other hand, in a 1969 Zollikon seminar at Medard Boss's house, Heidegger states the matter simply: 'Spatiality and temporality both belong to the clearing.' *Zollikoner Seminare* (Frankfurt am Main: Vittorio Klostermann, 2006), 188.

50 GA 16, 632; QDMT, our translation.

51 Martin Heidegger, *Zollikoner Seminare* (Frankfurt am Main: Vittorio Klostermann, 2006), 229. *Zollikon Seminars*, trans. Franz Mayr and Richard Askay (Evanston: Northwestern University Press, 1987), 183.

52 GA 15, 386–7; *Four Seminars*, 73.

53 *Zollikoner Seminare*, 223; *Zollikon Seminars*, 178.

54 Koichi Tsujimura, 'Martin Heidegger's Thinking and Japanese Philosophy,' trans. Richard Capobianco and Marie Göbel, *Epoché: A Journal for the History of Philosophy* 12, no. 2 (Spring 2008): 355 (his emphasis).

55 Martin Heidegger, *Der Satz vom Grund*, *Gesamtausgabe*, *Band* 10 (Frankfurt

am Main: Vittorio Klostermann, 1997), 169. Translated by Reginald Lilly as *The Principle of Reason* (Bloomington: Indiana University Press, 1991), 113.

7. Building: Centring, Decentring, Recentring

1 'Building Dwelling Thinking,' trans. Albert Hofstadter, in *Martin Heidegger: Basic Writings*, ed. David Farrell Krell (New York: HarperCollins, 1977), 323–39. 'Bauen Wohnen Denken,' in *Vorträge und Aufsätze, Gesamtausgabe, Band 7* (Frankfurt am Main: Vittorio Klostermann, 2000), 147–64. Originally delivered by Heidegger as a lecture in 1951; first published in 1952.
2 See especially his phenomenological descriptions of landscapes and places in *Genius Loci: Towards a Phenomenology of Architecture* (New York: Rizzoli International, 1980). Norberg-Schulz died in 2000 at the age of seventy-three.
3 See, for example, two collections of essays: *Dwelling, Place, and Environment: Towards a Phenomenology of Person and World*, ed. Robert Mugerauer and David Seamon (New York: Columbia University Press, 1989); and *Dwelling, Seeing, and Designing: Toward a Phenomenological Ecology*, ed. David Seamon (New York: SUNY Press, 1993). Related in spirit is the work of Christopher Alexander; cf., for example, his *The Timeless Way of Building* (London: Oxford University Press, 1979).
4 Norberg-Schulz, *Genius Loci*, 22–3.
5 For an overview of these positions, see Andrew Benjamin and Christopher Norris, *What Is Deconstruction?* (New York: St Martin's, 1988). See also Jacques Derrida, 'A Discussion of Architecture (with Christopher Norris),' in *Aesthetics: A Reader in Philosophy of the Arts*, ed. Lee B. Brown and David Goldblatt (Upper Saddle River: Prentice Hall, 1997), 179–88. Hereafter cited as *Aesthetics*. The interview with Derrida was originally published as 'Jacques Derrida in Discussion with Christopher Norris,' *Architectural Design* 59, nos. 1–2 (1989): 7–11.
6 For a discussion of the significance of the theme of 'not-at-homeness' in Heidegger's thinking, see chapter 3.
7 'Nolo Contendere,' in *Aesthetics*, 201. Originally in *Assemblage* 11 (1990): 57.
8 See Jeffrey Karl Ochsner, *H.H. Richardson: Complete Architectural Works* (Cambridge, MA: MIT Press, 1982). Gate Lodge, 217–19; Oakes Ames Memorial Hall, 204–7.
9 Norberg-Schulz, *Genius Loci*, 42.
10 'Building Dwelling Thinking,' 328 (Heidegger's emphasis; translation

modified). To gloss Heidegger's line: Only human beings know death *as* death, and they are always and essentially defined by death (finitude).

11 'The Dislocation of the Architectural Self,' in *Aesthetics,* especially at 191 and 197. Originally in *Journal of Aesthetics and Art Criticism* 49, no. 4 (Fall 1991): 339 and 346.

12 As transcribed in the interview with Christopher Norris; no text deleted. See *Aesthetics,* 185; *Architectural Design,* 10.

13 See, for example, Robert Venturi's theoretical and architectural work. One instructive essay is 'Architecture as Decorated Shelter,' in *Aesthetics,* 169–79. For an overview of 'postmodern' architectural thinking and work as a particular style, see Charles Jencks, *The Language of Post-Modern Architecture* (New York: Rizzoli International, 1987).

14 John Caputo uses the metaphor of 'surfaces' in lauding Derrida's radically disruptive, deconstructive readings: 'Derrida systematically explores all the "surfaces" of language, all the possible graphic, phonic, rhythmic, and psychoanalytic linkages between words. He wants to exploit every connection ... without regard to, in defiant reduction of, meaning.' *Radical Hermeneutics* (Bloomington: Indiana University Press, 1987), 148. Contrast this with Heidegger's words in 'Building Dwelling Thinking' that 'a boundary is not that at which something stops, but, as the Greeks recognized, the boundary is that from which something *begins its essencing (sein Wesen beginnt).*' Heidegger's emphasis; 'Building Dwelling Thinking,' 332.

8. Limit and Transgression

1 The richness of Heidegger's thinking is in evidence in that he returned to Sophocles' *Antigone* in a markedly different way in the 1940s. For a fuller discussion, see chapter 3.

2 See especially *The Birth of Tragedy,* Section 4, trans. Francis Golffing (New York: Anchor, 1956). In Section 15, Nietzsche is somewhat more charitable towards what the 'Apollonian Greek called *sophrosyne,*' offering only that it is a less life-denying ideal than the baneful 'Socratism.'

3 *Introduction to Metaphysics,* trans. Ralph Manheim (New York: Yale University Press, 1959). Hereafter IM. All references are collected from pages 144–65, with only minor modifications to the translation in some instances. Cf. the German text *Einführung in die Metaphysik, Gesamtausgabe, Band* 40 (Frankfurt am Main: Vittorio Klostermann, 1983). The corresponding pages are 153–74.

4 IM, 161.

5 IM, 165 and 157, respectively.

6 *The Oedipus Plays of Sophocles*, trans. Paul Roche (New York: Penguin, 1991), 222. See also the Greek text and translation in volume 21 of the Loeb Classical Library, *Sophocles*, trans. Hugh Lloyd-Jones (Cambridge, MA: Harvard University Press, 1994), 68–9.

7 *The Oedipus Plays of Sophocles*, 238 (slightly modified). See also Loeb Library, vol. 21, 98–9.

8 *The Oedipus Plays of Sophocles*, 252. See also Loeb Library, vol. 21, 126–7.

9 IM, 158.

10 *The Seminar of Jacques Lacan, Book VII: The Ethics of Psychoanalysis 1959– 1960*, trans. Dennis Porter (New York: W.W. Norton, 1992), 247–50. Hereafter *The Ethics of Psychoanalysis*. The French edition is *Le Seminaire, Livre VII: L'éthique de la psychanalyse* (Paris: Éditions du Seuil, 1986). Lacan takes up a reading of *Antigone* in Sections XIX, XX, and XXI; this corresponds to the seminars dated 25 May 1960, 1 June 1960, and 8 June 1960, with a supplementary note given on 15 June 1960.

11 *The Ethics of Psychoanalysis*, Section XXIV, 314.

12 Ibid., 319. Porter translates *cèdè sur* in this line as 'having given ground relative to one's desire.' I prefer William J. Richardson's translation: 'to have compromised one's desire,' in, among other places, his essay 'Ethics and Desire,' *American Journal of Psychoanalysis* 47, no. 4 (1987).

13 Ibid., 319f. Porter translates *l'homme du commun* as the 'ordinary man.' I opt for the more obvious translation 'common' and use it throughout.

14 Ibid., 321.

15 Ibid., 319.

16 Ibid., 314–15.

17 Ibid., 273.

18 Ibid., 277.

19 Charles Sheperdson, 'Of Love and Beauty in Lacan's *Antigone*,' *UMBR(a)* 1 (1999): 71.

20 IM, 152–3.

21 *The Ethics of Psychoanalysis*, 280.

22 Ibid., 322.

23 *The Iliad*, trans. Robert Fagles (New York: Viking Penguin, 1990), 211.

Afterword

1 Martin Heidegger, *Hebel – der Hausfreund* (Pfullingen: Günther Neske, 1957), 33. Translated by Bruce V. Foltz and Michael Heim as 'Hebel – Friend of the House,' in *Contemporary German Philosophy*, vol. 3 (University Park: Penn State University Press, 1983), 99, translation modified.

Index

New Studies in Phenomenology and Hermeneutics

General Editor: Kenneth Maly

Gail Stenstad, *Transformations: Thinking after Heidegger*
Parvis Emad, *On the Way to Heidegger's* Contributions to Philosophy
Bernhard Radloff, *Heidegger and the Question of National Socialism: Disclosure and Gestalt*
Kenneth Maly, *Heidegger's Possibility: Language, Emergence – Saying Be-ing*
Robert Mugerauer, *Heidegger and Homecoming: The Leitmotif in the Later Writings*
Graeme Nicholson, *Justifying Our Existence: An Essay in Applied Phenomenology*
Ladelle McWhorter and Gail Stenstad, eds., *Heidegger and the Earth: Essays in Environmental Philosophy*, Second, Expanded Edition
Richard Capobianco, *Engaging Heidegger*